a Book of Not Forgetting

A Book of Not Forgetting

or

Time is a Thief

FABIA TORY

First published in Australia in 2016

by Fabia Tory

Copyright © Fabia Tory 2016

ISBN 978-0-9945641-0-8 (print book) | 978-0-9945641-1-5 (epub) | 978-0-9945641-2-2 (Kindle)

The right of the author to be identified as the author of this work has been asserted in accordance with the Copyright Amendment (Moral Rights) Act 2000.

This work is copyright. Apart from any use as permitted under the Copyright Act 1968, no part may be reproduced, copied, scanned, stored in a retrieval system, recorded or transmitted in any form or by any means, without the prior written permission of the publisher.

All paintings are by Fabia Tory, except for *Poster for Lew's wake* by Gwyn Perkins.

Most photographs are by Fabia Tory. *Christmas 1974* is by Peter Laverty. *Shells, Clifton Beach, Tasmania* is by Amanda Thomson. Photos of Ursula and Peter are by unknown photographers. Photos of Fabia Tory are by unknown photographers.

Cover design – Simon Keck

Cover painting – Fabia Tory *By Shanks's Pony*

A Book of Not Forgetting Facebook Page:

https://www.facebook.com/abookofnotforgetting2016/

Direct enquiries to: abookofnotforgetting@yahoo.com

National Library of Australia Cataloguing-in-Publication entry:
Creator: Tory, Fabia, author, illustrator, photographer, book designer.
Title: A book of not forgetting, or, Time is a thief / by Fabia Tory.
ISBN: 9780994564115 (ebook : epub)
Subjects: Tory, Fabia.
Tory, Fabia--Marriage.
Tory, Fabia.--Travel.
Women artists--Australia--Biography.
Man-woman relationships.
Bereavement.
Dewey Number: 759.994

With love for Lewis

Bird Bliss

Preamble

Lewis did not marry until he was fifty. He was so chuffed his nose went red and tears rolled down his striking face. I was forty-nine and had not expected to remarry. But there we stood, over the moon that we had found each other and the rest of our lives were now entwined.

On our honeymoon we visited Monet's garden at Giverny. We swapped the jostle and tussle of Paris for the quiet of this tiny village where Monet had created a ravishing garden. Splashed in sunlight and holding hands, we meandered through the flowerbeds where scarlet, oranges, yellows and purples, clamoured for attention. Waterlilies perched on an exquisite pond, in daubs of crimson, pinks and white. The mirror surface rippled from dangles of willow.

Monet's pink and green-shuttered home was loved and open-hearted. Floorboards, furniture and wall hues all conveyed an endearing warmth. The kitchen tiles were a riot of patterned blue and white freshness, dappled with gleaming copper pots that shone like gold-leaf highlights. The lavishly yellow dining room was decorated with delicate Japanese woodblock prints and navy and white porcelain. The phrase 'less is more' had not yet come into vogue when this place was fashioned. How could you not be happy here? Our delight in each other's company resonated in this gem.

Eventually, saturated by the beauty of the place, we left to find a late lunch. At the nearby Musée d'Art Américain, under a trellis of wisteria mauves, my husband's tastebuds tingled from his smoked-fish lunch. And I was smitten by his pleasure.

Before we were married, we were dusted by the same magic, sardined on a Sydney peak-hour train as it made its way through the city. We stood facing each other, squished together and absolutely delighted at the physicality of our predicament, especially at our ages.

I looked up at you, and saw in your twinkling eyes your darling love for me.

Such warmth, it was hard to pull back as the crowds eased.

A Beginning

I was born in 1956 and grew up in Wahroonga, about 22 kilometres north-west from the not-so-dead centre of Sydney. Our land had once been a market garden, so down the back was a field of undulations splodged by a myriad of fruit trees. You could see, in rainbow order, small plums, oranges, persimmons, bush lemons, loquats, quinces, pears, Granny Smith apples, large plums, and somewhere on that list you would place mulberries. In autumn the leaf colours danced. In spring the ground was scented, and shimmered with ixias, freesias, snowdrops and jonquils. When I was tiny, the odd cow and horse loitered through. I was astonished at how big they were, but I'm jumping ahead …

Peter, and his sisters were born and grew up in Winchester, England. It's an architecturally enchanting city and if you're lucky enough to visit you can easily see why it lingered in his heart. His father's people were wood carvers, teachers and furniture makers. His mother, Beatrice, had a beautiful singing voice and gave solo concerts for charities and for the troops. Peter's sister Janet said he was a talented boy soprano and people came a long way to hear him sing in Winchester Cathedral, which has (as he occasionally imparted to his children) the longest nave of a Gothic cathedral.

In 1936, when Peter was ten, his mother died from an abscess on her lung. His father, who'd never recovered from serving in the tanks in the Great War, was unable to care for his children. Peter drew the long straw and went to live with his kindly grandmother, Kate. His younger sisters, Janet and Margaret, were fostered out to a caring couple who wanted to adopt them, but their interfering aunts didn't like the cut of the couple's jib, so the girls spent their childhoods unkindly dressed in identical clothes being shuffled between indifferent relations.

During the Second World War, at seventeen, Peter joined the RAF. He was extremely disappointed that his poor eyesight and hearing loss – the latter, a gift from childhood measles – prevented him from training as a pilot. So he worked in the RAF as a photographer. At some point Laurence Olivier was his liaison officer and apparently the poor man was bored out of his mind. After the war ended Peter had to remain in the Air Force for, I believe, eighteen months. The upside of this – and to Peter it was a big upside – was that members of the Armed Services could obtain free tickets to the London Royal Opera, Ballet, Theatre and Symphony Orchestra. Most nights he would attend a marvellous production.

When he was finally demobbed he started a painting course at Winchester School of Art, where his father had taught and where he met Ursula. She was sixteen, a talented drawer and rather lovely, and the first thing she said to him was, 'May I borrow your rubber?'

Ursula was the eldest of five children. She was followed by Julian, Camilla, Venetia and Virginia. The first three were born and grew up in London until the war started; then they moved south into the country, where the twins were born. Ursula's father, Lynd, had been orphaned at three. He was an Australian who had studied in England and then lived in London. Her mother, Vera, a South African, came to London on a primary school teacher's exchange. She later studied to be a sculptor. She was talented, but gave it up after she had her first two children. She found all the interruptions while working difficult, and her quick-tempered husband said if she wanted more children she would have to stop being a sculptor. Lynd's mother had died having him at the age of forty-six in 1901, so he didn't know what women were capable of, and sadly Vera didn't pursue it.

A Beginning

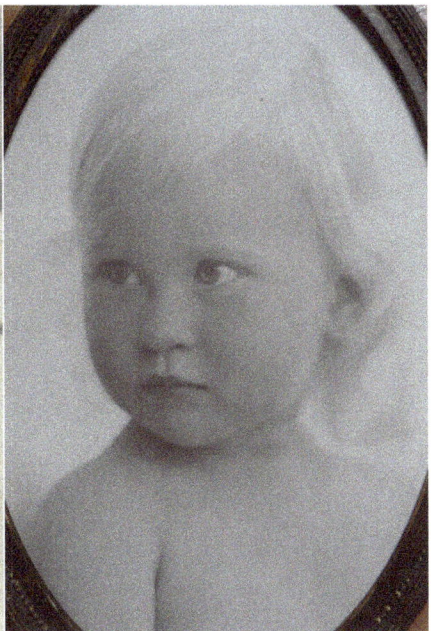

Peter, a student at Winchester School of Art

Ursula as a child, London

When Ursula was eighteen and at the end of her second year at art school, her parents, after too many years of war, rationing and rain, packed the family up and returned to her father's country. She gave Peter a leather and vellum copy of Shakespeare's complete works. That's when he knew: she was The One. They wrote to each other twice a week for two years.

When Peter completed his art course, he was extremely fortunate to obtain a rare passage on a ship to Australia. He left England before he had his final results, which was a very un-Peter thing to do. On board, quite a few Australians asked what he did for a crust and he told them he was a painter. 'Oh, you'll have no trouble getting work in Australia as a painter. There's plenty of work for painters over there.'

His first port of call in Australia was Fremantle, where his enthusiasm for architecture was rewarded when he asked the locals if there were any interesting buildings around. 'Oh yes,' they replied with much pride and gave him directions to their brand-new abattoir.

He was also keen to try the local food and purchased his first 'Pie Floater', a meat pie floating in pea soup. He must have loved Ursula very much.

When Ursula's family came to Australia in 1949, she continued her diploma at the National Art School in Sydney. Peter had planned to work as a portrait painter when he first arrived, but he obtained a four-day-a-week position as a teacher at the same art school. Sometime later he became Head of the Painting School. He was always able to paint part-time.

Peter and Ursula – or Mum and Dad as I called them – married and had three high-spirited children in two and three-quarter years: Simon, Piers and Fabia – that's me.

Our family, Wahroonga

When we were children, our Mum painted, was a printmaker, exhibited regularly, drew, read, nibbled on barley sugar or caramels, dreaded the dentist, wrote and later published poetry, cooked delicious meals on plates we regularly licked, went to church, worried not so much, loved our Dad and us, and admirably avoided much of the dreary aspects of housework. She was a painter who never stopped painting. She said she occasionally put herself in the children's playpen so she could paint, and we played outside it. Other friends' mums told me they did that with their sewing. She only ever wore flat shoes, bit her fingernails, had thick wavy flaxen hair and, apart from face powder, used no make-up. I admire her tremendously. I was surprised to later discover a few friends had Difficult Mothers. I didn't know there was such a thing. She rarely burdened me with advice, except to be particularly clear that she thought gossip was unacceptable and to always close the curtains at night when you're getting changed. Oh, and that it's important to drive defensively. Everyone liked our Mum enormously. She radiated kindness and gentleness, which made her an impressive oasis in a family of 'robust' personalities.

Mum and Dad in their studio

Each evening she would dash off and comb her hair just before Dad came home. They would take a glass of wine and walk around their large and private garden as he unwound and talk about their day. Often at night as I was drifting to sleep, I could hear them choking with laughter at one of those side-splitting English television comedies. Noisy detonations of unrestrained hilarity. I loved it.

'Wahroonga' is an Aboriginal word, most likely originated from the Kuringgai language group that means 'our home'. The architect Sydney Ancher designed our house in the early fifties. Skillion roof, floor-to-ceiling glass, tallowwood floors and built around three sides of a courtyard. The sun would come in for the winter and stay out in the summer. It was a home to be in love with. A friend lived climb-three-fences-away in an intriguing stone, glass and white Harry Seidler house.

Our front garden, bordered by a greyed slip-rail fence and a five-rail gate, was a tangle of crackly Australian bush. To see it properly you had to peer close. The back garden was a formal English garden with hedges, lawns, a ha-ha wall and a field of fruit trees. You needed to step back to better see this part. Through a giant telescope in a shed with a roll-off roof Dad would look at and photograph the stars, the moon and the planets in the night sky. Throughout the garden were two cats, a dog, blue-tongue lizards, ants, skinks, bandicoots, pee-wees, magpies, black wrens, kookaburras, and red-back and funnel-web spiders, but it was for the bindi-eyes in the grass that we kept our thongs on.

And drifting above us were the cries in the skies of the not-yet-faded moon. That was all I could see in the sky to explain the sound. It was disappointing to discover some years later that the moon didn't call out to us in a shrieking-to-fade voice. It was the unseen ravens.

One day, as a very small child, I found some vivid red paint. I smeared it generously onto the white wall in one corner of my bedroom: a solid red circle. I still recall the pulsating strength of the swirls of paint on that stark wall. Dad made us all show him our hands. Simon's were grubby with dirt from playing outside; Piers's were covered in all colours of paint. Mine were bright red. *I think I can get away with this*, I thought. 'I promise I didn't do it,' I said. Apart from this hiccup, I drew and painted on paper non-stop until I learnt to read.

As a young child I was happy and optimistic by nature. Life was fun and there was much to discover. I remember it was always sparkly hot summer. I remember the light, and the sun tinted by bushfires. And that we were thrilled by the regular southerly busters.

I was lucky our parents were devoted to their vocations and each other. It gave me a freedom – which probably also came with being the youngest – to range out all day, exploring the bush, making forts and cubbyhouses, playing baseball or cricket with stacks of local children, and daydreaming. I had two ways to travel apart from my feet: either on my bicycle or underground through the stormwater drains in our neighbourhood. I loved the echoing sound my feet made slapping through the water-trickles in these pipes. Sadly for me, this covert life came to an end when I rapidly grew too tall to be comfortable inside the pipes.

I've been 170 centimetres since I was twelve, which was a bit alarming at the time, being the tallest girl in primary school. We were arranged in an all-inclusive (otherwise I would never have been in it) choir according to height and I was at the very end of the back row, although it was debatable as to whether Kim Coldrake should have been behind me. Many of my friends eventually caught up to or overtook me. Now it appears I'm not so tall.

Every night of our childhood Mum turned down our beds for us to climb into. Far into the future I discovered she did this because occasionally a funnel-web spider would detour through our house. Mum only smacked me once. I remember her chasing me down the hall – maybe I was six – and I remember a red mottled handprint on my leg and how much it stung. I don't remember what I did, just that I very strongly deserved it. She says she also smacked me when I was about three, distraught after I'd gleefully run straight across a busy road.

One family of seven cousins and another of five lived within a couple of blocks of us. All younger, they were great kids. Their mothers, Diana and Camilla, were remarkable and capable and I liked them tremendously. We were three points of a family triangle. Six more cousins lived elsewhere in Sydney. Their mothers were twins and we weren't as close to them in age or feeling. There were always babies in our childhood to be besotted by. This was all Mum's family. Dad's family remained in England.

Our parents travelled to Europe when we were children. When they were in Greece, Mikis Theodorakis's music was everywhere. They returned home, relieved us of our cranky babysitter, and this astonishing music filled the house; mostly it was joyful and life affirming. Otherwise Mum's favourites, Handel, Haydn or Purcell, would be industriously playing on the stereo. Our childhoods were peppered with slide shows of magnificent architecture from Europe. I have to say I absolutely loved it.

Dad was an excellent photographer. Four things I am keen on because of his enthusiasms: art history, travel, photography and gardening. He used to treat our Citroën DS car like a horse that needed a good run out in the country. 'Weeeee!' he would exclaim as the car flew along unsurfaced gravel roads. He was a speedy-fast-reflexes driver.

Because Dad had teaching holidays, every year we would pile into that car and travel over 800 kilometres north to Cabarita Beach, which in those days was a sleepy and elemental place. Always the same families with stacks of children would come together, some from Sydney, most from Brisbane and one from Toowoomba, for the month of January. To this day I believe you have rocks in your head if you don't find time to go away as a family each year. And there's nothing like the seaside. Dad would fish to his heart's content, the fridge would bulge with seafood, watermelon and runny Camembert, and Mum would collect ocean oddments and draw.

When we returned home we listened to the silence from no more crashing waves. And the grass was always a foot high. And the pussycats' fleas would jump and tickle your legs when you walked on the Finnish rugs, until Mum discovered sprinkling flea powder on the rugs before we departed.

We had Finnish rugs, Finnish chairs, Finnish wall hangings, Finnish curtains and Finnish glassware. What wasn't Finnish, Dad had skilfully designed and had made, apart from a scattering of lush antique furniture passed down through the family. It would be years later that I realised Finland was the country these beautiful things came from and not some extra good final design 'finish' that made something look special. Eero Saarinen, Tapio Wirkkala, Marimekko and Iittala were wonderful names from our childhood.

One day, my eldest brother Simon and I were horsing around, laughing and full of fun. To our horror we knocked the lovely deep green Finnish bottle off the mantelpiece. It bounced off the brick hearth and onto the timber floor. To our titanic relief it didn't smash. Now I had a firm understanding of what a miracle was – the ones we kept hearing about at Sunday school.

Our maternal grandmother, Vera, was responsible for the feminine side of my nature. I adored her; she was a huge part of my life. A lifetime out of the sun meant her skin was oh so white and soft. She smelt wonderful from Elizabeth Arden's Blue Grass dusting powder, had beautiful hands, was often formidable to her own five children, but much gentler to her twenty-one grandchildren. She had a fulsome gift for domesticity and her home was always fresh and welcoming – a conglomeration of striking antique furniture, Persian rugs, Asian ceramics, paintings and books. She was proud of her father's French ancestry and she dressed exquisitely. Much later in life she remarked, 'You can put me in my coffin when I lose interest in clothes.' This turned out to be true.

She handmade beautiful clothes for the bride doll and other dolls she gave me. She carefully taught me how to sew and knit well, which I did with great perseVERAnce. She encouraged my reading, sometimes with wonderful books, other times with romantic trash. I was happy gobbling up both. She had a large library from which you could borrow. You had to write your name and the title of the book in pencil in a little notebook she had sitting on one of her bookshelves. 'Over the years I've lost so many books,' she lamented.

'The nuns were the worst for not returning them.' She was a vibrant communicator and believed we all were obliged to make interesting conversation, and you sensed her disappointment if you didn't.

Granny died aged eighty-nine, in 1989. My whole life I visited her every Tuesday afternoon with a small bunch of flowers and some delicious little cakes, plus for the last ten years of her life with whoever was my youngest. The last few months I only visited her fortnightly because life was hectic. I'd told her I was going to do this, but she'd misunderstood me and thought I wasn't going to see her any more. We sorted that out.

'Goodbye, I'll see you when we get back from our holiday,' I said to her at the door of her apartment, with a gentle hug and a soft warm kiss.

'This old age is not what it's cracked up to be, darling,' she said. 'I hope it really is goodbye.'

It was. Ever after, I've always told people if I love them, because I was achingly sorry I'd never said that to Granny. Dear Aunt Camilla said she would have known.

School Haze

I understood how the behaviour system worked in our home, but in primary school I had no idea I was often being naughty. Probably daydreaming or chatting – both have held me in good and bad stead throughout my life. Funny that good qualities can also be bad; just depends on your location and what the circumstances are. The unexpected stinging smacks on my legs and sometimes hands rained down thick and fast from my teachers.

It was at school that I learnt to eat with my mouth shut, as one day I crunched on a crackly fly while eating a tomato sandwich. I'd had no idea that was possible.

I loved playing on the metal monkey bars. Hanging by the knees upside down, hair standing on end, or one knee hooked over and around and around I'd go. Climbing, stretching, running, so much energy. Always my knees were scabby.

In fourth class I started a new school, which had no boys and where they didn't smack. Elastics, skipping, swap cards and knucklebones abounded. They also had a grassy playground and here too, much of my playtime was spent willingly the wrong way up, reversing myself into bridges, headstands, handstands, and flinging myself into cartwheels.

In sixth class my teacher did not like me, even the littlest bit. My happiness, no doubt doused by puberty, came to a screeching halt. And one day late in that year, I noticed with surprise that the permanent grazes on my knees had disappeared.

Luckily, at this school the following year I met thirteen-year-old Prudence, and we began a boisterous forty-five-year allegiance. We dressed up, made books, sewed, knitted, drew, painted, were in plays and found gales of laughter in most things. We hung on to every moment of Peter Cook's and Dudley Moore's weekly television show *Not Only... But Also* and Somerset Maugham's dramatised short stories. When I asked Prue about those times, this is what she remembers: we shared an unfortunately unrestrained passion for flares, exuberantly plucked eyebrows and scads of garish make-up. Or was that just me? Prue's mum sometimes joined in. My Mum tried to keep a straight face, but you could easily read the suppressed laughter. One day Prue overheard my Mum say to her mum, 'It wouldn't be so bad if they weren't so funny.' We took that as a huge compliment.

By 1970, Dad was Head of the National Art School. The following year he became Director of the Art Gallery of New South Wales. This last job was very busy and he had to stop painting.

In high school I relished, in order of preference, boys, dancing classes, art, drama, athletics, modern and ancient history; and was horribly lazy in the single year I studied Latin. I thought BOYS were a magical creation and didn't know why I hadn't noticed them before. They were in no way similar to my brothers and their friends.

Every Tuesday afternoon after school, I did special art classes. We had a wonderful fierce art teacher called Jana Bruce. Luckily she liked me, because she was quite explosive and some if she didn't. She gave me access to all sorts of unusual materials and their possibilities.

I loved clothes and made most of my own. I considered studying fashion design, but Dad's disparaging comments about the difficulties of the 'rag trade' possibly lanced that idea.

After seeing Judi Dench performing in the Royal Shakespeare Company's Australian tour of *Twelfth Night* and *A Winter's Tale* when I was fourteen, I thought acting was the most illuminating profession in the world. Prue and I burnt up a lot of energy being involved in plays with our school. I also participated in plays with the boys' school down the road, where John Turnbull was their rousing drama teacher. Several times he told me and a cast member that we were 'upstaging each other'. I kept pushing my chair backwards until I almost fell off the back of the little side stage. Again, it was years later that I found out what 'upstaged' meant. Dylan Thomas's *Under Milk Wood* was my favourite of the plays we performed.

Granny took us to see the Royal Shakespeare Company again. This time it was Peter Brook's fanciful production of *A Midsummer Night's Dream*. When I mentioned to Granny I wouldn't mind being an actress, her expression wasn't promising, even though I'd been named after an English actress friend of hers, Fabia Drake.

I never realised that being young we were mostly lovely; instead my 'flaws' loomed large. If ever I complained about one of my body parts, Mum would dismiss it with, 'At least you have feet, ears', or whatever. And they all worked. Some more than others. She is the least shallow person I know, by a long way. Granny, sporadically sharp of tongue, one day said to me, 'You know, you don't have to smile all the time.' So it would seem that I smile a lot.

My brothers' teenage years were pretty grim. So many very loud arguments. They disliked their school, cadets and the nasty short haircuts their school enforced upon them. Dad clashed with Simon over his wonderful music choices – Johnny Winter, Muddy Waters, Bob Dylan, Jimi Hendrix and The Rolling Stones. Late in high school, my brothers changed schools. I couldn't understand why they had to confront my parents on everything. *For goodness sake, do what you want, but just don't tell them*, I thought. This attitude wouldn't have helped at all in the first three of their disputes.

There are photographs of Mum at this time looking sad. I remember Dad looked cross. Mum had spent her teenage years in boarding school, away from the bombs of London; Dad had spent his living with his grandmother. There was a much bigger, scarier reality in those days. They say the first child breaks the parents in for the rest; in our case it was the first and second, and they nearly broke the parents. Within a couple of years, my brothers had left home and a scarred peace reigned in our home. I decided that I would never, for any reason whatsoever, send my children to private schools, that short hair on boys was hideous, and that I would be open to my children's choices in music come hell or high water.

Christmas 1974

How to sum up my teenage years? Of course there were painful, regretful and angsty stints, and I developed a mental habit of wanting to bolt. It was only later in life that I realised those raw times were periods of change and growth, that my friends probably felt the same way, and that I shouldn't have been so hard on myself in some instances and perhaps could've been tougher in others. It took me years to work out that in a day or two I would feel much better. And yet there were plenty of marvellous, challenging and new experiences, lots of fun and parties, a particularly dear boyfriend called Cameron, and plenty of local and school friends. Luckily I liked my school, we didn't have idiotic cadets, and I could wear my hair, tied up, as long as I liked.

In August of my last school year I went overseas with Mum and Dad for two months. I took quite a few heavy school textbooks, which I did not open, but I do believe they enjoyed the change of scenery. I returned two and a half weeks before my Higher School Certificate and stayed with Granny as my parents were still travelling. I did okay in my final exams, but ungratefully sometimes I wish I'd been able to give them my best shot. And that possibly explains why I still occasionally have dreams about redoing those damn exams. On the other hand, the artistic treasures I saw when travelling with my knowledgeable and eager parents were irreplaceable and I really enjoyed their company. When I was seeing something glorious for the first time, let's say Monreale Cathedral in Sicily, I saw the delight in Dad's face at my response. In our family, you could never travel without being given a lengthy list of the finest buildings and museums in the cities you were about to visit. Dad was always generous with his knowledge.

On the last day of school I couldn't comprehend why so many people were upset. I was so excited to be at last climbing into REAL LIFE! Occasionally at school I'd been troubled by the sense that I was with some people I didn't have much in common with, and no doubt vice versa. And there were a few whose mums hadn't taught them that to gossip was nasty. What a relief that out in the real world these two issues would no longer be the case. We had a special final-year dance to celebrate school finishing. For no particularly strong reason I didn't go.

Art School

The visual world of birds, buildings, cats, circuses, clouds, colours, fabrics, fishes, flowers, fruit, humans, insects, landscapes, patterns, plants, pottery, seascapes, shells and trees had always given me delicious delight. Like my parents and oldest brother, and with the added input from my high school art teacher, in my last year of school I decided I wanted to go to art school to become a painter. My early works were colourful, decorative, naive and prolific. When I was asked by the entrance interrogators what I would like to do if I wasn't accepted into the art school, I was mortified that I had no answer. Eventually I mumbled that *m a y b e* I could study history at university … But I didn't want to go to university. I much preferred making things.

In 1975 I was accepted into the foundation year of a new art school. Using the Division of Fine Arts section of the National Art School as its core, the poetic bureaucrats had created Alexander Mackie College of Advanced Education (!). Dad was very sad to see the mangling of the National Art School.

In my first year we were housed in a comparatively soulless multistorey building in the soulful Rocks area of Sydney. Dad would drop me there each morning on his way to work. He was always great to chat with. I'd make my own way home, struggling to stay awake on the train. They hadn't yet organised chairs for the students, so we were asked to bring in a cushion to sit on. Painting was now known as Graphic Communications I, and sculpture was called Wood and Metal

Technology. First year was a general introduction to many disciplines and my work was conservative. More than half of the students were mature age and had already done a heap of interesting things. I felt painfully shy at times; however, I studied hard and loved it.

At art school I met Barbara and a sparkling and heady friendship began. She was a dark-haired, blazingly becoming, mature age student of thirty-one; I was eighteen. She was keen for culture! One of our first animated conversations was about the music of Vivaldi and Lawrence Durrell's *Alexandria Quartet*. She introduced me to the novels of John Paul Sartre, which I loved. She had grown up in a warm family that loved the beach, camping, reading, music, horse racing and travel. She had travelled widely and lived and worked overseas. Barbs also studied singing at the Conservatorium and had a rich voice that would have made an excellent vivacious black-haired Carmen. These days Barbara's greatest passion is art-related travel and she's pursued that with gusto, particularly giving the Venice Biennale a thorough thrashing. Her love of books comes an immeasurably close second, but I think it's her joie de vivre I love the most. If there's a marvellous film, travel experience, exhibition, scent or ice cream shop, she dives in. She introduced me to light Italian panettone splashed with amaretto and French vanilla ice cream.

At the beginning of second year and now a vegetarian, I callously bolted from home without a backwards glance, and lived in a share house in inner-city Darlinghurst with two friends of my brothers' and my blond bombshell boyfriend, Jonathon, an architecture student. (Jonathon gave me the loveliest present I have ever been given. In a small white paper bag were five thick velvet ribbons – crimson, orange, viridian, cobalt and yellow – to tie up my long hair.) My brother Simon was also living in Darlinghurst. The first time he visited, he checked if I was okay and then told me that if there was anything I needed, he was there to help, which he did frequently.

In the spirit of not confronting my parents with things that would cause arguments, I didn't tell them I was living with my boyfriend. My Dad, of whom I was so fond, was no fool and countered this situation by not speaking to me for a year. I discovered there are worse things than arguments.

But in many ways, second year was a Grand Adventure. Painting was my major and over three years my teachers included Roy Jackson, Kevin Connor, Terry O'Donnell and Syd Ball. Ceramics was my minor for that year, with June Lord, and I loved making pots. I regretfully switched my minor to life drawing (Graphic Communications II) for my last two years, as my drawing was weak and those classes would strengthen my paintings. Alan Oldfield and Margaret McLellan were my teachers in this subject. I liked to use splotchy black ink and broken twigs as a pen. My paintings, still colourful, became big, bold, loose and abstract. I worked on raw canvas with my hands, brushes, squirting sauce bottles filled with watered-down paint, and sometimes attached torn-up chunks of my black-on-white ink drawings. And oodles of energy was let loose. It would be interesting to know if I hit the kilometre mark in canvas covered, and how many buildings I could have papered with my life drawings. This was a time of great freedom and I'm very grateful to have had it.

On weekends I worked in a nursing home, making beds, serving morning and afternoon teas, washing up and putting away laundry. This gave me a skewed view that we live well into our nineties and, conversely, sometimes to an overripe old age. For the first time, I saw up close dementia, incarceration and colostomy bags failing. One day when I was in a two-bedroom ward, a gentle woman was quietly crying and I asked her what was wrong. She said she'd never been to Paris and now it was too late. Another time, a patient had died and the matron called me into her office as I was one of the last people in her room. The patient's wedding ring had disappeared and I was asked if I knew anything about that. Matron was one of the types of people I'd thought I would never have to see again after leaving school.

Two Alzheimer patients hooked up and would be found wandering the corridors looking and asking for a double bed. We didn't have any. Bonking was important to me and I felt very sorry for them. The nursing sister who told me she was a Good Presbyterian caught them in a single bed together and was scandalised.

I didn't know before I worked there that a mum in her ninties, could have the sudden terrible blow of her seventy-year old daughter's death. That some patients were tied to their chairs so they wouldn't wander off or fall and break a limb. Nor that women keep their handbags close even when they'd lost their minds. Or that having all the patients showered before breakfast wasn't always possible. I saw one incontinent diabetic woman being sprayed with deodorant before she was wheeled off unwashed to her brekkie. And I was devastated to see that some people at the end of their lives were bedridden, their minds and their most basic abilities extinguished. All these dear elderly patients were Jewish and most were European, so this was not their first experience of the harshness of life.

After a year of this weekend work, I changed to house painting, developed a lifelong aversion to painting ceilings, and then worked nights as a waitress.

Second and third years were taught in the former gaol buildings of the National Art School in Darlinghurst, where Mum had studied and Dad had taught. Many of my teachers had been taught by Dad and spoke of him warmly. I used to paint in my roomy studio space in the old golden sandstone buildings at night. No one was around and I was in heaven. Big abstract splashy canvases. Someone asked me if I was scared to paint alone in a place that had once been a gaol and possibly had some unhappy spirits shiftily drifting around. I continued for a few more nights, looking over my shoulder with straining ears, then took to working evenings in my room in our lively and vehemently grotty terrace in Thomson Street.

Just after I'd finished my four-year course, the art school's name changed to the City Art Institute. Eventually in 1990 it became COFA (College of Fine Arts) under the auspices of the University of New South Wales. It was a time of change for change's sake, and unless you were involved with Sydney art schools in the seventies you would have no idea who or what Alexander Mackie College was. The old

National Art School was revived in the late nineties and, despite bungling bureaucratic meddling, is in existence today and highly regarded.

Student Work

In my third year of art school, when I was twenty and Jonathon was twenty-one, we married. My parents thought we were way too young and should at least wait until we'd finished our courses. But we weren't waiters, and I'm still not one, though I can ruefully see now that there are many benefits to being one. My parents graciously organised a beautiful wedding for us.

Jonathon and I had much in common and so much happiness. We moved to Surry Hills and lived there for two years. We studied hard and life was very satisfying. Jonathon designed and made me a work table and us a couch, and I made a glass-mosaic top for our coffee table. Our record-player resounded with Bach, Beethoven,

Bob Dylan, John Lee Hooker, Rachmaninoff and Van Morrison. I didn't know what a workaholic was, and didn't realise I had married one.

At the age of fifty, in 1977, just after we were married, Dad left his job and returned with a passion to full-time painting. He told me that others could be the director of the state gallery, but only he could do his paintings. I remember being so proud of his choice and that his works from this period were exploding with energy. We never spoke about us not speaking.

And Babies Make Five

Jonathon and I moved to Drummoyne, a pretty inner suburb of Sydney with harbour inlet views abounding, but partially disfigured by a mega-busy six-lane road. We were expecting our first child. I'd been working at night as a waitress. I looked about fifteen and my tips when pregnant were impressive. I'd finished my course, but Jonathon was still studying.

After Nicholas was born, I sat up in my hospital bed reading a review of a group show I was in. To my exasperation the *Herald* critic said I painted as if I were running out of time. Certainly I had worked in the back shed, which in summer was like a sauna. Here's a conundrum for you: which is worse – being affronted by the critics or being ignored by them?

But I had far bigger fish to fry than worrying about art critics. I was twenty-two and absolutely besotted by our adorable babe. Even though I grew up surrounded by babies, when I brought Nicky home from hospital I hadn't realised I had to feed him in the middle of the night. Such a shock. So there was always a part of my nature that wasn't paying attention.

None of my friends had babies, nor were any married. Those who eventually had children waited until their mid-thirties. Gradually I made new friends who had small children. The isolation of being home alone with a little one who was a great sleeper was relieved by reading. Books were an irresistible escape, particularly novels with their insights into being human. In my twenties, despite young children, or perhaps because of them, I read voraciously. Balzac, Dickens and Stendhal were my favourites. I found *The Charterhouse of Parma* haunting, and some years later did a series of works loosely based on the book.

By the time I had two little boys just under two, my own work went onto the back burner. Mum had told me she painted late into the night when we were tiny. I just couldn't do that. By 9.30 pm I couldn't wait to go to bed. I was definitely a human first and an artist second. Nevertheless, I loved being a mum, except of course when it drove me spare. I was pretty bloody sick with morning sickness and each time was a little worse. And yet being pregnant was a sustaining time in my life when I felt I had to prove nothing to nobody. I sometimes wish I were able to revisit my children when they were little and so appealing and hold them close.

When Nicky was two weeks old, we took him on a sleepy ferry ride on Pittwater in Sydney's northern beaches. The ferry stopped at a Scotland Island wharf, and four coltish children with same-family features stamped upon their faces came running down a dirt and stony hill and jumped off the wharf and into the ferry's wake. No hovering parents in sight. We never forgot that magical carefree image. In 1980, when we were expecting Hugh, we bought a block of land on that same beautiful treed island with the intention of building a house of Jonathon's design. The sense of place was overwhelming and we were excited that we would be giving our children a wonderful childhood. We'd both grown up surrounded by bushland, which had given us lots of freedom. Jonathon was working as an architect and also writing his thesis when Hughie made his entrance.

We had obviously become much more realistic by the time number three was born. Claudia arrived just before we were about to start building our home. Jonathon ended up with pneumonia. He was working full-time, had designed our house and got it through council. So we decided to wait for a year before building and just enjoy our family. We had a lovely year. Nicky had started school, Hughie was at preschool two days a week, and Claudie, although not such a good night sleeper, was a lovely placid baby. I believe this was the only time in our marriage that we ever slowed down. That is, if you can call being the parents of two young children and a baby slowing down.

We took a seaside holiday. A woman came up to me at a shopping centre and seemed to know me. 'Hello,' she said. 'Hi,' I replied. 'I know you!' she said. 'Do you?' I answered, worried that my lack of sleep due to Claudie had wiped my memory. 'Yes. You're on television.' 'No ... No, I'm not,' I replied, feeling rather flattered. 'Yes. Yes, you are. You're on *Prisoner*, aren't you?' In the late 1970s and '80s, *Prisoner* was a grim Australian TV soapie set in a women's prison. The women were tough and mean and ugly.

It was hard to find time to paint and my brain wasn't its normally alert self. However I managed to do quite a few endearing watercolour, black ink and crayon drawings of the children and us as a family. My desire to make things was strong and in those early years the sewing machine ran hot as I made much of our clothing, culminating in making Jonathon a silk suit, which wasn't bad until I washed the pants and shrank them. I often made Granny cool and simple summer frocks. Because I was so busy I had trouble getting them started, so I developed a habit of calling her and saying I'd drop in the next day with her dress. That night I would stay up and make the outfit to a soundtrack of the sewing machine whirring. I've always worked better to a deadline. The next day she'd wear her new dress. Her animated conversations, with a blue and white Spode Italian teacup waving in her hand, occasionally left tiny splashes of tea down her front. I took a lot of pleasure in knitting too, and made numerous patterned and colourful jumpers for our little tribe.

In 1985 we started to build. Jonathon was working full-time in the city and spent the weekends on the island, digging by hand thirty-six 2-metre-deep holes for the foundations of our house. This was so as not to disturb the scraggly natural bush of the block, which we both loved – spotted gums, casuarinas, wattles, blueberry ash, fine-leaf geebungs, hardenbergias, lomandras and native grasses. Jonathon's dear dad, Bruce, who always helped him, renamed him Hard-Way and enquired whether our children were conceived standing up in a canoe.

One day some islanders gave Jonathon a lift across the water. When he told them he was building a house they said, 'Are you married?' 'Yes,' he replied. 'Be careful,' they told him. 'Some people who build their own houses here end up getting divorced. As long as you have no children, we're sure your marriage will last.' He didn't mention we had three.

During a brief respite from the rain, and after many a pump-out, the foundations were finally poured into those holes and masses of materials bought over from the mainland. We were both pretty stretched, and finding a place to rent nearby was tricky. We moved four times in eighteen months – hiring a small truck, making multiple trips, like millions before us doing it ourselves. That can really shave off the pleasantries of a person's character.

I have a picture imprinted on my brain of Jonathon working on the tallowwood frame of the house, before there were walls or floorboards. He is sitting on a temporary plywood platform two storeys up, with six-year-old white-haired Hughie, who also has his own leather tool belt. They are toiling away in the sunshine with commendable concentration.

Little Claudie patiently travelled all over Sydney with me while I picked up various materials. I would reward her at the end of each day with a little Bertie Beetle chocolate, which she nibbled on the ferry on the way home. One day a local friend suggested to me that bribery was a very poor way to bring up a child. So I stopped buying dear long-suffering Claudie a beetle on the way home. She yelled from the car to the ferry, yelled while waiting for the ferry, yelled on the ferry and yelled all the way home. It crossed my mind to toss her off the ferry and then perhaps I could live quietly in gaol and do my paintings. The poor little creature never asked for a chocolate beetle again.

Eventually, as Claudie approached three, I was able to help with the building. The boys were both at school, and kind island friends would often mind Claudie with their children. We clad the external walls with cedar hammered in with copper nails, then spent two weeks drilling and then hammering in the tallowwood floors. Our poor neighbours! Mum and I filled, sealed and painted the internal gyprock walls and glazed some of the windows. I sealed and varnished all the cedar doors and windows.

Utterly worn out from commuting to the city and from house building, Jonathon decided to go out on his own as an architect. This added erratic income to our strains.

After two years of building and when the 'baby' was three, our fourth move was into our own beloved home. The beauty of our timber house was a huge credit to Jonathon's creativity. On this final move I had a car full of rolls and rolls of unstretched canvases. They filled the car, were tied to the roof racks and I could barely move. Passing the local tip, beyond exasperation, I turned in, dumped the lot and returned with another carload. There were one or two I miss, but there weren't any masterpieces.

A builder had put together the house frame for us and sometime later he joked that architects never finish their own houses. I could barely suppress my fuming. The frame he'd erected cost us exactly twice the rough quote he'd given. We had used up all our owner-builder loan and couldn't afford to continue renting, so we moved into our house in the middle of winter with the stern August westerlies blowing. We had no kitchen, no bathroom and no stairs to the bedrooms. Not all the windows were in. I would do battle with the intractable possums to protect our food. Luckily, we had an unusable clothes dryer that I could keep our fruit in.

The only power we had was an extension cord running from the back of the block, which gave us a fridge, a couple of lights and an electric frypan. When we plugged in a heater it melted the power board, so no heating, but I don't remember being cold *that* year. We had no internal doors. There were twenty concertinaing doors along the front and twelve along the back of the house. The external doors were closed by timber wedges and the strong westerlies every now and again would blast one of the doors open, which in turn would blow out one on the other side of the house. I remember going out the back one day and YELLING at the doors, 'If you do that one more time I'm going to get stuck into you with a mattock!' Our neighbours were close by and I was worried they might think I was shouting at our children when actually I was only shrieking at the doors. Either way, it didn't look good.

We had a metal garbage bin out the back with a hessian frame around it for a toilet. Our dear generous neighbours Ross and Sue let us use their bathroom to wash the children and ourselves. We were all on tank water. So Jonathon washed at his parents' place as that was near his work, and I limited myself to one quick shower a week. I took our washing to Mum and Dad's as bedwetting was burgeoning.

Four weeks later the plumber informed us that he couldn't connect the toilet until the bathroom floor was tiled. Another two weeks passed while Mum and I tiled the bathroom and laundry floors and walls, and then the plumber set in the toilet, connected the water and we had a bathroom. I could now use the washing machine and we had a laundry sink, which doubled as a 'kitchen' sink.

I would like to say I faced this time with grace, but that would be a big fat lie. I was sooo strained. I lost a lot of weight, was regularly unreasonable and life stopped being an adventure and became irksome. Jonathon was mostly unable to help me with the children because he was so busy with study, work, trying to finish the house and now setting up his own practice. Eventually I blamed him for our predicament, but really we were in it together. We'd both made choices that made things extra difficult; we both seemed expertly skilled at taking on too much. It took me some years to like myself again. What doesn't kill you makes you stronger. Who the hell said that?

Money was really tight – I had to get a job. No more painting. I felt trapped and distraught. I couldn't accept how Jonathon could work as an architect but I couldn't work as a painter. I was incapable of seeing the bigger picture. I tore up many of the colourful pictures I'd done of the family, but that was the last time I ever destroyed my own work if it wasn't poor quality. I was so worn out that I felt like bolting. My darling parents hauled me off with them for a ten-day holiday in Central Australia. That helped to restore my equilibrium and also unexpectedly gave me some inspiring subject matter for a new body of work. When I returned, nothing had been miraculously finished in the house, but I'd been given some good breathing space.

Gradually the house came together. Mum and Dad gave us a stove, and somehow the electrician wired it in separately from the rest of the not-connected power. Bruce continued to help on many a weekend, and Jonathon's generous Mum took the children for several days each school holidays. We discovered we really liked each other if we just temporarily removed one of our stresses.

When Claudie started preschool, my brain returned and I was finally able to get my teeth back into part-time painting. I tended to paint in the same manner as before I went to art school – celebratory, naive, with a passion for colour and often leaning towards the decorative; my subject matter usually objects or places that delighted me, especially Pittwater, or now and then an emotion that had tripped me up.

Two years later my Granny died. We were away on the north coast of New South Wales at the time, the first holiday our rocks-in-the-head, over-extended, overwrought, house-building family had had in years. I'd had a successful exhibition and we had enough money to take off to the seaside and also have the power connected. Granny left us her comfy couch, one of which we did not have – and Mum gave each of her children part of her inheritance. So the following year we were able to build a kitchen, buy a slow-combustion stove, and build some stairs up the cliff face that we'd been scrambling up with the shopping.

I noticed the island locals always called a house by the name of the people who'd built it, not the name of the people who currently lived there. I understood this. Just getting your materials on site was tough enough, let alone using them. They had to be delivered to the mainland wharf, barged across the water, delivered to the back of the block and then carried down, or to the front of the block and carried up.

Despite the self-inflicted toughness of our lives on Scotland Island, it has a huge tenderness in all our hearts. It's a completely different subject to talk about the wonders of the island and that we were able to give our children a mostly terrific childhood. The obvious inconveniences were nothing compared to the extraordinary ragged beauty of the place and its community of dear and interesting people. Big enough to be private, small enough to be intimate.

We had a sense of living outdoors because the elements were so evident – the bush, the water and the sky in all their moods. The water at the bottom of our garden, so benign like in a children's story book – kids jumping off wharves, asking the ferry for some buoyantly bubbly wake to jump into, boys fishing, little tinnies going backwards and forwards, graceful and not-so-graceful sailing boats, barges, workboats and the ferry all day, reliably going around and around the island and the offshore bays. The occasionally wild and unpredictably angry sea – if possible, better left to its own bad temper. We endured rapacious bushfires and mini cyclones. But the rain was always a gift because we were living on tank water.

We took magical bushwalks, sailed with friends, had no locks on our doors, and the children camped. Wednesday twilight and Saturday afternoon sailing races made a picturesque backdrop to our veranda, with a soundtrack of sails and spinnakers flapping, flocks of galahs screeching overhead in the dawning mornings, and those damn nocturnal possums fighting and thudding across our roof. One of my favourite things was walking around the island at night, no streetlights, no torch, a huge delicate black lacy canopy of spotted gums way above your head, the moonlight peeping through. Somehow I never tripped on the uneven dirt roads. Muddy clay, rain, ticks, mozzies, the smell of eucalypts and septic tanks, trees way outnumbering the houses, the moulting bark of spotted gums, an echidna rustling by, hurtling ourselves into the water on a blazingly hot day, fairy penguins darting, vivid but shy king parrots, and fine friends.

I thought the teenage years of our children were the best, and found it exciting seeing them slowly becoming the adults they were going to be. We each had a spell at being a pain, although for some it was longer than others. It was lucky that they all have a strong sense of humour.

When our boys were teenagers, we sat them down and asked them if it would be easier to rent for a while on the mainland because of all the to-ing and fro-ing. 'No!' they protested. 'We love it here.'

When Claudie was a teenager, she sat us down and said, 'Could we rent on the mainland? It's too inconvenient.' And we said, 'No. We love it here.'

It was on the island that effervescent Ellie and I formed a friendship that flittered from inconsequential to insightful in an instant. Ellie is such a fun person. Cooking, clothes, books, gardening and painting are all enthusiasms of hers. Her creativity filters through her whole life. She always looks so marvellous you can't be jealous – such a delight to the eye. But it's her two contrasting qualities I like the most: her sparkly, bubbly sense of spontaneous fun; and when one is really in trouble, she speaks most intelligently with considered objective empathy.

Warts And Some

Some years later, working full-time in a wholesale jewellery business, I took on a second mortgage to complete the house. My husband spent way too much of the money restoring a beautiful dilapidated timber putt-putt boat. The house wasn't able to be finished and we just stopped working as team. I would not enjoy this charming boat and I'm ashamed I was so petty. A snake-in-the-grass developer refused to pay Jonathon for a group of townhouses he'd designed for him. After too much angst and arguments, and because we had teenagers who needed our full attention, we decided to walk away. Jonathon was flattened by this experience, and we were financially and emotionally drained. I had to continue working away from home and not painting.

I wouldn't agree to a third mortgage to finish the house as we didn't have the income to repay it. Jonathon was always working. When he came home at night he'd be asleep within the hour. Sometime after 1 am he'd wake and start working again in the home office that was in our bedroom. It was no kind of life for either of us. Things had broken down and I had no idea how to fix them. We had tried counselling, but there were subjects he refused to speak about and no wonder: I was angry and sometimes lost the tact to talk about them gently. Various other shitty things happened.

I'd managed to sell a lot of work overseas, thanks to the efforts of my English cousin's wife, Fiona. Uncle Phil, husband of my father's sister Janet, was much loved by our family and was seriously unwell with cancer. I decided to use the money I'd earned to go to England and see them all, and also catch up with Prue who was now living in Rome, instead of ploughing it into my husband's business. Jonathon wouldn't travel with me, so I went alone for four weeks.

When I returned, my husband said he was leaving. He stated that he wouldn't change his mind and told me that he'd felt abandoned by me. This, despite me spending most of my weekends alone for years while he worked on his career. His love for me was gone and probably had been for some time.

I'd always thought we could fix things: again, I hadn't been paying attention. Twenty-seven years together, many of them very happy, but a slow build-up of too many quarrels with insults not left unsaid, too much unforgiven and too many money worries – and to Jonathon, the bad times outweighed the good. I stood on our veranda and hurled my beautiful twisted gold and silver wedding ring – a replica of Mum's – as far as I could, into the water. And later I threw away all but the crimson and cobalt velvet ribbons he'd given me.

Jonathon left. I continued living in the house for a year, mostly skittish, shocked and feeling solitary. This was the first time in my adult life I'd been without a partner, if you didn't count the weekends. I painted up a storm – some of my most beautiful work. I was anguished and angry and bloody well going to prove that I was a worthwhile person.

But I needed to leave. I felt such a failure and humiliated. I wanted to start a new life somewhere else, with the stimulation that the city had to offer. The reverse of a sea change. Nick had moved out a few years before; and by the time the house was sold, Hugh had moved also.

At our divorce hearing, I cried and cried. Jonathon was stony-faced. The judge asked me if this was what I wanted. I said yes. But I still had trouble letting go. It now occurs to me that I was a goose and had been for some time.

The night before moving, I spent several hours writing a long letter to the house's new owners, letting them know the best things in and around the area. My way, I guess, of saying goodbye to our much-loved home.

Begin Again

In the inner west of Sydney, I bought a tiny Victorian house in a tree-lined street with a strong sense of place, and moved in with Claudie and our two black cats. The first year there was pretty miserable and Claudie, at nineteen, had far more to deal with than she should have. She was studying at the University of Technology Sydney by this time, and her studies were affected by our divorce and the move and my lack of bouncing back. She had to ask for a couple of extensions for assignments. In the end the university wanted a copy of our divorce certificate, the sale of the house and the purchase of the new house, which I meekly supplied. Most of the children's lives we'd put them first, but I was a mess and all I can say is poor Claudie. I didn't seek emotional support from my parents, but Ellie was a darling, even though I was Misery Incorporated. Prue was too far away, and my constant woe became understandably too much for Barbara.

However, I managed to have a large exhibition with masses of colourful work, much of it based on the Chelsea Flower Show, which, thanks to Aunt Janet, I had attended just before Jonathon bolted. Joyful exuberant work that in no way reflected how I felt.

I used the sales from that show to return to Europe, where I saw Dad's dear sisters and Prue again, but this time without darling Uncle Phil, and spent some glorious time in Barcelona with Fiona and Cousin Jane. That helped to revive me. For some pitiful reason I asked Jonathon if he wanted to travel with me, but he did not. And the despair that had almost downed me did not also.

Thoughtful Claudie talked me into taking a hand-building pottery evening course with her at the University of New South Wales, which I took pleasure in. I'd only done wheel work at art school. The pots I made were appallingly bad, but I couldn't wait to get stuck into that clay, to daub or dip it in glazes, and even my lopsided disastrously ugly kiln shocks didn't deter me. The following semester, this time with Hugh's girlfriend, I continued making hideous pots with gusto. I even made quite a decent large vase that I hoped would be a lovely present for Jonathon's fiftieth birthday, but I managed to not give it to him.

Claudie also wrangled me into a pet shop. I told her we weren't getting any more animals; in our tiny joint and tiny garden, two cats were enough. I saw a little Tenterfield terrier puppy in a cage, who looked at me with her head tilted sideways, and I asked the assistant if I could hold her. She quivered with nervousness and I was smitten with her. *Struth*, I thought, *do I want to take on a dog?* So I asked the assistant if I could go away and think about the little dog, and if anyone else wanted her could I have first refusal? But in the blink of a head tilt I had fallen in love with her, so I returned. When I bought her home, she was so nervous that her tiny body was aquiver. I placed her down the front of my V-necked jumper with her head peeping out and spoke oh so gently to her for a long time.

Molly-Dog could also take a bow for helping me to snap out of it. She has the elegant proportions of a miniature horse, is short-haired, and a child's colouring-in of black, tan and white with black spots. She tilts her head to one side when you speak to her, as if English is her second language and she's carefully trying to translate. As a puppy she was ridiculously affectionate, mischievous and occasionally destructive, and mostly I didn't mind. My daily walks with her in a huge park nearby were a lifesaver for me.

The park gives a 360-degree view, fringed with brush box trees, of the sky, with all its variations from sun-up to sun-down, in all kinds of weather and seasonal changes. Next to the park and always in view is an enormous jacaranda tree. Each year it loses its leaves and becomes covered in radiant mauve flowers that are so intense you can almost taste them. I imagine they taste like liquorice. The feeling of living outdoors that I'd had on the island returned.

At least five times around the outside of the oval with this enthusiastic creature was such a tonic. With all her speedy dashes, loops and zigzags, three of my laps would have equalled one of hers. Her antics brought a smile to my face. She would roll down a grassy hill on her back, pushing off with her back leg. The galling barks at another dog that was six times her size, her spirited joy in chasing and returning a ball, leaping into the air to catch it, the endless sniff, sniff, sniffing, her friendliness to other dogs and their owners, and most of all the grin on her face while she scampered or bolted.

I discovered, at the age of forty-eight, that a dog has an admirable attitude to life. They enjoy each moment as it comes, are very easily pleased, and slather you in an unconditional love that is effortless to return. Early one morning, around eighteen months after my move, I awoke, annoyed with one cattie curled around my head for warmth, another sitting on my feet, and the little dog snuggled into my side. I lay there looking out my bedroom window at the flourishing plants in the garden, and it dawned upon me that I was enjoying my life again.

Hugh moved in, temporarily camping in the living room. He'd been thoroughly upset by the divorce and hoped we'd reconcile. Claudie felt that would be a disaster, and Nick wanted for us whatever made us happy. I was glad to have Hugh with us. He is tall, fair and very likable. His perceptions are of great depth, and he often thinks about concepts many of us are too busy or shallow to give enough time to. He works well with his hands with three-dimensional things, is a fantastic fisherman, a long, strong walker and particularly enjoys the natural world. I share his last two traits. When he was a little boy he said, 'Mum, you don't always do as you say.' I told him that was a perfect example of a hypocrite. (Hopefully this was relating to chocolate consumption.)

Claudie's boyfriend, Pete, also moved in so he could save for the overseas trip they were planning.

I slept and worked in my studio/bedroom and life was better than okay. I was working part-time in a furniture business, designing and selling furniture. AT LAST, the past was where it should be.

A New Chapter

Two years after I'd left the island, a former neighbour, Kerry, rang for a catch-up.

I liked this family. We'd lived next door to each other on the island and had both built houses of our own design. Similarly, we'd had two little boys and a baby girl. You don't endure being neighbouring islander owner-builders with three small children without making a strong bond. Kerry's husband, Pete, a former farmer, had lost his hands in a wheat-thresher accident some years before. The doctors had been clever enough to cobble back together one hand, but it had little movement. Remarkably, he had built their house by welding together a steel frame.

Kerry chatted about a friend of theirs who was recently single and had been renting from them for a while. His name was Lewis. I remembered him. He'd lived on the island for some years and was rather lovely; in looks, I thought, a cross between a young Albert Einstein and Plácido Domingo. My Aunt Camilla would have called him dishy.

The conversation ambled on and Kerry asked if I would like to come to dinner at their other house in North Sydney with a couple of friends I knew. I said I'd love to. It wasn't clear if Lewis would be there and I was too shy to ask. But I noticed I took extraordinary care getting ready that evening and I'd bought an alluring pair of caramel suede boots. Well, Lewis was there and we were a little timid to talk to each other, but each time we did, conversation stopped and everyone listened. What a set-up.

I'd driven to the dinner, but had too much wine to drive home, so was going to catch a taxi. Kerry said it was impossible to catch one from their place, but a couple of blocks away there was a taxi stand and Lewis would walk me there. Red-haired Kerry was the headmistress of a primary school and she managed to have us out the door without my realising how honed was her ability to make people do just as she wished.

We shyly walked together to the taxi stand – well, really I was floating. I don't recall what we spoke of, just that it was lovely walking next to this gentle man and I was disappointed that the taxi rank turned out to be so close. And then time slowed down as we shared a brief, gentle kiss goodbye, as unfortunately there was a taxi waiting.

Now the ironic thing is, when you've been married since twenty to someone you met when you were nineteen, you've probably spent a bit of time recommending to friends who really like someone to 'call them, for God's sake'. When you're finally in this situation yourself, aged forty-eight, it occurs to you – how tricky is this?

I called Kerry and thanked her for such a great night. Then I said, 'I thought Lewis was lovely.'

'Yes, he's lots of fun,' said Kerry.

Pause. 'Do you think he'd be interested in seeing me again?'

Her deadpan reply was, 'Do you really want to know?'

Bugger, I thought, *he's not interested.* 'Y…y…es …?'

'Fabe, he's besotted!'

I spoke like a fourteen year old. 'Really? Oh. Wow! Gosh …' At this mature age you would expect a certain amount of restraint, but I was deliriously hip-hoppity-happy to hear this. As a teenager I'd been able to do back flips and front flips. That was just how I felt. 'Do you think … it would be okay … if I called him?'

'Yes, Fabe, I think that would be a good idea.'

'Umm … do you … have his number?'

'Sure. Just a moment …' The number was given.

'Thanks so much, Kerry!'

The phones were hung up. I sat down. *Aaahhhhh!*

Working up the courage to call was excruciating. I remember exactly where I was in my living room when I made that call, on which part of the rug, head down, looking abstractedly at the tan, deep blue and crimson pattern.

Lewis's phone rang. *Shit. Shit. Deep breath, Fabie* ... But it was his answering machine ... *What a beautiful voice he has* ...

Trying to sound calm, and in a voice a little lower than normal, I said, 'Hi, Lewis, Fabia here. It was really nice catching up with you the other night ... Um ... When you're free, could you give me a call on this number? Ahh ... I thought maybe we could go on a picnic some time? Byeee.'

Piece of cake to be brave when you're not actually talking to someone. Damn it, that 'byeee' sounded a bit high.

The phone rang within five minutes. *Oh yes, he wants to go on a picnic!*

But no, it was Lewis calling and he'd received a call from this number, which he was returning. I guess he thought it was a business call. Why don't people listen to their messages? So I had to start all over again. Speaking directly to Lewis was much harder and higher and there were more ums and pauses than speaking to his answering machine.

'Yes,' he said in his warm voice, 'that would be great. How about next Saturday?'

After we hung up I had to sit down again.

The nicest thing was that several times that week he rang me in the evening, and I rang him, and we happily chatted, me sitting on the floor, my back leaning against the bed, looking forward to Saturday. Molly-Dog, still a puppy, was sitting next to me, misbehaving with exuberant jealousy.

On Saturday it was raining. Lewis said, 'Never mind, I've booked a table at a restaurant by the sea. We'll go there instead.' And feeling exactly thirty-two years younger, I thought, *Yippee!*

This first time we went out together, we had a giddy meal with heavenly champagne by the water. He didn't know I don't like seafood.

The restaurant served seafood only. I hoped fish in batter would taste less like fish, so I ordered that. For Lewis I ate fish (drenched in lemon juice, salt and pepper and tartar sauce), I was so happy in his darling company. When he said his fish was delicious, I said he just had to try mine as it was tremendous too! So I managed to pass half my fish over to him.

No awkward silences, just easy conversation rambling on. Kim Beazley, the politician, walked past. I joked I'd had trouble with him stalking me. We were 'caught' by an island friend Beth and her partner, who joined us for coffee. I could sense my face dancing with happiness.

The weather fined up and the light on the water sparkled. We left our friends and walked alongside the shimmering harbour. It was as if nature was striving to be her loveliest. How wonderful the world looks in sunshine after rain.

I found myself saying randomly, 'I like your deep blue trousers.'
Lewis replied, 'I just bought them.'
(*You buy new pants if you really like someone, don't you?*)

The glittering afternoon was fragrant with sunshine, salt water, happiness, blues, greens and promise. I was looking at Lewis walking next to me in that park by the sea. He was wearing a blue and white checked shirt. The sunlight was on his curls. He turned and smiled a beautiful soft crinkly-eyed smile at me. I dropped deeply and joyfully into love.

We sat on a sandy concrete step by the glassy water. Distant, seemingly little sailing boats drifted by. Lewis looked so lush. I was utterly happy and life had never been so uncomplicated. And glorious. I was hoping we might kiss, but Lewis jumped up and said we'd better be going. My heart sank. I thought I'd misread his liking for me.

We went to Kerry's place at North Sydney and had a coffee with her, and then I thought, *This is all too much, I'd better go.*

Lewis walked me to my car.

I nervously said, 'Thank you so much for a lovely day.'

He responded, 'Let's get together next week?'

'I would love to,' I gladly replied.

He looked like he wanted to kiss me. I certainly wanted to kiss him. How do you kiss when you've primly only kissed one man in the last thirty years? So I awkwardly dived at Lewis and gave him a kiss on the mouth, possibly like a kookaburra stealing a chicken bone out of your hand on a picnic. Then I jumped into the car and drove off.

Again through the week we talked on the phone. Lewis on the island; me near the city, sitting on the floor with the puppy being a pest. He told me that living on Scotland Island felt like he'd been on a ten-year holiday. I loved that he appreciated the beauty of the place.

The second time we went out, I wanted to take him to an inner-city restaurant that I'd liked. Me being me, I wasn't sure of its name so I drove to Leichhardt a few days before and booked a table for Friday night. My joy spilling over, I told the waitress that I was meeting a really lovely man there. The staff were warm to us and made it a memorable night. Lew ordered lamb shanks, and the way it was presented – raunchily launched on a bed of mashed potatoes – amused him no end.

He was being very cuddly and suggested we go back to my place. We drove back and Lew sat on the couch. I sat on a different couch, so awkward with this dating thing. He asked me to come and sit next to him. I gently asked him why he'd left the waterfront so suddenly last week when we were getting on so well? He laughed and said he'd needed a bathroom. And I remembered he'd ducked into one that was near the car.

After lots of delicious kissing, I said to Lew that I hadn't done this for a while and could we just keep to kissing? He said, of course. Well, what a wally I was. Imagine not doing the wild thing for almost three years and then spending the night with someone as luscious as Lew and thinking you would be able just to kiss? I've been told that the first time you go to bed with someone is not so good, but with Lewy it was so magically perfect that this woman who loves her sleep did not.

From that night on, Lew and I were together every day. For love to be returned whole-heartedly – what a joy. Everything else was trivial, everything else was wonderful. The rangy branches of the nearby jacaranda tree were delicately embroidered with tiny green leaves.

On several occasions, Mum and Claudie (who was overseas with her boyfriend) each cautioned me, saying, 'Just take things slowly.'

Usually I valued their opinions; especially with Claudie – over the last three years her maturity had been impressive. But this time I said, 'I don't think so,' (*and why?* I thought). I was forty-eight for not much longer, and Lew was forty-nine.

To be clear, Lew pretty much moved in two weeks after we met, bringing a large flagon of exquisite olive oil, Italian cheeses – including an enticing goat's cheese – and olives, all from his favourite Italian deli, Lavoti's, and bright red pyjamas. There were no uncertainties, no second thoughts.

I went to work on the days I had to, but by 3 pm my eyes would be hanging out of my head because we slept so little. One day my boss burst out laughing and told me to go home. The next day I felt the same, but there's only so much leeway you can give your employees.

I vividly remember Lew standing in the kitchen at the workbench, happily relaxed and generously putting together some delicious concoction for our dinner. He was using all sorts of ambitious spices and extravagant ingredients. Time stood still. It's so clear in my head the revelation I had: *You are a really, really NICE man.*

Something my Grandmother Vera told me: 'You should only use the word nice pertaining to food.' Well, with Lew there was always a connection, and luckily I was not oVERAwed by her occasional remarks.

From small local businesses, Lew brought home giant bunches of flowers made up of lively wired-to-attention gerberas, cheery sunflowers, purpley-crimson chrysanthemums, bottomless blue irises and headily-scented rich oriental lilies. In the living room such a riot of colours bouncing off their green leaves and stems, which had been wrapped in a fat orange bow and arranged in a large Chinese vase covered in delicate flower patterns. This room is tiny and they always looked double-takingly out of scale.

The living room also hummed with our shared delight in music.

Lew loved Beethoven's Piano Concertos, conducted by Claudio Abbado with Maurizio Pollini on the piano. Listening to the quieter sections of the Emperor's first movement, I told him that was how my heart felt being in love with him. And Leonard Cohen – his resonant music filled the house with his own deep allure.

And what was Lew feeling? When friends asked him how he was, he'd glowingly respond, 'Oh, I'm a Happy Man!'

How do I describe Lew's face? His personality was written upon it, but there were qualities to discover that weren't immediately evident. First mentioned must be his glorious riotous silver curly hair. As he passed fifty, his eyebrows grew like those of a villain in a pantomime. Near the end of each the hint of a pointy devilish horn, which gave his sparkly-blue-eyed smile a wicked look. This look matched his laugh. I trimmed his eyebrows sporadically. But no one could trim his love of music, food, wine, touch and all things pertaining to the senses. Lew's generous moustache hid his top lip. His bottom lip was full and sensual. Occasionally he had his moustache cut back and this was when I first saw his defenceless upper lip, which was pursed in an adorable and secret sensitivity. He had a strong jaw and a great beak. His face was as warm as his colouring.

Whenever I think of Lew's face, I can't leave out the strings of his glasses. His reading/work glasses were attached around his neck by a leather cord. And there were always his sunglasses on a nylon string, probably propped up in his curly hair. Many nights after dark I took his sunglasses out of his hair as he'd forgotten they were still there. There's hardly a photograph of him without his two pairs of glasses dangling around his neck. And he was way too handsome for them to look daggy.

Lew was an electrician by trade. In the eighties he became a gaffer and did lighting for television, advertisements and film. As that work was periodic he also did electrical jobs. Sometimes he would be particularly busy with work, but when I'd ask if he had time to see a film or whatever, he'd always say, 'I'll make time.' I couldn't get over that: for Lew, spending time together was a priority. I felt so valued. And when we did spend that time together I never felt that he was thinking about other pressing things. He was just happy in the moment. I treasured that quality in him mightily.

Claudie and Pete were still away, and Hugh was living at home and was sometimes cranky. He'd hoped his parents' divorce wasn't permanent. He was sad we'd sold our house and he was cross with his Dad.

One day after Hugh had been particularly surly, Lew said to me, 'Have you had lots of blokes back here since your divorce and Hugh is sick to death of them?'

'No!' I replied, mortified. 'I believe he's grumpy about me moving on relationship-wise. It's a big change to take on board.'

Lew's parents had divorced when he was approximately Hugh's age. His father had died very soon after, and his youngest brother had a serious motorbike accident that resulted in the loss of his arm. Lew had found it a ghastly time, so he had quite a lot of empathy for Hugh.

When Claudie and Pete returned from their trip, she was surprised that Lew had moved in. Now in our two-bedroom house there were five adults – one sleeping on a mattress on the living room floor – two cats and a puppy. But despite the squish and my children's adjustments, for me it was a particularly happy time, as every member, be they two-legged or four, I liked tremendously.

One morning, early on in our relationship, I was really cross with Lew. He was meeting Nick and his not-yet-wife Jess for the first time and had kindly offered to give a dinner party for them and my other kids and their partners. Lew shopped and cooked while I was at work. When I walked in, the kids were all lounging in the living room chatting.

I said, 'I hope you've been helping Lew?'

'We've all offered, but he says he's happy in the kitchen doing the cooking himself,' they said.

'I am!' he called out.

He'd also been happy in the kitchen steadying his nerves with whisky. By the time we all sat down to a sumptuous dinner, he was plastered and had to go to bed. Hugh was amused, but Nick looked at me quizzically, and I missed Claudie's expression.

The next morning I started to have a go at Lew and he stood in the kitchen looking hurt but taking it on the chin. He knew that he'd behaved badly. I stopped. I wanted scolding and recriminations out of my life for good.

It was lucky I was magnanimous, because I ended up being quite squiffy myself when I nervously first met Lew's Mum, brother and sister-in-law.

Aunt Camilla had gently said after my divorce that she was sure one day I'd meet a terrific man and have a great new life. I told her archly that I'd rather have a red-hot poker up the bottom than go out with another bloke. And now here we were, as irresistibly happy and cherished as could be. After not much more than three months of being together, we planned to be married on the first anniversary of the day we met. That was sort of taking things slowly.

Six months later, Claudie and Pete found their own apartment. Our whole lives Claudie and I had been attuned, but now she rarely contacted me. It took her around twelve months to accept that Mum had a new life. I understood her feelings, but she was twenty-one when I met Lew and I knew I was allowed to be happy.

Hugh was the last to move out. He moved into a flat with his Dad just near Claudie. This was a chance to repair their relationship. Loading up the last of his things I was taken by surprise when I started sobbing. The family life that I'd known for so long was over. It took me a while to recover.

One night Lew and I were at a dinner with friends. They were all complaining about their well-into-adulthood children still living at home, often with boy or girl friends.

I piped up, 'Actually it's pretty distressing when they all finally leave.'

A cool draught of silence hit the table and everyone turned to look at me – like I was cracked and should be enjoying the freedom.

From that dinner onwards, I embraced the change and got over myself. Lew was so patient with me. I knew I'd found an adorable gem.

Idyll

Lewy revelled in our inner-west home with its closeness to numerous possibilities. We'd jump on an express train and end up at Circular Quay, where the giant harbour expanse throws itself at you like a magnificent gift. We'd wander around The Rocks, where the intimate scale is charming. First stop would be the challenges of the innovative at the Museum of Contemporary Art. Nearby we could recharge with fancy French cakes and pastries at La Renaissance café. Sitting in their sunshined courtyard was a sweet oasis from the hustle of the city. Up the hill and round the corner is the Hero of Waterloo pub, where Lew loved listening to jazz. He couldn't wait to take me there, and I was so tickled when I unexpectedly knew the drummer, Chris, a painter and teacher of mine from art school thirty years ago. Alternatively, from the Quay we would stroll around to that celebrated sculpture known as the Sydney Opera House. Then we'd continue our amble through the Botanic Gardens, with its immigrant trees whose startling silhouettes stand before a backdrop of Port Jackson, and end up at the Art Gallery of New South Wales, where we'd always find something to enjoy.

Sometimes we'd catch the light rail from Leichhardt, which deposited us at Darling Harbour's Maritime Museum and the exquisitely crafted wooden boat show, or my favourite, the Sydney Aquarium, where fanciful sea creatures drift, fluorescent sea plants undulate and flamboyantly coloured tiny fishes laze.

How many times did we walk the Bondi-to-Bronte-and-Back-Again path along the squeaky beaches and dazzling cliff faces and watch the massive ocean heave and swell below us? Molly would be skipping and beaming with delight at the scents of a new place, her two humans with similar outlook. You know, I could go on and on with more places where the beauty of Sydney can smite you. I've not mentioned catching the RiverCat to Parramatta or the ferry to Manly, or Balmoral beach, Jubilee Park, or Observatory Hill …

We saw thoughtful Australian and foreign films in Leichhardt and Newtown. One day, we were enjoying ourselves on an up-high outdoor veranda in Leichhardt. I'd changed into a rarity of freshly ironed white clothes, with colourful embroidered flowers on my skirt. The wind picked up the froth of my coffee and splattered it all down my front, and all we could do was giggle.

Even after a hot hard day working in someone's roof, Lew was happy to go to an exhibition opening that I'd forgotten to mention to him. I would not have been so obliging – well, not before I met him.

Before I met Lewy, I'd been with my children's father since I was nineteen, and despite our miserable ending I had an accumulation of happy memories. Conscious of holding back some past experiences that were trying to elbow themselves into my and Lew's conversations, I realised we needed to accrue precious new memories together. At the same time, Lewy spoke of his regret of never having taken holidays. Well, he only needed to say that once to set me on a course of planning some adventurous overseas trips and travels around our own vast and varied country.

Φ

Our first trip together was our honeymoon.

We had a small wedding in our garden. (Charming Prue was living in Rome at the time and said she couldn't make it, but promised she'd make my next one …) We went to the flower markets the day before and filled the car with as many vibrant bunches as we could. However, heaps of things did NOT fall into place on our wedding day. Lew realised he didn't have a tie for the service so bolted out to buy one. He was *not* gone for half an hour. It had been raining for days before and our house was too small to have the ceremony inside. So Plan B was a white covering over the top of the garden. The weather cleared at the last minute so the covering was taken down, but many of the flowers were left in the house instead of brought into the garden. The waiters – who were supposed to move the flowers and serve hors d'oeuvres and champagne after the ceremony – wafted in an hour and a half late.

At Nick and Jess's wedding

A couple of key guests were also late, so we held our horses for them. If only I'd taken a horse tranquiliser. I had yet to master another quality of Lew's that was admirable – that of not being a jittery-fluttery wreck at your own wedding. I felt beside myself. Also beside me was Lew, who wasn't anxious at all, just blazingly happy. Despite all my flusterings, I was able to U-turn joyously into the part of our day where I became Lew's wife and he became my husband.

There is a heavy-duty reason why you should not be married at home. Our guests had arrived around noon and the last of them left around 11 pm. From 7 pm all I wanted to do was be alone with this glorious man … We should have booked a hotel for the night to sneak off to.

I guess it depends on how you look at things: either I have absolutely no skills in organising a wedding; or nobody stresses over a perfectly lovely wedding better than me. Mum told me it was the happiest wedding she'd ever been to. So there you go.

On our honeymoon, we travelled around enchanting Italy and stayed in sophisticated Paris. In Italy we went to Rome, Florence, Pisa, the Cinque Terre, Genoa, Ravenna and Venice. All places that Lew hadn't been to; all places that were ravishing and we loved. It was a tenderly miraculous time.

In Florence, we found a little hotel up four flights of stairs, unburdened by the pretensions of a lift. They had a tiny roof terrace. I had to forget any fear of heights and climb a narrow stairway on the outside of the building with a single thin rail only 50 centimetres high. You could see the non-bounceable paving five floors below. There were no chairs in this tiny space. Each evening we'd take a bottle of wine and two glasses, sit on our bottoms and, delighting in each other's company, watch the glowing sunset over the rich terracotta rooftops.

Lew and I blissed out on the dreamy Cinque Terre. We swam in the Mediterranean off a steep and rocky shore, giggled at the oiled sunbakers who took themselves so seriously, and took hot long walks from town to town through the steep and stepped vineyards. We were happily kissing on one of these walks, the Via dell'Amore, when a friendly American tourist called out, 'Get a room!' In this paradise I turned fifty. Lew had secretly brought a badge from Sydney saying '50' for me to wear that day.

In Vernazza, still damp from the sea, our dishevelled clothes over our swimmers, we wandered into a pretty church. A heavily pregnant beauty was rehearsing her exquisite singing for a wedding taking place that afternoon. Lew's eyes brimmed with tears at the loveliness of her voice resonating in the quiet of the church. In Manarola, we jumped off the huge, hot, black rocks into the clear, deep, dark water of the northern Italian Mediterranean. We weren't particularly fit or young or suntanned or bejewelled or wearing spectacular swimming costumes, nor were we stylish swimmers, but our delight in each other's company was heavenly.

Lew had a passion for train travel. We were leaving the Cinque Terre on a fast train to Genoa when he went looking for a glass of water and ended up in the sociable driver's cabin. He saw workmen scattering as the train raced in and out of black tunnels and along the bedazzling coastline. Lew's face was glowing with happiness when he returned.

I know Lew also adored Ravenna with those glittering Byzantine mosaics and its friendly inhabitants. And in Venice, we were walking down a too crowded laneway and another American tourist cried out, 'Oh my Gaad! It's Albert Einstein!' Lewy really liked that.

But he preferred Paris to Italy, where he shone with the happiest I'd ever seen him. Visiting the Parisian icons of the Arc de Triomphe, the Eiffel Tower and the Champs-Élysées captured his heart. He loved gargoyles and they were in abundance in Paris. He was bowled over by French cuisine and local wines. Our little hotel overlooked Notre-Dame Cathedral and the Seine. Lew would stand at the open French windows late each night, the lace curtains lightly billowing, a glass of red wine in his hand, a little park below us, and become a little teary, unable to believe his good fortune at being in Paris with his new wife.

It's a wonderful feeling knowing you are making someone very happy. I favoured Italy, but Lew's delight made me see Paris in a new light.

On our way home I asked him, 'What did you enjoy the most on our honeymoon?'

'The bonking!' he immediately said.

Which only goes to show, the best memories can be the least grand.

Lewy at the Louvre

After we'd returned to Sydney, we had a few days together before work began. That first morning, I woke up as Lew walked into the bedroom with a tray of toasted Turkish bread laden with fine slices of Italian goat's cheese and artichokes, and a pot of tea. He held that little feast he'd made for us with his head shyly tilted to one side and radiated me with his contentment.

Φ

Central and Northern Australia were just as magical. Hot, infinitely spacious, with incongruously tough and fragile landscapes that knock you out with their saturated beauty. In Kakadu and Arnhem Land, the delicate rock paintings dating from twenty thousand years ago by the Oenpelli Aborigines were outstanding.

We took many long and breathtaking walks in the Northern Territory and these were our favourites only by a whisker: exploring Nourlangie Rock at Kakadu, sauntering the rim of Kings Canyon, trekking the Valley of the Winds at Kata Tjuta, hiking to and around Ormiston Pound, and meandering the perimeter of Uluru.

Lew was so blown away by the scratchy-dried-lichen rain trails on Uluru that he said we should keep an ear out for when it was raining in that area and extravagantly jump on a plane and try to see it 'raining on the Rock'. Lew was like a human vacuum cleaner, sucking up each new experience with gusto. I produced a body of work from this trip, which filled an exhibition that I was delighted with.

Arnhem Land

Floating

Valley of the Winds

On another trip, we crisscrossed Spain and Morocco. Spain is a place I could live in. It's also a place to run away to. For these two decorative, colourful and sizzling countries and their peoples we fell. Completely under their spell.

Rory, a dear friend of Claudie's who lived in Madrid, made herself completely available to us. I'd done lots of homework on the cultural side of the city and Rory was glad to come and see these gems with us, and she knew lots of gorgeous restaurants that served extra good Spanish fare. Lew was in heaven and made little notes about the dishes so he could recreate them at home.

We bussed and trained our way around sunny Spain and it was like being on our honeymoon again. Barcelona, Toledo, Cuenca, Almagro, Jaén, Granada, Córdoba and Seville. We acquired vibrant ceramic jugs on our way and carried them in a small backpack. We took turns wearing it through airports and placed an expression on our faces that implied it was weightless.

In Almagro, we went looking for some notable sixteenth-century houses that had been built by prosperous townsfolk. Like most of the town's private homes, the outsides were fairly inscrutable – the usual beautiful curling ironwork on the lower windows, which were set in plain masonry walls a little bigger than in less wealthy homes. Only a subdued stone coat of arms above the front door indicated the importance of the dwelling. It was conspicuously different from the 'aren't we wealthy' outward display that you sometimes find in Australia.

One of the best feasts Lew and I had was in Barcelona. We bought fresh figs and imported French Camembert wrapped in straw from the famous La Boqueria market, plus a bottle of soft Spanish wine. We ate these delicacies picnicking on our bed in the hotel, grinning at each other on our own softest cloud nine.

In the last rooms of the Nazarene Palace, part of the Alhambra in Granada, Lew sang. The sounds resonated, bouncing off the stone paving, low arched roof and columns, taking on a life of their own. We looked at each other in amazement – a bubbling secret conversation with our eyes. Much of the happiness of our time together was made up of returned happily tender gawps.

We decided to go on a tour of Morocco rather than travel around independently. We met so many dear fellow passengers from all over the world that Lewy Have-a-Chat was in heaven. Like Hugh, he was completely at home striking up a conversation with new people.

One of the tour members asked our guide if there was much oil industry in Morocco? 'No, madame, fortunately there is not,' he replied with a knowing look.

Lew looking sheik

In the medina of Fès, where I was careful to avoid the snake charmers, we sensed medieval times, especially when visiting the tannery. We dawdled in the glorious cacti gardens of Jacques Majorelle in Marrakesh. Along the roads of the Middle and High Atlas Mountains we travelled, mesmerised by the spectacular scenery – ancient cedar forests, vast ranges peaked with snow, river panoramas, oases, date palms ready to harvest, lone shepherds tending their goat or sheep flocks, impressive kasbahs and minimal Berber tents. In the desert we rode a camel – which was bloody uncomfortable – saw wondrous fossils and sped along part of the Paris-Dakar Rally route in off-road vehicles, as if we were in a Toyota advertisement. We relished flavourful seasonal fruits and vegetables and the smiling friendly Moroccans. And again Lewy was sometimes teary with delight.

We adored Morocco. I have two words for that Muslim country – GO THERE!

Morocco

We also had, thank goodness, a relaxed holiday halfway up the New South Wales coast, at Trial Bay, not far from Kempsey.

'But there's nothing to do here,' Lew said.

How much did I savour showing him how to do 'nothing' – bushwalking, enjoying the fauna and stunted flora of the coastal headland and its magnificent 360-degree views, and swimming in the huge unpopulated and sheltered bay.

We walked up to the historic lighthouse, gazed at the unguarded sea fringed by empty beaches, had great coffees at Trial Bay Kiosk or at nearby South West Rocks, and visited many pretty little towns around and about, delighting in the flourishing countryside of the mighty Macleay River.

We stayed upstairs in a historic house, drinking tea on our iron-roofed veranda, which was nestled in huge oak trees, elderly frangipanis and poinciana trees. And hanging in the air all around us was birdsong.

The works I created from this holiday were not so successful and I didn't exhibit them. I eventually painted over all but one – a vivid reminder of an enchanting landscape.

Lew was a joy to travel with. Of course mostly we saw the sights with raring-to-go enthusiasm, but he was also an animated shopper, buying gifts for friends, souvenirs, clothes and postcards. He wrote with thoughtful concentration of the wonders he was seeing. I'd slap together a few words coasting on the beauty of the postcard. He'd send a postcard to Jack the butcher in our street whom he liked, who supplied the munificent meats for Lew's barbeques. Had Lew's father been alive, he and Jack would have been similar in age.

In Paris, Lew bought the best bright red trousers to wear with his yellow T-shirt. He was just as generous to me. I have so many lush presents from Lew. It was a pleasure for me to shower him with gifts too.

Luminous memories from our new life stockpiled rapidly. The present was a joy. I'm hugely grateful that we dived into life and relished all the delight to be found.

At the end of January 2009, Claudie moved from Sydney to Melbourne to study for three years. We held a heavenly farewell party for her one summery evening. Dishes of delicacies, wines, perfect weather, family, Claudie's friends and mine who were close to her. Captivatingly patterned dresses and laughter. Lew looked marvellous. He had an innate sense of what colours suited him – a quality much appreciated by a painter. My darling husband had bedecked our tiny garden with candled lanterns, softly glowing and shimmering in the darkness.

My art school friend Barbara said to me the next day, 'My God, Lewis sitting there last night, I've never seen such a happy man.'

Uphill

I was now working two shifts a week at a Returned and Services League (RSL) club. Australian RSL clubs were created in 1916 for the welfare of Australians serving or who have served in the Army, Navy or Air Force. It's also a social club that includes folk with no military background. You can catch up for a meal or a drink, sit all afternoon in the lounge escaping the heat or the cold and read a book, enjoy lawn bowls, a game of pool, snooker or darts, play bingo, enter the meat raffles, join in the trivia quizzes, hear lots of live music, dance or play the ubiquitous poker machines. Friday and Saturday nights can be full-on with plenty of young people socialising.

Over the years I've met some striking Second World War, Korean and Vietnam veterans who belonged to the Sub-Branch of the RSL. Jim, aged ninety-five, told me with tears in his eyes about his comrade who, alongside him, survived ghastly years as a prisoner of the Japanese, only to discover that his wife back home had thought him dead and was remarried with children. Tom, ninety, who fought for the liberation of France during the Second World War was awarded the Legion of Honour some seventy years later. Wal's wartime horrors – surviving the construction of the Thai-Burma railway and the Japanse prisoner of war camps associated with it, twice being bombed out of POW ships into the Pacific Ocean, enforced labour camps in a freezing Japan and the subsequent firestorms there created by Allied bombings – were extraordinary. And I recall one

Second World War veteran with the softest eyes, who never marched on Anzac Day, nor belonged to the Sub-Branch, because he needed to forget his experiences.

I've seen middle-aged daughters, year after year, be incredibly kind to their aged parents, and very rarely I've seen horrible impatient family members with their frail relatives. You may see sneaky seventeen year olds trying to pose as eighteen year olds. Sometimes when I've greeted elderly people and asked them how their day's been so far, they'll say, oh we're exhausted, we've just been to see Mum. Mum must be a hundred and seven. Some years ago, a gentleman who was ninety-nine joined the club with a five-year membership. He lasted until he was almost one hundred and two.

Although politically the RSL organisation is a conservative bunch, there's a warmth and kindness in these varied, dear and interesting people and it's a treat to know them. Rarely do you have a nasty customer, but when it does happen it's like a slap in the face and an excruciating workout in not saying what you really think.

Φ

I arrived home frayed at 2 am after a full-on Friday night at work. On Saturday morning, Lewy and I were curled up together, sleeping in. The phone was ringing in the kitchen and Lew went to answer it.

He came back with the phone and stood next to me on the side of the bed near the two tall windows. It was his doctor calling with the results of a biopsy of a lump under his left armpit. The lump had appeared five years before and at that time Lew had an ultrasound and a biopsy. No sign of cancer. His GP had told him it was up to him whether he wanted to have it removed or not. Lew decided to leave it. Why have unnecessary surgery? Then in July 2008 he felt it change and he went back to his doctor. The doctor requested another ultrasound. The ultrasound report said that the lump was actually slightly smaller. At that time Lewy's doctor said it didn't appear to have changed so there was no need to do anything. Lew didn't agree with the report but thought these people must know what they're talking about.

Now, Lewy was quite still, his face didn't give away much, he spoke just the occasional acknowledgement. My mind was pitching with unease. After he hung up I asked him, 'What did the doctor say?'

He said in a deliberate and un-Lewy way, 'The pathology of the biopsy showed a squamous secondary cancer and that the primary was a skin cancer.'

I didn't know what primary or secondary cancer meant, let alone squamous. We were shocked. What do you say to that information?

At first we agreed to see the doctor on Monday, but then I said, 'I think we should go now and find out what we need to do.'

Lewy hadn't been aware of any skin cancer or melanoma; he had beautiful skin, always wore an Akubra hat and was proud of his ability to cover up under the sun. He was rattled by his doctor's phone call, and my sudden change of mind didn't help, especially as we had to get out the door fast as his GP, who was far away, would be closing soon.

Lew's doctor said he was very sorry and gave him a referral to a specialist. It was Saturday 7th February 2009, and so smothered were we by this awful news that we hardly registered the appalling bushfires in Victoria that day.

The specialist Lew was referred to was brilliant. He was all you could hope for in a cancer surgeon: caring, informative and available – no deadpan detachment there. Let's call him Dr Kindheart. On Monday I called to make an appointment for Lew; he said he would see us that same day. I picked up Lew from a job he was working on and off we went to see Dr Kindheart, taking Lewy's referral and entering a huge unknown.

The specialist couldn't find anything on Lew's skin. We were told that it's possible for a primary squamous skin cancer to never be found, or to have disappeared and then resurface as a secondary.

Significantly we were told that the lump under his armpit should have been removed five years ago, and that it shouldn't have been an optional decision.

Dr Kindheart scheduled Lew to have all sorts of tests and a scan of his head and upper body that day to try and find the primary site and to see if the cancer had spread to anywhere else. When a secondary appears, it apparently usually means the primary cancer is or was in that half of the body.

Just to be thorough, Lew went to see a skin specialist he'd seen a few years earlier and asked him to check him again, but he couldn't find anything either.

Lew was booked in for an operation to remove his tumour on 4th March. He was a public patient and Dr Kindheart had a list of patients to operate on at a large public hospital. Lew would have to wait three weeks and three days for his operation.

I blurted out, 'But that is so far away!'

Dr Kindheart replied, 'I know. I have a list of public patients who are scheduled for their operations. Sometimes my list is cancelled and my patients have to wait even longer. I can't stand it when that happens.'

I suggested, 'We have some savings. Would it make a difference if we paid for the operation to be earlier at the private hospital?'

'I don't believe it would make a difference,' he said.

The initial scans gave no clue as to where the primary was, but some nodes in Lew's chest looked suspicious so they gave him a different scan for those. This PET scan revealed Lew had had a fractured vertebra high up in his spine.

Dr Kindheart asked how he'd done it, and Lew explained that in April 1983 he'd had a bad car accident south of Goulburn in his Buick, and his neck and back had given him grief for a long while afterwards. When he complained to the doctor he'd been seeing at the time, he'd sneered, 'Are you after compo?' so Lew left it at that. I have no idea who that doctor was, but I would like to tell him those results.

Fortunately the lymph nodes in Lew's chest were only minorly suspect, so a separate biopsy on them was planned for when he was in hospital. Radiation therapy would begin a month later, when his wound had healed.

The waiting was awful. I wish Lew had had the operation sooner.

When I look back, I hear those well-worn words by Dickens: *It was the best of times, it was the worst of times* … You can say cancer is malevolent, but from the moment Lew was first diagnosed our relationship became magical.

We had always adored each other and it was fun just being together, enhanced no doubt by that feeling of freedom when the last offspring has left home. If I were unexpectedly late, Lew would be in the front garden waiting for me, and vice versa. How divine was that? Whenever I arrived home, my heart would hop to see his navy blue car, ladder perched on top, parked outside. He was my dearest best friend.

But now everything was heightened. Everything we did together – buying flowers from extravagantly colourful scent-filled florists, rambling walks, the endless generous sky that watched over us, never indifferent I believe with its changing exhibition of clouds, soft frothy coffees, hot breakfasts whose enticing aromas lazed in our kitchen (I became a vivacious short-order cook), burbling banter, dear and empathetic friends, many a kindness and sweet kisses – were bathed in a beautiful luminosity.

Lew had always been good at living in the moment, and somehow those moments really shone. It was a radiant time.

Flowers and Scallop Shells

Denial

Strangely, Lew looked healthy. Thick, curly silvery-white hair, golden skin, a great appetite and a lovely naughty twinkle in his blue eyes. However he wasn't sleeping well. He had a permanent fever and he felt hot to cuddle. Some nights he was dripping in sweat even though the weather wasn't hot. He was often tired, working most days, but just short days. He never complained. It was only when I asked that he quietly told me. Gradually I realised he didn't like to be asked, so I learnt to be sparing with my enquiries. We took each day as it came, and of course he was being spoilt rotten.

Lew began to experience pain under his arm. At first he swallowed paracetamol, but that wasn't strong enough. We rang Dr Kindheart, who said go to the doctor for some stronger prescription painkillers. They helped. Lew was able to sleep and was less uncomfortable, but the increasing pain scared us because it possibly meant that what was under his arm was growing rapidly.

We saw the specialist three times before the operation and he too thought the tumour was growing, but said it wasn't long now until the operation. We kept forgetting to ask the doctor questions because we were so stunned. I noticed that when the doctor questioned Lew he would sometimes answer with something unrelated. This was big stuff. I could see Lew was rocked by what was happening, as normally he was a great listener. I realised the obvious: you need someone with you when you have tests and meetings, because between the two of you, you can piece together what was said. And nothing would have kept me away from these appointments.

A secondary cancer diagnosis with an unknown primary is grim news for anyone. Lew wasn't asking questions, but I'd read denial wasn't a problem as long as it didn't stop a patient from having the right treatment. In fact, denial gave a person time to come to terms with their illness. This was Lew's illness and he could deal with it however he liked, and as far as we knew he was having all the right treatment.

I looked up a few things on the internet about cancer with an unknown primary and didn't like what I saw. I didn't talk to Lew, or my friends, about what I'd read. Something inside of me wouldn't believe it. I put it in a file in my head marked *Do Not Open*. It was hard for me to face the truth as well.

Lew was overloaded by his diagnosis and needed time to deal with it. It was such a shock. I understood this, but felt concerned that he hadn't told his family he was seriously ill. His youngest brother, Andrew, had died suddenly at forty. The damage done to him in a serious motorbike accident when he was twenty had shortened his life considerably.

I emailed Lew's younger brother, Tim, who lived in the country, and told him what had been happening. He was very uneasy and took the time to email a cancer specialist he'd known from high school. He agreed with the advice we'd been given about Lew waiting for his operation.

Then I emailed Lew's Mum, who also lives in the country, and let her know about Lew's health. She was reassuring and bought him some new pyjamas for his hospital stay. She planned to visit him in hospital the week after the operation.

Apart from one other time in July, emailing his family were the only times I went against Lewy's wishes. When I told him what I'd done, he appeared relieved that they knew. He just didn't want any emotional conversations at the moment.

At our last visit to the specialist before the operation, Dr Kindheart mentioned that Lew would lose some muscle tissue around his arm, which in turn would affect his arm's mobility.

After the appointment, Lew was so positive, but I felt shattered. I went to do the weekly shop for my parents. My Mum hadn't been well, and Dad no longer drove. Claudie was having trouble getting a job in Melbourne so I wanted to send some money to her, and I was struggling to find a birthday present for Hugh. I attended to everything, but secretly I wanted to forget about everyone else and just hold Lew. Tight.

From our friends there was an outpouring of kindness: they offered to help Lew in any way that was needed. Helen and Fred, Claudie's godparents, took us to dinner at our favourite northern Chinese restaurant at Ashfield. Helen is the older sister I never had and she has always looked after my well-being. She is the listener from heaven. We met in Drummoyne, and our children were babies together.

We had a wonderful evening. They asked Lew how he was going with his illness.

He said, 'Well, it looks like I'm going to win the Big Screen TV Battle.'

He wanted one of those large flat-screen televisions, and previously I'd been against it. Now, what baby wants, baby gets.

Because day-to-day life was so tender, I wasn't fearful for the future.

Two Operations And Two Friends

On 4th March, Lew went to the hospital just before 7 am. We were told to be there at that time, eat nothing, etc. He wasn't wheeled off to surgery for another six hours. We watched everyone else go and I started to panic, knowing that if he wasn't operated on today it would be another week to wait, if not more. Finally Lew was taken away.

Around 4 pm Dr Kindheart came and spoke to me. 'The tumour was large, the size of a small football, and was growing around Lewis's nerves and veins. That's why he was having so much pain. I've also removed the underarm lymph nodes. I believe I've taken out most of the tumour, but there are microscopic traces left attached to the veins that I was unable to remove. If I took the veins out, his arm would be significantly affected.'

I said, 'I don't think Lew would mind that.'

'I'm afraid it wouldn't make any difference to his long-term prognosis.'

'Oh no, this is really serious,' I said. And a huge clunk fell through my body, like the dreams I'd had of the vast unexpected drop of an elevator.

Dr Kindheart then said, 'I wanted to talk with you. Lewis isn't asking any of the questions he should be … That's okay … He's entitled to deal with this in the way he wants, but one of you should have a realistic knowledge of the situation.'

I started to cry as the dear doctor told me the seriousness of Lew's cancer.

'Because it's a secondary cancer it's just a matter of time before it reappears somewhere else … I'm sorry …'

I replied, 'I've been desperately hoping the fevers, sweating and tiredness were related to a lymphatic primary cancer and not secondaries?'

The doctor said, 'The way the cancer has grown around the veins and nerves indicates secondary cancer. Primary lymphatic cancer pushes away the nerves and veins …'

'How long does Lewy have?' I asked.

'Lewis probably has two years to live …'

I remember most things that happened with Lew, but I can't remember much of this conversation from here on. Only that the doctor took me into a quiet room and was hugely kind. I was sobbing and he stayed with me for a long time and said any questions I had he would answer. He said Lew struck him as one of those 'top blokes'. After a lengthy time and when there was no more talking, he said he had to go and do another operation.

I stayed in that room for a while, and then I called my neighbour at work because I was worried about Molly – for goodness sake. Who would look after her, as I wouldn't be home until late? Poor Liz – apparently I was hysterical. She asked me whether I had someone to pick me up from the hospital because I shouldn't drive in that state, and said that she'd look after the dog.

When I returned to the almost empty waiting room, another patient's wife said, 'Are you all right?'

I said, 'I've had the worst news about my husband who is only fifty-three.'

She said, 'My husband had a stroke at thirty-six and is now seventy-two. That's a tragedy because I've had to look after him all that time.'

Fuck off, I silently thought as I walked away.

I called Barbara, who lived sort of near the hospital, and asked if her husband could drop her off and would she be able to drive me home in my car later that evening? And then out in a little garden I called Mum and Dad. I tried to explain what was happening, but I began to cry again and ended up incoherent. Poor Mum. And Dad. Barbara arrived. How lucky I was to have such a great friend.

I asked at the nurses' station several times if Lew was out of recovery.

'No,' they said. 'We'll let you know.'

Finally I said, 'Please will you check again?'

And they said, 'Oh yes, he's been out for about an hour.' The dour sister who told me that could have made an effortless career move to the prison system.

When Barbara and I found Lew, he wasn't looking ghastly, nor dead or gone, but sitting up in bed smiling at me, looking vulnerable and kissable. With his white hospital gown and white curls, he was a picture of a cruising happy angel.

I said, 'I've been worried about you, how are you?'

He looked a little shyly embarrassed as if he had been causing too much trouble. 'I'm fine,' he gently said.

The next day, Lew's aunt and a favourite cousin, Gabrielle, visited. His Mum and brother were driving down from the country and would be arriving soon. Lew began to sweat, became agitated and started vomiting, which we couldn't stop. So I called his Mum and brother and asked them to come later. I've always been a sympathetic vomiter, but Lew being sick didn't worry me.

The ward was closed so patients could rest, so I left a calmer Lew to sleep and went down to the lobby. His cousin Guy was there, along with Lew's Mum and brother Tim. We sat and chatted in those large, soft, enveloping chairs until the wards were reopened.

My days were spent with Lew at the hospital, chatting, listening, buying newspapers and fruit juices, and watching him enjoy his visitors. He had a tube coming out of a large neat wound in his side, which drained into a container. Several friends had recommended that a positive attitude, the conviction that he could successfully fight his cancer, was important. Lew was optimistic, and I was fiercely strong and positive for him.

He dozed sometimes and then I'd read *Harry Potter*. I love to read, but my concentration was shot, so these books were a gentle escape for me.

The nurses were appallingly overworked and Lew was sorry for them. He told me that one night an elderly man in the bed opposite had been buzzing the nurses for ages as he needed to go to the toilet. Finally he couldn't wait any more. As he left his bed, he started to fall. The nurse who'd just arrived caught him, and was in tears because she was so stretched and the patient had almost had a nasty accident.

'Can you bring in a big box of biscuits from Pasticceria Papa at Haberfield for the nurses?' he asked me.

'That would be a pleasure, treasure!'

Lew had the best yellow leather slippers he'd bought at the Marrakesh markets in Morocco. He had some cool pyjama pants and asked me to bring in a T-shirt, then insisted we sneak out to the Thai restaurant over the road from the hospital and have some real food, albeit at the sophisticated nursing-home hour of 5 pm. He hid his hideous full-of-red-liquid drain in a green shopping bag by his side. He was determined to escape. It was fun, but I was expecting a disciplinary hand on my shoulder at any time.

Two days later, my darling boy had another operation to check the suspicious lymph nodes in his chest, as that was where the cancer was likely to spread. I reminded the nurses to put on his pressure stockings as they wheeled him off. The hospital staff were so overworked that you really had to keep an eye on the patient. I had cancelled work as I wanted to wait until Lew came out of surgery, hang out with him, make sure he had his painkillers and anything else he needed. And he was lovely to just sit with.

After his surgery, Lew looked so defenceless. I felt an overwhelming surge of love for him. He was running a temperature and looking a bit flushed, which the nurse said was not unusual after two lots of surgery.

Dr Kindheart came and spoke to us and said the results would be in in five days. He wasn't sure when Lew would be going home. They still had to keep eye on the drain from his underarm wound. Possibly he could go home in a few days' time.

That night was Hughie's birthday. I didn't go to the celebrations. I needed some stillness and was worried I would start crying. When I arrived home, my always kindly neighbour Liz popped in and asked me to have dinner with them. I wasn't up to eating, but we had some drinks together and I came home.

Molly-Dog sat with me as I replied to most-welcome supportive emails and wrote group emails to let family and friends know where Lew was up to.

EMAIL to Lew's Mum and brother: Just wanted to let you guys know that I am overwhelmed with good wishes for Lewy. At least twelve messages a day from the phone and about the same on email. So many people love that Lewy, it is very heart-warming! Thanks again for driving all that way to see him ...

EMAIL to Prue who lives in Rome: Thank you adorable girl, have printed that out. These are the ones [from the list Prue sent] we eat all the time: avocados, carrots, chillies, garlic, green leafy veggies, mushrooms, pawpaw, red wine and rosemary. Will add others to list. Your dear mum rang with best wishes. Do you remember how much she used to laugh when we were being silly? Love ya.

Later that night, overtired and home alone, a wave of desperation swamped me and I cried and cried.

Φ

EMAIL from Prue: I've been busy and I didn't check my emails for ages. Did you need to emotionally throw up on me? Next time I promise to check more often. Hope you're OK? Love you. P

EMAIL to Prue: I went to bed, best place for me, feeling good this morning. Sorry about that, darling. Fabe xxxxxxxxxxxxxxxxxxxx xxxxxxxxxxxxxxxxxxxxxxxxxxxxxx

Home Again

On Sunday I called Lew from work only to find … he'd called Barbara and asked if she could pick him up and bring him home. He was meant to stay in hospital a bit longer, but he didn't like it there at all. Unbeknownst to Lew I'd organised for Pete and Kerry to visit him in hospital because I couldn't be there that day. Lew had often said to me communication is everything. But it was so good to have him home, especially for Lewy.

He was happily reading a hideous biography about a Mafia hit man that one of his friends had lent him. A slight contrast to the first *Harry Potter* book I'd bought him. He managed his drain by placing it in a bag attached to his belt, and looked a bit like a gay man with bad taste in man bags. The wheat grass that a friend had recommended we plant was growing well; and our house had plenty of veggies as always. And we were overwhelmed by kindness and good wishes.

The following day, Lewy was about to have his first shower at home. Our shower is over the bath, and I was standing next to him because he'd had two anaesthetics in the last six days. He told me I was fussing and he was fine. I turned around to walk away and he lost his balance and fell over in the shower and fractured a rib. A broken rib is very painful, but luckily only when you breathe or move … It was awful. As if the drain and the large and small wounds weren't enough.

We found a new GP, as Lew didn't want to go back to the one

he'd been seeing for years. The doctor said the bone hadn't separated and there was nothing to be done for a fractured rib except rest and take prescription painkillers in order to breathe deeply to avoid a chest infection.

Lewy had a lot of pain from his rib. It was such bad luck. I went to a nearby hospital and hired a bench that sat firmly on top of the bath, and bought a hand-held hose to attach to the bath tap. Lew would be safe now.

His night sweating was getting worse, which was perhaps a reaction to painkillers, although lovely fresh sheets each day were a bonus. I ended up with a lousy cold that had me dragging my feet, but it kept me quiet, which was also a bonus.

One night, when Lew was cooking for the first time since hospital, Liz dropped in. There was Lew, his Italian apron covering his drain, cooking a homemade pesto sauce and marinated chicken with wholemeal pasta, and I was sitting there doing nothing. I tried to say I'd been making three gorgeous meals a day for that man, but it didn't look good.

A much appreciated part of Lew's convalescence was having the Home Nursing Service come to our place each day. They were kind, and never made you feel they were rushed or busy. Their chats and friendliness gave Lew a hefty boost, and their visits took the pressure off me as I was nervous about dealing with the wound and drain that Lew took in his stride. Our favourite was Gake, who lit up our home whenever she came. She was a champion!

Lew's drain became blocked sometimes, and it was easier said than done going all the way back to the Emergency Department of the hospital where he'd had his operations for an unblockage. We lived in the Near West of Sydney and that hospital was in the Far East.

Φ

In the past, emailing had been an instant and enjoyable way of keeping in touch with overseas family and friends, but now there was a shift. It became an indispensable communicator with friends, often simultaneously, letting them know how Lew was.

Sometimes I was emotionally heaving, and composing emails to those who cared about us helped me to make sense of the latest news. I could consider my words in my own time, which was usually at the end of the day. It was a contradiction of desperately wanting to connect with and hear from friends, but needing a calm space around me.

EMAIL to my English cousin Sue (who had spent some time in America): He is a gazillion times happier at home than in hospital of course. We've had a few hiccups and had to go back to hospital, but he's here now. Had a wonderful laugh when you said you were all rooting for us. In Australia this word has only two meanings: one is that you are completely exhausted, i.e. rooted; the other is ... When we hear Americans are rooting for their team we can only admire their stamina!

Not What We Thought

We turned up to see Dr Kindheart for a post-op check-up and to find out the test results. Lew looked a bit tired, sore and not such a fabulous colour, but otherwise his same cruisey self with a hearty appetite.

Unexpectedly, the pathology results for Lew's large tumour said that his secondary cancer was not related to a skin cancer, but may be related to stomach or bowel cancer. The three lymph nodes in his chest that they took out were clear!

So another round of tests began. Lew prepared for an endoscopy and a colonoscopy.

The stomach and bowel surgeon asked him to bring a list of any medications he was using. When Lew also mentioned some naturopathic medicines he was taking, the delightful doctor said, 'I don't want to know about that crap.'

> *EMAIL to Barbara: After stomach doc appointment we waited two hours in Emergency to have Lew's blocked drain cleared and later another three-quarters of an hour to have the doc sign off. Then we went to the vet and waited forty-five minutes to pick up the cat as the vet wanted to talk to me. Because I was stressed he explained … s l o w l y … the problem … with the … cat. Meanwhile Lew is waiting in the car. You can only guess at my suppressed stress … Bought a bottle of sparkling on the way home. Liz dropped in to say keep the cat box as long as we need*

it, meanwhile huge furry cat has weed in the box, jumped out when we arrived home, and floor, box and cat are all saturated. I'm thinking who needs a glass? Will drink straight from bottle … Had a great five-lap wobbly walk with Molly around the outside of oval …

Lew was on a fluids-only diet for a few days before these investigations. He accidentally ate a piece of lettuce after all the special liquids he'd been taking. I couldn't believe how outwardly cross and secretly furious I felt about a piece of lettuce. Poor Lew.

So another, this time mild anaesthetic, and absolutely no complaints from Lew.

Dr Kindheart had said there was a five to ten percent chance they wouldn't be able to find the primary source, and we thought, *well, if they don't, at least there'll be no more operations.* This is not a good way to think. Cancer treatment is much more effective if they know the primary.

You could describe me as a woman who likes to daydream at home drinking tea. Family, career and life are draped over this fundamental me. The pattern of our days became a sequence of zigzags. We went east, west and north to four hospitals six times in six days. This crisscrossing became more frequent, and there were fewer and fewer spaces on the cloth of our lives as my tea-drinking days drew to a close.

EMAIL to Claudie: Hi darling, how's it all going? How's the new job? Have you made new friends? How's Simon? I went to visit Hugh the other day and was so sad I couldn't drop in and say hello to you too! Saw Nick for about an hour last night. I was too tired to stay longer. He's such a gem, hard to believe he's thirty. We gave him a huge fabulous cactus with big pretty umber and white pebbles around the bottom. And a card made by Gwyn Perkins. He looks adorable and calm as always and Jess looks great too. Please let me know your latest when you have time. A family group email?

We saw a naturopath again as Lew has had three general anaesthetics and will have burns from radiation, etc, so we thought we'd try a bit of

> *alternative therapy. I told the naturopath I drank about four cups of tea a day (actually it's probably more). She looked horrified. Gosh, you'd have thought I'd said heroin not tea! I feel so sorry for Lew and it's hard not to fuss. He's lost some mobility in his arm and will lose more from radiation. His colour is a bit odd.*
>
> *Please email me your news – I need cheering up. Hope you're OK?*

Φ

Gradually, Lew's wounds were healing and his drain was drying up. Two weeks and two days after the first operation we went to a different hospital to see the radiation professor – let's call him Professor Hopeful – to learn about the radiation procedure. Professor Hopeful was capable and thorough without the deeply caring manner of Dr Kindheart.

The professor warned Lew that radiation could affect his teeth. Lew's teeth had never been that good. He organised a check-up and some treatments with his dentist before radiation began on 6th April for six weeks.

> *EMAIL to Tim and Lew's Mum: Drain has gone. It kept getting blocked. My darling Dad who is hard of hearing said why don't we call a plumber?*

The result for Lew's bowel test was all clear. A couple of areas in his stomach were biopsied and the results would be available in a few days. The doctor believed the results were more than likely to be okay.

This was all good news, but we still didn't know the primary.

Confidence

I was feeling optimistic, but sometimes there would be a catch in my throat. In the night I would snuggle up to Lew and he'd make the loveliest sounds in his sleep. I'd think, *I am so lucky*. We took each day as it came and we made the most of them.

We went to the hospital clinic for Lew to have some tiny tattoos for the radiation treatment. He showed the specialist how high he could move his left arm – straight up – and I nearly burst into tears. I'd been thinking that I should be badgering him to move it more, because he would lose some mobility after radiation, and he'd been quietly doing his exercises unbeknownst to me. We were tickled pink.

That night we had a silly, happy walk with Molly, a fun drink with our neighbours Liz and Graham, and then a great healthy dinner. Our perfect day was topped off by lots of emails splashed with good wishes and a couple of recipes.

Life was strangely sweet and tender, and Lew was a champion for never complaining. We were bumbling along very happily.

> *EMAIL to Lew's family: Lew will see the stomach specialist again tomorrow. We had the loveliest day today. We went to see the movie Dean Spanley at Leichhardt, which was endearingly terrific, and then had a delicious Italian lunch at Newtown. Lewy's gone off to Medicare and I'm doing a bit of a clean-up. I'd say a top day!*

Lew had the finest of qualities to live with. He was always so relaxed. He'd walk into a room with a dear expectant smile on his face. He gave off the most easygoing energy that filled our house with contentment. He criticised me once, saying my only fault was that I didn't like seafood (there's no doubt love is blind), which was no mean feat in itself, and he loved me for who I am. It was especially easy to be devoted to him. Effortless.

Φ

I was managing to paint. I was looking forward to staying at Uluru as an Artist in Residence for the month of November. As well as the residency, you had to bring a large amount of work, which would be exhibited and hopefully sold during your stay. I'd been working in my studio for this residency for some time and had more than half the works completed.

Between Kata Tjuta and Uluru

Central Australia had been so inspiring, it was a pleasure creating new works. Fragile floras on a background of richly pigmented soil. Ancient weathered rocks protruding from a landscape where the climate was harsh and evidence of humans was minimal. I was using glowing watercolours, black ink and crayon on heavy watercolour paper.

> *EMAIL to Barbara: Thanks for your email, Babs. My painting's going well. Have started this rousing-so-far picture of casuarinas at Uluru. Plenty of time for it to skew off in the wrong direction ...*
>
> *We took a beautiful walk along the curly Glebe foreshore with Molly today. Tonight Lew cooked a delicious dinner of lush baked veggies swathed in garlic and rosemary. He's such a treasure and never complains, but to me he's looking quite tired. I'm so hoping docs, life, etc are wrong, would really like to go next year with Lew to the south of France ... He loved Paris so much, I think he'd be very happy in the south ...*

> *EMAIL to Claudie: Lewy had his first radiation treatment today ... He's such a champion. Gosh those nurses were kind and considerate ...*
>
> *We arrived in separate cars as he came from work and I came from painting. I was blowing him kisses when we stopped at traffic lights on the way home. He looked like the responsible one. I looked like an idiot. Only twenty-seven treatments to go. The MRI in three months is the important one ...*

Lew's night sweats had stopped, thank goodness, which enabled him to sleep and feel better. He was working in the mornings and radiation was in the afternoon. Each zap was quite quick. He planned to work for as long as he could. Because radiation caused cumulative tiredness, maybe in a few weeks it would be harder for him.

I only went to some of these treatments, and while Lew was at work and busy I was painting. Things were looking up.

> *EMAIL to Lew's Mum: Lewy's going well ... He's working on Sat and Sun on a student film. On Sat I'm going to see a film of the Royal*

Ballet's version of Beatrix Potter as I've a strong desire to see dancing frogs. Have a great safe trip to US! Have put a blanket on the bed, so yes it is cooler. March is still my favourite month. Even though all this has been pretty gruelling, especially for Lew, it's also been a very loving time when all good moments seem extra good …

Ire

EMAIL to Lew's family, mine, Prue and Kerry: Having a grim time. Lew has a lump the size of an egg where he had the tumour removed. He felt it on Sunday. Rang doc on Monday – public holiday! So saw radiation doctor and professor of radiology Tuesday. They checked it out and will check again on Friday to see if size changes. We always knew tiny amounts were left after the op. Professor says at best it could be a swelling of fluid as so much tissue was removed. We are seeing Dr Kindheart on Thursday morning. Very stressful ... Lewy of course is pretty together. My heart is heavy ...

Normally we were such a chatty pair. There was nothing to say as fear slunk in.

At last Thursday came and we were so thankful to see Dr Kindheart. He recommended an ultrasound, which Lew had straight away. He said they wouldn't do a biopsy because of the risk of infection with the ongoing radiation.

Unfortunately, the ultrasound looked sinister and it was recommended to immediately do a biopsy, which was done. The results would be available in twenty-four to thirty-six hours. We were full of dread.

The biopsy results were not good for the lump that had returned under Lew's arm six days into radiation. So they increased the level of radiation and also gave it to him twice a day, early morning and last thing in the afternoon for seven days, which was spread over two weeks. After that there would be five more single treatments. Radiation would now finish earlier than originally planned, because of the increased intensity. A CT scan was booked to see if the cancer had spread any further.

During this time, I was reminded that there is always someone else worse off. When Lew was having his radiation treatment, twice I saw, silent in the background, a tall man who was being treated for cancer of the face. A more pitiless disfiguring disease I've not seen.

> *EMAIL to Cousin Sue, Granada Jane and Helen: So in two weeks they'll operate again to remove the tumour. It's scary because it has grown back so fast, which means it's a very aggressive form of cancer. I have to say I feel quite aggressive myself. Lew is his usual self, enjoying one day at a time, with his beautiful smile. Thanks for asking …*

Well, Lew wasn't his usual self.

We were meeting Barbara at Newtown on Saturday for lunch and to see the award-winning film *Tulpan*, which was set in Kazakhstan. Rattled about Lew's latest news and tired from Friday night at work, I was driving like a fool. In one of those narrow back streets of Newtown I managed to jam the car's wheels against the footpath. An oncoming car couldn't pass and the car behind me was also trapped. Lew said he'd hop out and tell me which way to turn the wheel as I couldn't work it out. The other car was beeping.

Lew jumped out and they thought he wanted to fight them. The passenger leapt out to threaten Lewy, who completely lost it and threatened him back in a most ridiculously aggressive way, as if he didn't care that this imposing Polynesian could come to blows with him. The man backed off, somehow I unstuck the wheels, and if we hadn't been meeting Barbs for lunch I would have shakily driven home, leaving Lew there, it had been so ugly. There was a large Saturday audience to all this and I was mortified.

Finally I got a grip and managed to park, and we joined Barbs for lunch. I was shattered and Lew was utterly unnerved by what had overtaken him.

When I spoke to Dr Kindheart about it a few days later, he looked extra directly at me and gently said, 'Of course Lewis has every reason to be really angry.'

> *EMAIL from Barbara: I always have a great time with you – no need to be sorry for anything on Saturday – except for that so called 'joyful' film! Two of my former neighbours both work for the Cancer Council – and one survived bad breast cancer a few years ago. Think I'll have a talk with her about how to support. With Lewy on Saturday after such bad news, I didn't know whether to talk about it, or just try to take one's mind away from it for a brief period. This is such a punishing time for both of you and I wish I could help/make it all better. Sounds perfectly reasonable and a normal reaction to vent anger into a road rage mode – and he must need to express anger I should imagine.*
>
> *The sun is shining and everything is revealed as layered with dust! Ho hum! Take special care of yourself and love to you both …*

> *EMAIL to Barbara: Thanks Babsie, I'm angry too … Can't imagine how we'll be if more turns up in CT? … The most reliable thing to turn up in the universe … DUST! Torn between cleaning everything in sight and not giving a damn about the mess …*

A cruel side effect of the high doses of radiation, apart from the cumulative tiredness, were the burns Lew received on his shoulder and chest. They were painful, but the burn in his armpit was splitting, raw and horrid. Twice a day the clinic put a layer of sorbolene over all this and let it sit for twenty minutes, then gently removed it and put on two treatment creams, Jelonet, a padded dressing and a sort of stretchy netting that fitted over Lew's chest and kept it all in place. Much to Lew's delight, this netting was made from revamped women's undies – of a style, in my Brief Experience, I'd never seen before.

He really liked these becoming nurses doing this treatment for him. We were told that after the radiation treatment ended, the burns would continue to worsen, like an internal microwave.

On weekends, when there was no radiation treatment, we again had the capable Home Nursing Service visiting us. The areas the nurses visited were rotated and this time Lew particularly liked Matt. Lew would have his shower, dress to the waist, and then in our cosy and steamy yellow bathroom that smelt of soapy freshness I would gently put a thick layer of sorbolene on his burns. Despite the circumstances I could see Lew really enjoyed this. Then a clean towel more than dampened in warm water went over his back and chest, and a small warm damp towel was placed in his armpit. I put a large, hot, clean, dry towel over that, and Lew would sit in the living room by the heater with a cup of tea. Half an hour later, the home nurse would arrive, take it all off and carefully dress the burns.

These visits, (which became daily after radiation finished) were such a help, both practically and emotionally. We enjoyed the nurses' calls, and as a result of this support I was never burdened by my responsibilities. A couple of times a sweet young female nurse arrived to do the dressings and I could see Lew was pretty chuffed.

Unfortunately, Lew's teeth started to crumble – I guess the quadrupled doses of radiation affected them badly – but he always had such warmth and beauty in his eyes.

EMAIL to Tim: Lewy had a CT scan yesterday and unfortunately the cancer has spread to his lungs. Do you want me to stop sending all this bad news?

EMAIL from Tim: Fabes, keep sending it. It's easier to receive it this way rather than you or Lewy having to tell me over the phone.

So because the cancer had spread, Lew immediately had another full body scan, not three months after the radiation as planned. He also had a brain scan as his vision was occasionally kaleidoscoping.

The cancer had not only spread to his lungs, but to his brain, liver and to the lymph nodes of his trachea. WE WERE STUNNED.

I was horrified that it had spread to his brain; the thought of gentle Lew not being the same person because of cancer in his brain made me secretly utterly despondent.

Despite the high doses of radiation, a third lump appeared. Each day was bringing more bad news. The radiation specialist also suggested another type of more detailed brain scan.

A friend said, 'You know, once cancer is exposed to the air it spreads rapidly.' But Lew's cancer had been growing scarily fast in those three weeks and three days before he'd been operated on. It was strange that this horrible cancer was spreading so quickly and yet Lew's wounds had healed, and his radiation burns would heal fairly swiftly and well. I think from this time onwards my brain started to find dealing with anything out of the ordinary hard. I definitely was panicked.

We saw Dr Kindheart. At the end of the appointment I asked Lew if I could speak to the doctor alone. After Lew had left the room, I simply said, 'How long do you think Lew has left?'

He quietly replied, 'About six months.'

I went out to the full-of-people waiting room. While Lew was paying his bill I started to cry. I just couldn't stop. Lew looked at me with an indulgent smile. I went out into the corridor. A doctor walked past and looked so sorry for me. It wasn't me I was crying for.

Later that night Lew said to me, 'How long have I got?'

I could not tell him. I just shook my head and mumbled, 'I don't know.'

Φ

EMAIL from Prue: Hi, does that mean they've stopped the chemo, or that after this next two weeks they won't give him more? Quality of Life is a very salient issue in all this.

... Yesterday I was directing seven Italians to act a 5-minute version of Hamlet (or Omelette as the Italians pronounce it) on a terrace near Piazza di Spagna. Very funny. My work held a party for Billy Waggledagger's birthday. I managed to consume five Pimms and was more boisterous than the situation allowed ... Love you terribly. P

EMAIL to Prue: Lewy is doing radiation not chemo. For his type of cancer in the lymph nodes, radiation is more effective ... but aggressive radiation hasn't worked so far ... I am devastated. They won't do chemo because it needs to be specific. We don't know the primary source despite a gazillion tests. It would only make him sick. He is weirdly well (and wonderfully). Also as cancer is so aggressive maybe even if they knew the primary it might not work. I can't have enough cuddles. And I really need my Mum.

EMAIL from Prue: Oh Jesus. Keep Lew Lew happy. I am so proud of having you as my friend. Your strength and humour are just amazing. I'm sorry I mixed up radiation with chemo, I don't know enough about the treatments to hide my ignorance sometimes ... P

EMAIL to Prue: Please don't apologise for not knowing medical terms. We have done a crash course in all this. This week was just one terrible blow after another. I didn't go to work tonight because I couldn't stop crying.

Lew has done so many tests. He is brave and positive and just delighted to be surrounded by loving friends.

... Unconservative doc recommended no overseas travel and I can see his point. When radiation finishes we may go to Hill End and Sofala, where Lew has always wanted to take me. I always liked Canberra and we haven't been there together. Maybe we will go to the south of France but I can't see it. Lewy has such a sweet and loving personality, I can't bear the thought of him losing that ...

EMAIL to Laraine, an RSL workmate: Hello dear friend, thanks for asking. Lewy is not so good ... His spirits are positive and I'm sorry to say sometimes he has to comfort me. I knew it was unnatural to be this happy in a marriage. Anyway we are bumbling along as best we can, and every good moment, especially the small ones, seems very precious.

EMAIL to Tim: Lew finished his two-a-day high-dose radiation yesterday, so now just once a day until mid or late next week. Sadly the tumour hasn't shrunk and is starting to be quite uncomfortable. He's tired, but that could also be all the lush visitors he's been having. Now that the treatment is only once a day we can probably do more fun things.

Feeling Low

Because the cancer was spreading so fast, less than three months since Lew had been diagnosed, he wanted to give chemotherapy a try. Early on Dr Kindheart had told us that for chemo to be effective it had to be based on the primary cancer. Although we had already done this, we were again desperately racking our brains for some way to find the primary cancer. Maybe there was SOMETHING we'd forgotten to tell the doctor?

When Lew's Dad had died from a sudden heart attack thirty years ago, a doctor had told Lew that his father's body was riddled with cancer. I guessed that because his death happened just after he and Lew's Mum had divorced, no one in the family had the autopsy report or, apart from Lew, knew about the cancer. So I went to the hospital, where the autopsy had been done, to see if we could obtain a copy. It was all impossible until they realised that Lew was sick and we were trying to find a connection. All we needed was a letter from Lew's specialist, which he gave us immediately, and about a week later, on 1st May, the report was ready for pick-up from the coroner's office in Glebe.

> *EMAIL to Barbara: Thank you for your always-grand hospitality. Sorry Lew was a bit out of it. So much to process at the moment, but also he's tired from radiation. We are just trying to do our best ... Tomorrow we pick up Lew's Dad's autopsy (erk, but maybe helpful) report, then off*

to work via Mum and Dad ... Trying to make sense of parts of today, five phone calls to state coroner, Lew's step-uncle, Hugh, Dad, Home Nursing Service and God knows who else ...

EMAIL to Prue: So much difficult stuff today and then all ended with us in our kitchen with my foots on darling Lew's lap, he drinking a beer and me wine, so happy. So there you go. The skin on Lew's chest and underarm is blistered and splitting, he's sooo tired, etc. Don't know when op is. We have a 360-degree turnaround and we see the specialist tomorrow re chemo ... Had lovely walk with dancing-happy ball-chasing dog tonight and then we had a drink with temporary-next-door Ailsa ...

(Our dear neighbours Liz, Graham and their son were travelling overseas for six weeks and hoping to catch up with Prue in Rome. Ailsa, a friend of ours, was house-sitting for them.)

Unfortunately, the autopsy report only dealt with Lew's Dad's heart attack. I can't tell you how disappointed we were. Straw-clutching is such a bad feeling.

On the same day we picked up the report, we saw the chemo specialist. The registrar saw Lew first and asked him lots of questions that he found difficult to answer, so I did much of the talking. Lew was overwhelmed.

I asked him if it bothered him that I was asking and answering a lot of the questions and he said, 'Oh no, please do.'

I was agitated. Here he was considering doing chemo and no clue as to the primary, and it was all moving too fast. The information in our heads, our understanding and the questions we should be asking were way behind this rapidly advancing demon. Getting information from Lew's original GP was trying, and why did we want it they wanted to know? Because he was doing chemo and we needed all the clues we could get. Racking our brains and the past for anything of significance was stressful, and all the time Lew was running out of time.

Such frustration I'd never experienced before. I was quite curt with the particularly nice registrar, which was completely uncalled for.

I imagine the poor man had seen all this before. He was kindly and calming.

When we first saw the chemo specialist – from now on known as Professor Bleak – he had his finger on his lips; not a good sign, I worried. He wasn't a cold man, just scrupulously professional. He had read Lew's file, the registrar's notes and had spoken to Professor Hopeful, and said he thought he could make Lew a cocktail of chemo. The only thing Lew had to lose was the quality of life in what time he had left …

Φ

We were lying in bed, this time with Lew wrapped around me, always so comfortable, like two pieces of a matched puzzle – his kneecaps in the crook of my knees, my calves against his shins, the arches of my feet resting on top of his, his tummy in the curve of my back, my shoulders cradled in his chest. His arms enfolding my breasts and our hands entwined. Lew had lots of muscles and yet the overall feeling was of an enveloping gentleness.

'I don't want to leave you,' he said.

What comforting words did I say? I just started to cry in big choking sobs. He held me tight.

In the kitchen, I tripped over a chair and really stubbed my toe. I started to show Lew and tell him how much it hurt. He looked kindly amused. I was embarrassed. He'd never complained about anything, and here I was letting fly about a toe. I don't quite know how he did it – managed to not criticise me. There was a wealth of material.

Another time when we were holding each other, I asked Lew if he was afraid.

'Yes,' he said.

I said, 'I think dying is like going to sleep, and sleep is lovely, and when you die you go to sleep and you just don't wake up.'

Lew didn't say anything.

Feeling Low

On her way back to the country after a holiday in the US, Lew's Mum stopped in for a visit. She arrived just as Lew was having treatments for his burns, and I was stressed because an unfamiliar weekend nurse needed to be clear on the hospital's written instructions about Lew's creams and dressings and needed a little help taping up the padding and netting.

Lew's Mum was full of her trip, as you are when you arrive home, and she brought him a bottle of Glenfiddich whisky, which he loved.

In the kitchen she asked me how he was going, and became quiet as I updated her with the latest devastating news. I also told her Lewy had been so brave and positive about everything. After lunch and while Lew was napping, I drove her to her friend's house.

> *EMAIL to Lew's Mum the following evening: Great photos. What fun! Today was much better – my soul caught up with my brain or vice versa. As far as we know there are only two more treatments to go. I was a bit panicked by the dreadful smell and colour of Lew's dressings, but the nurse said that's how radiation-burn dressings smell and it's not infected, thank goodness. Apparently the skin continues to burn for ten days after radiation finishes.*
>
> *We received stronger painkillers today for Lew. We have really slowed down, as last week was gruelling with two hospital trips per day, etc. We've cancelled all visits this week. I can't believe how fast the days go …*

Dear Dr Kindheart,

I just wanted to let you know that Lew has decided he would like to take a gamble with chemo. He wants to try and have a bit more time. I have made it clear to him that this must be about what he wants and not about me or anyone else.

I have also put in this letter his Dad's autopsy report, which doesn't seem to mention anything about cancer sadly. Maybe you can conjure something out of it?

... We are seeing a professor at the hospital to arrange chemo ... Because this doc is twice removed from you, and as Lew and I are a bit shell-shocked, I am nervous that he may not fully understand Lew's case ... He says he can make some sort of cocktail for Lew ...

Another professor said the other day in passing to me that because Lew had been a smoker he thought the primary might have been lung. I thought there was only one tiny uncertain spot on Lewy's lung when you first had the PET scan done at [hospital] or prior scanning at [hospital] way back in Feb. So I'm nervous of this opinion, although obviously I have absolutely no training. Could a tiny spot like that have been the primary while the secondary was so much more developed?

Lewy has had three biopsies, all of which you have the results for. Could you call Professor Hopeful with your opinion of what the primary may have been?

Then I desperately repeated seven possible causes of Lew's cancer, which may not have had any relevance.

... I know you advised Lewis that chemo would make an otherwise feeling pretty healthy man feel pretty bad, and that we do not even know which primary is to be targeted, but because he is fifty-three and really enjoying his life he wants to try. Should we make an appointment to see you? Can you call either Professor Bleak or Hopeful and give them your best estimation of the primary?

Thank you so much ...

Φ

EMAIL to Prue: *Hi. This is how we are. For the first time Lew is a bit down. Radiation finishes tomorrow. He's very tired and has lots of raw patches on his skin. Must be excruciating. We have a meeting tomorrow with radiation doc about whether tumour has shrunk, etc.*

I didn't go to radiation today, as I wanted to fill in four lots of forms, each about twenty pages, so Lew can receive a disability pension (erk!) and I a tiny carer's allowance. I'll still work at the club. There've been lots of photocopies, looking into info and no privacy – merde!

I wrote a letter to the original specialist doc on Monday ... Glorious doc rang tonight and had a talk to me about letter and autopsy report from Lew's Dad I sent him. He said Lewy should try chemo, as it was important that we believe we've given it our best shot. He said there were certainly some cancers they could rule out with this chemo. He said autopsy reports at that time would have only dealt with the direct cause of his Dad's death.

Prue, when I'm with Lewy I'm so happy, but when he's not here I have the heaviest pressure in the chest and my oesophagus feels like there is a big hand around it squeezing so tightly …

Financials

EMAIL to Prue: Thanks for Roman food parcel. Lew was sooo delighted, and me too.

We are having a drink (how unusual) to celebrate Radiation Ending, although we are strangely flat today. Maybe knowing burns will continue to burn sort of takes the edge off. And whether or not chemo will work is a shit. However Lew has decided to sell his land and says if the docs say it's OK, which maybe they won't, we'll be back overseas this year catching up with you. Otherwise a bit of travel in Australia. Whatever. When I cuddle up to Lew at night it's the best time ...

Am about to download seven years of bank statements so Lew can put his tax in order ... I seem to be oddly attracted to men who don't like Scrabble and won't do their tax!

Have finally finished filling out forms for Lew's disability pension, a minuscule carer's allowance for me, asset and means test forms, small business forms ... shit, shit, shit! So much paperwork, so many pieces of paperwork required to look up and attach to them. Hopefully tomorrow will be better. Keep in touch. I so look forward to your emails ...

EMAIL from Ellie: Hello dear friend, this is a quick note to say goodnight and that I hope your evening improved out of sight after we spoke, and that you and Lewy Baby had a restful and deep sleep ... a bit of that is very healing!

Hang on in there, don't let the bureaucracy get to you ... it's not worth *it, and you are doing such a brilliant job in the most awful and trying circumstances ... bravo, Fabie!!! Anyhow say the word and I'll be there any day you both have the need for diversion!!*

EMAIL to Ellie: Thanks, dearest friend, have finished Centrelink forms as far as I know. Feel a little better. Will give to elusive social worker tomorrow if we can find her ...

Sort out tax next ... I want to tackle that tomorrow so we can put it behind us. Poor Lewy.

I'm just not on top of everything, but Hugh rang tonight which was lovely.

Made beautiful lettuce, corn, avocado, Spanish onion, butter bean, caper, Italian cheese, sun-dried tomato salad with marinated chops for dinner ...

EMAIL to Barbara: Because Lew has savings I don't believe we're eligible for financial help. So almost a week wasted filling in forms, etc, to find that out. GRRR ...!

Thanks so much for all your good wishes. It really helps ...

I decided to leave Lew's tax alone after this, as I'd already wasted too much precious fun-with-Lewy time filling in forms.

EMAIL to Prue: Last week has been the worst for me. No extra bad news, just ground down by it all and Lew's burns slowly getting worse. I guess the reality of it for Lew has been particularly awful. We tried backing off from everyone as we were feeling so dreadful, but realised it was the situation that was crap ...

Φ

I had informed the Uluru residency folk that Lew's health was not good. The next day I emailed them and cancelled the residency. My paintings had to be completed before November, but producing work now became impossible with the heaviness of Lew's illness and the pressure was too much. I only wanted to be with and help Lewy.

And then out of the blue, Lew organised a Mother's Day dinner for me with Hugh, Nick and Jess. He made a scrumptious salad and ordered lush Italian pizzas from Five Dock.

Jess and Nick have an equanimity about them, which was mightily appreciated this night. It's hard to describe Nick. He's so affable that neither his father nor I are quite sure where he came from. He has the most delicious sense of humour, can be a great mimic, is ridiculously artistically talented and so very reasonable. A Genuine Throwback.

Jess's dark hair is a wild and woolly mass of curls, an endearing contradiction to her personality. Her clear blue eyes reflect her qualities. She is intelligent, capable, patient and without neurosis, all talents which we heartily welcome into our little gene pool.

Hugh and I are more volatile and bubbly; within the family we possibly have the artistic temperaments … Hugh can always toss in a few yarns about fascinating peoples he has randomly chatted with.

The night was topped off by Prue ringing, and she was also able to talk to the kids whom she really likes. We were thoroughly cheered by the evening, especially Mr Lewy.

Chemotherapy

Nine days after radiation finished, on 15th May, Lew started his cocktail of chemo. He'd been feeling overwhelmed and wasn't going to start until the Monday, but the registrar had said, 'Lewis, this is serious, you would be better off starting as soon as possible.' So we rang after we arrived home and they kindly changed the start back to the Friday. Poor Lewy.

Normally they give one drug the first time, and two drugs the following week, but because the cancer was particularly aggressive, they did it the other way around. Lewy's treatment was every Friday.

We didn't know how fast or bad the side effects would be. I was only working two days a week away from home but we needed the income. I worked on Friday nights, so I would take Lew to chemo and then bring him home, and dear Ellie would drive all the way over from the other side of Sydney to cook him dinner and just hang out. Ellie is an outstanding cook and great company. She supported us all the way through Lew's treatments with the warmest encouraging phone calls.

Φ

> *EMAIL to everyone: Lewy has started his four-week chemo cycle. They give him blood tests before each one to see if the chemo is having any effect. They will repeat the cycle according to effectiveness. Possibly try a different type if not working …?*

Look, the wonderful news is, he has responded to the first dose of two drugs well. We were up at 7 am. I gave his radiation burns the 30-min preliminaries, and then a nurse arrived to do the follow-up … Getting ALL the right equipment out is like that game we played as children at parties — you know, the crap one where they had a tray of items and then covered it up and you had to write down everything you could remember?

We went to the hospital where Lew had his tests and we talked to the doc and then nurses. Lew then sat in a comfy chair in a day clinic reading Barry Humphries' autobiography (thanks Tim) and intravenously they gave him chemo over about 2½ hours.

I picked up his anti-nausea drugs from the most depressing hospital pharmacy I've ever waited in — in my life. Boy, are some people sick! The pharmacy gives you a nasty-looking hand-drawn number. No, I didn't have Lewis's Medicare card so back across two roads, into the building, up several levels and into the cancer wing to retrieve his card, and etc, etc back to the pharmacy. The women's magazine I read was even more miserable than the other patients. Man, are those magazines Bitchy!

Then I went and bought some new music — Bob Dylan, Leonard Cohen and Geoffrey Gurrumul Yunupingu's new albums, the last two are fabulous!

Arrived home before three where Ellie is waiting for us. I have to leave for work. She is looking after Lew this night and our thoughtful temporary neighbour Ailsa has cooked laksa for the three of them. Someone else drops in a pot plant and a card arrives in the mail from Prue's mum. No wonder Lew has such a good response to chemo — So Much Kindness.

Work was good, crazily busy at first, thank goodness, and then ridiculously quiet for the last two hours. The person I work with from 5 to 8 was sick and not replaced. A lovely customer gave me a chocolate.

Lewy's burns are much better, only under his arm is raw now. His colour is a bit odd sometimes, but his spirits are good.

We have to be careful of infection, so if you have a cold, flu, etc, keep away until you're better because his immune system is vulnerable at present, otherwise he would love to see you …

EMAIL to Lewy's Mum: I was premature saying Lewy had a good response to chemo. It's 11 am and he was feeling so ill he's now in bed asleep. This is the second time (I think) that he has been beaten down by cancer/treatment. He did have a lovely brekkie of baked beans and pumpkin bread toast, but he looks the colour of the bread now. I'll be really worried when he loses that wonderful appetite. I am so sorry for him. Thanks so much for the flowers. They look lovely ...

EMAIL to Tim: Lewy emerged about five o'clock. He didn't know what he wanted food-wise so I made him lamb chops, half a corn cob and new potatoes with butter, chives and pepper. Probably minimal is best, maybe things we liked as kids? He drank ginger beer. We watched Chocolat (Lasse Hallström) on our new big bold TV, which was heavenly. He's tucked up in bed now with fresh sheets, aired pillows and an extra blanket. He is so very, very lovable ...

Helen has had many jobs, but originally she trained as a hairdresser. She rang Lew and said could she come over and give him the treat of a haircut – to be one jump ahead of the chemo. He was tickled pink! She gave him a brilliant shorter-than-usual cut and he was like a pussycat, taking pleasure in the luxury of it.

Lew had an acquaintance whose father was involved in cancer research. They told him they could possibly tell the primary cancer from hair testing, so Lew swept up his hair and popped it in a postbag and sent it off to be tested. Hopefully without too much dog and cat hair in there. I didn't say to him they may not need that much.

Later Barbara said, 'Wow! Lew looks fantastic!' Whereas Ellie said, 'Why did he cut off so much of his lovely hair?' Contradictions – life is full of them.

EMAIL to Prim, an old friend: Fri chemo went well ... Brain scan on Mon, to see if or how much has spread. Hugely have fingers crossed to see if chemo is having effect, also checking maybe how much longer Lew can drive.

We had a lovely day today. We met my Mum, who is having a painting exhibition nearby, and drank great coffee. I took Lew home and dropped Mum at the station. Later we went to Haberfield and picked up a gorgeous ricotta cake for Lew's cousin Guy and his wife, who visited this afternoon. They are particularly nice people, positive, kind and helpful. Lewy really enjoyed their visit. We then took Molly for an energetic walk. Finally had drinks with neighbours Liz and Graham, who have just returned from six weeks in Europe. At 7.30 pm we arrived home tired and so Glad to be here. Looking forward to dinner on Sat, dear friend, and sorry I haven't rung back ...

Prim gave a dinner at her place for Lew, with lots of old friends. We had a beaut night and amiable Lew was touched that she had gone to such trouble for him.

Φ

EMAIL to Barbara: It's 9.06 pm and I'm sleepy. Just returned from great striding walk with Molly. Lew's asleep, tired but happy. He has a brain scan tomorrow; quite lucky they're not doing mine ... Keep those emails coming, they are such a lifeline to me ... Sorry I haven't rung. It's easier for me to email as all a bit overwhelming at present, however we're living in the moment and very happy together. Still lots of fun to be found ...

Ursula's show looks good. She has sold two so far and an offer on a third. A fourth is my favourite and I'm going to buy it after the show ... It's called 'The Book of Leaves' and has a really strong sense of the paintings Mum has done over the years, right back to when I was little.

More Desperate

I was impressed at how positive, uncomplaining and brave Lew was. His radiation burns no longer needed dressing by the nurse, who was pleased by how fast and well they'd healed. His tanned armpit and shoulder now looked like they'd been on holiday to Cairns with a hair-removal specialist.

Lew had a brain MRI to see if the cancer there had worsened. We would have the results in about a week. We asked them to contact us right away if Lew should stop driving. Previously we had wanted to know test results ASAP, but they were always so bad that now we preferred to wait.

Lew was, however, being knocked around by the chemo and I remembered Dr Kindheart's comment that chemo was a poison. He spent a day in bed, exhausted. He wasn't one to give in, so he must have been wrecked. His mouth was full of ulcers. He vomited occasionally and sometimes couldn't make it to the bathroom. Even water tasted awful.

I bought and cooked the healthiest things – avocados, cashews, yoghurt and pork – so that he wouldn't lose weight during chemo. Lew lost only a little weight during the treatment, but I stacked it on.

He started having a lot of pain deep inside his thigh. What the hell that was from we'd find out soon enough. So far with this cancer, the treatment had been far worse than the disease. I could understand people stopping treatment.

EMAIL to Prue: Hi darling, thanks so much for your phone call. Prue, I'm quite low sometimes. I just need to know that if things go badly here, if you know what I mean, I can take off and be with you in Rome for a few weeks. I can't bear the thought of Lewy not being around. If I have the possibility to stay with you it would help me. Sorry to be so gloomy. I realise you would have to work, but I believe Rome would have plenty of daytime diversions, as long as we could hang out at night and on weekends.

Look, maybe things will turn around, certainly Lewy is very positive. And maybe the chemo will work, but if I can see you if things go pear-shaped, it would help me to be stronger. What do you think?

Now I felt like I was going down the drain and it did not feel good.

Ф

Lewy had two weeks of chemotherapy and then a week off. On 1st June, at the beginning of the fourth week, when the side effects had subsided somewhat and before the next dose, we jumped on a plane and went to Tasmania for four days. This was Lew's choice of nearby possibilities. It was the first time we'd been able to leave; prior to that there were always tests, operations, dressings and drains to check, radiation, burns to dress, and now chemo. We were bursting to escape, to exist with no more bad news, no doctors, nurses and hospitals. Since 9th February Lew had undergone nearly a hundred tests and treatments.

We stayed with Prue's bubbly and talented sister Amanda, and visited their parents whom I have known since I was thirteen. Amanda had stayed with us in Sydney in January, on her way home to Tasmania after seeing Prue in Rome.

Lew had worked in Hobart briefly in the seventies. He was flown in and out and had had no time to explore. I'd never been. It's a beautiful city, and Amanda was hugely hospitable to us, with enough food to feed an army – Tasmanian cheeses, yoghurt, Belgian chocolates – and she had sprouted mung beans especially for Lew.

It was wintry and we weren't aware that chemo could make you more sensitive to the cold. At least Lew had his Merino Country fine woollen underwear, tops, scarves and beanies so he wasn't too uncomfortable. Every winter he was a cosy walking advertisement for that firm and always recommended their clothes. When Claudie moved to Melbourne and Hugh's girlfriend was going to Cradle Mountain in Tasmania, Lew bought them each a light woollen spencer to keep them warm, and just to be kind he gave me one too. Fortunately, warming coffees trickled through our Tasmanian time.

Amanda is a gorgeous person, quite different in personality to Prue, but both are gems and immensely attractive.

I said to Lew, 'Should I be worried about you and Amanda?'

'No way,' he said, 'not enough bench space.'

Lew loved to cook, and Amanda's kitchen and whole house were piled high with her books, hobbies and photos, as well as her laughter and enthusiasm.

Amanda took us everywhere. When we first arrived, she dropped us at Barilla Bay Restaurant, a fabulous seafood joint near the airport, as she had to return to the airport to pick up one of her children. Lew happily tucked into smoked salmon and the biggest oysters and scallops you've ever seen.

She drove us to the top of Mount Wellington, which was mightily chilly and blanketed by fog, with vivid, stunted alpine vegetation. In our layered spencers, tops, jumpers, vests, jackets, parkas, beanies and gloves we looked like a couple of Teletubbies. We drove further down the mountain and stopped at the Organ Pipes track just above the Springs and the Chalet. The track gave us magnificent views and we walked through the most amazing rocks, gum trees and white burnt-out skeletons of trees. Hobart was way below us and so appealing. The mountains stretched off into the misty distance. The space, colours and light were astonishing.

We walked for a long time, stopping to eat some luscious cake, and after we'd seen the famous Pipes we finally turned around and walked back. I'd not thought of the obvious – that gradually going downhill meant going back uphill – and Lew began to sweat heavily and found it hard going. He was such a non-complainer that sometimes you could forget he was sick.

From on high Amanda pointed out Ralphs Bay, which was a tiny piece of the endless expanse beneath us. A local community action group was trying to stop a developer from constructing a canal-style housing estate in the bay. Another day, she took us to that beautiful, hazy, bird- and light-filled bay. She was so available for us, always asking what we would like to do.

We went to Salamanca to explore the harbour area, which was covered with perfectly proportioned Georgian stone buildings housing irresistible arts and craft shops. Inside we saw glowing photographs of Tasmania's natural world, paintings, vibrant glass, local timber furniture, sculptures and colourful hand-knitted garments. Lew took us to lunch at Maldini, a delicious Italian restaurant.

The Tasmanian Museum and Art Gallery displayed the works of one of my favourite painters, the exquisite John Glover. There was a fascinating Antarctic exhibition with elemental black and white photographs, which included Douglas Mawson's and Scott's expeditions, a film with 3D glasses, birds and sea wildlife and model ships.

On Clifton Beach we collected some large colourful striped scallop shells that I put in a rich green striped bowl when we arrived home. The shells didn't jump out of the bowl, but the colours did. An over-enthusiastic girl was swimming at this beach with no wetsuit in a Tasmanian winter – unlike the board-riders, who did wear them. She was a bright shivery red when she came out of the water.

We caught up with Prue and Amanda's mum and dad, whose personalities, like their daughters', were as larger than life as ever. 'Faaabeeaaarrr, daarrrrling! Hooow wuunnderful to seeee you again!!! Aand yooou mussst be Lluuuuuw!!!'

Seesaw

We arrived back in Sydney on Thursday night quite late. Lewy was having his chemo the next morning, the last for this four-week cycle. The following Friday he would begin another.

He collected the more detailed brain scan and report and we discovered that the marks on his brain were not from cancer but possibly some damage from a past injury. Oh, some good news! Lewy would still be Lewy.

> *EMAIL from Barbara: Hi, Fabes – I spoke to Lew this morning – he sounded great and full of energy. Told me the anti-nausea tablets were effective, which is good news …*

But by Sunday he was crook again.

A thoughtful friend had made Lewy some biscuits with marijuana in them, which were exceedingly helpful with relaxation and pain. They didn't use all the mixture, so I could cook more when he ran out. One night when Ellie came over, I thought I'd bake up more of this concoction. I was fifty-two years old and had never had one, so after more than a couple of drinks, and when they came out of the oven before our dinner did, I decided to give one a go. They tasted unbelievable!

Lew gently said, 'You should stop at one. You're not used to them, they're quite strong.'

But did I listen? No, greedy me dived in. I only had another two – although Lew and Ellie said I had three more. Suddenly I was unwell. I couldn't climb onto our bed. I was slumped on the floor like a heap of discarded clothes, as if there were no bones in my body, and oh so charmingly massively throwing up into a bucket. I was thinking, *I need an ambulance. And what will I say to the doctors?*

Lew was mortified; he thought he should have protected me better from myself.

Darling Ellie said, 'Okay … well … I think … I'll … go … to bed now …'

I was unable to speak. Shows how sick I was.

Could-do-without-this Lew was looking after me, despite him being the legitimately ill one. Unexpectedly there was a loud scream from the bathroom. Lew rushed off to see what had happened to Ellie. She had tried to brush her teeth with tinea cream. Poor Lewy.

The next morning I remembered an old saying that I hadn't identified with: *Beer and grass, you're on your arse. Grass and beer, you're in the clear.* I made up my own:

A lady of unstinting class
On grog had gorged and then grass.
As everything numbed,
This bilious blancmange
Slid onto the floor and out passed.

Φ

Before the new chemo cycle began, Lew had an appointment with Professor Bleak. We feared the thigh pain he'd been experiencing might mean the cancer had spread to his bones, so the week before the appointment he had an X-ray of his thigh as well as his lungs.

After some discussion with Professor Bleak of various crap symptoms, including bad headaches, Lew asked for the results of his thigh X-ray.

His thigh was clear! *Oh my, more good news. Don't cry, Fabie.*

However, despite being hammered by huge doses of radiation, heartbreakingly there were, the professor agreed, some new small lumps under Lew's arm.

And then it happened. The professor was looking for Lew's lung X-rays on his computer and they came up automatically in front of us, before he'd looked at them himself.

'Fuck …' I quietly said.

They were a golf-ball snowstorm of tumours. In six weeks, Lew's lungs had gone from a couple of small spots to this. The chemo hadn't worked; it had just made Lew sick, as Dr Kindheart had suggested all those months ago.

Lew decided not to do the chemo that week, but to go home and think about it and see Professor Bleak in two weeks. At least he would start to feel better from the foul chemo symptoms.

Lew had to do some thinking about what he wanted. If the cancer had spread in his lungs this quickly, I couldn't see how he could breathe in another six weeks. I thought, *it's going to be that quick*. I just couldn't believe it.

Lew didn't bring the subject up and I couldn't bear to. I decided I would find a counsellor for him to see. He wasn't interested in seeing a minister, but he was facing his mortality and issues from his past were distressing him. He really needed to talk to someone. Straight away.

Home again, we snuggled on our bed and gently talked. Lew's love of life was palpable.

He told me that the professor had asked him, 'Do you want to be revived if you have a heart attack from a pain breakthrough?'

He said he'd answered, 'Yes! I've had a lousy life for forty-eight years and now that I'm happy I want to have as much time as possible.'

Oh, Lewy …

Φ

I'd stopped painting in May, and now I emailed the club to see if I could take compassionate leave starting the next day. They immediately confirmed my leave and asked if there was anything else they could do.

I thanked them for their kindness. It was quietly appearing to me that there was nothing that anybody could do to save Lew.

Downhill Is Worse

After our wonderful time in Paris, Lew had always wanted to go to the south of France. We had asked the chemo specialist and registrar if this was possible. They thought not. I called Dr Kindheart and promised myself I would accept what he said. He said that Lew's lungs were full of tumours and couldn't take the cabin pressure of a long flight. They could rupture, and it was really hard to bring a body back from Europe. I didn't tell Lew the last bit.

There was nowhere to run away to now. So we let go of that idea, and as we did we finally accepted the reality of Lew's condition. We thought how good it would be to go to Broken Hill, or Canberra, but even that was too difficult and home was looking grand.

We went to the naturopath again to belatedly try to counteract the remnants of chemo. But from here on, Lewy's decline became relentlessly rapid.

Φ

We were invited to a wedding on Scotland Island, which Lew was really looking forward to.

Unheeding of how unwell he was, Lew couldn't stay away from Pittwater. Sometimes, when I was at work, he'd drive all the way there on a Friday afternoon to have a few drinks, a chinwag and to absorb the tranquil beauty of the place. Or I would drop him off before work, and he would return home by himself after several hours on public transport.

The tension of driving across Sydney in the Saturday morning traffic made me realise how strained and anxious we were. Again, my driving was lame. If this was hard, then going to the south of France was absurd. The possibility of going had just made the future look much brighter. The possibility of a future …

Lew looked really lovely in the soft blue shirt I'd bought him in Ravenna on our honeymoon, along with his bright red Parisian trousers and the leather Moroccan sleeveless jacket bartered for in the Medina in Fez for his birthday.

The service was down by the water, and the bride was late. The mother of the groom was in a panic because storm clouds were gathering. I was painfully panicked myself. Lew and I hadn't even been married for three years.

Lew started to feel ill and was trying not to throw up; he went for a little walk. He didn't understand people who weren't on time, especially to their own wedding. After the service, we climbed many steep stairs up to the house. Lew became really unwell and went and lay down. This was so unlike him – the party boy. Later, he was well enough to come and have dinner, but sadly we missed the speeches as it was best to leave, slipping out quietly, me trying not to cry.

Kerry and Pete's daughter Lizzie drove us back across the water and was very kind. I have known her since she was nine months old. Now she was a beautiful woman of twenty-four.

Φ

Some years ago, Lew's married childhood friends, Elizabeth and Roy, had organised for him to go gliding and he'd absolutely loved it. He'd never forgotten the beauty and silence of cruising through the air and he'd mentioned it dreamily to me several times. Now they organised for Lew and his fifteen-year-old nephew David to go gliding again from Mangrove Mountain, about 60 kilometres north of Sydney. Lew was thrilled to do this and had a marvellous day.

While Lew was gliding, Nick rang and I was so teary. I wanted to be strong for Lew, who was being hugely courageous. *Stop it! Stop it!* I'd silently cry to myself and the cancer, but nothing could make any difference. Everything was so overwhelming, particularly visits to doctors with the most heart-rending news. Nick called me back ten minutes later and said he was on his way from work to spend a few hours with me. God, it helped so much. Whenever I hang out with Nick, I feel better. He's such a darling.

I would look at my beautiful Lew and couldn't quite believe it. He was coughing up blood, coughing and sweating at night, and quite unwell. It had dawned on me that Lewy wouldn't make another bright and sparkly Summer. That thought filled me with utter despair.

Φ

Lew's cousin Guy and his wife asked us over for a meal. Lew was really looking forward to it. That evening they gave us so much kindness. They had friends who ran a well-known French restaurant and they promised to take Lew there as soon as he was up to it, to compensate for not going to France. We were so grateful.

Another night, when Lew's brother Tim was staying with us, their cousin Kristen and her husband came for dinner with Ellie. I was so worn from broken sleep and the grimness of things that I cooked the worst dinner ever. Lewy had a good night with his family, but photos show him looking exhausted. It was easy to feel overprotective at this time

> *EMAIL to Tim: Lew had a horrendous night last night. Terrible stabbing pains in the lungs and shortness of breath, dripping night sweats, not much sleep. We went to the hospital this morning, thinking the worst. His X-rays revealed he has completely separated a rib from coughing; he has a temperature and is exhausted. We will have to be more careful with visitors and tiredness. He now has stronger painkillers. We*

have also organised palliative care so he can stay here if possible rather than be in hospital when needed in the future ... Today is four years that we have been together.

Lew was so sick, the idea of going anywhere was impossible. Then later in the afternoon he picked up, so we drove to our favourite little restaurant in Newtown, The Italian Bowl, and had a delicious meal. Unexpectedly, a bad day had become a good day. We were together and happy; the waiters always so friendly.

I had so much love for this man who could reverse the worst of times.

Φ

Just over a week later, Lew had his appointment with Professor Bleak. He'd always wanted to be an organ donor. The professor told him because of his cancer that wouldn't be feasible, apart from his corneas.

Lew also wanted to donate his body to science. For me, that thought was hard to bear, but whatever Lew wanted was important – he had so few choices left. However, he said to the professor that maybe he didn't want to leave his body to science as they had been so unable to help him. Privately, Lew believed the fact that the cancer hadn't been caught early had cost him his life, and that the painful 'scientific' treatments had been useless. Certainly with chemo, we had been warned that could be the case.

Broaching the topic for the first time Lew said, 'Will I be here for Christmas?'

Without hesitating the professor firmly said, 'No.'

I asked, 'Will Lew be here for his birthday?'

'No,' he said again, then, 'I can't keep answering that question.'

Neither of us was going to ask again.

I had been so excited to discover Lew's favourite Gilbert and Sullivan, *The Mikado*, was being performed at the Sydney Opera House and on his birthday. It didn't commence until late August and I wanted to buy tickets for 13th October. What a stupid reason to ask the professor that question. But it was asked out of a heartfelt longing to give Lewy more of life's great joys.

I realised we didn't have much time; all those miracles people kept telling us about weren't for Lew. The concept of being positive was bullshit. Lew couldn't have been more positive or optimistic. It hadn't slowed anything down, but it had certainly given us a great quality of life. And of course, that's all that really counts.

Φ

EMAIL to Tim: Lew had a bad night. Bed/pillows/blankets are saturated from sweating. He was in a lot of pain. Broken sleep again. John and Ziggy came over this morning whom he adores, so he was cheered. When he's OK he loves to see people. I'm good. It's such a pleasure to look after Lew. Racing out the door to organise finances after your helpful advice. I also managed to turn down the phones.

Our clamorous phone rang constantly. Friends calling Lew, or me to see how he was. Even though he was extremely ill, exhausted and suffering numerous miserable cancer treatment side effects, he would say, 'I'm good. I'm surrounded by so much love that I can only be happy.'

It took me some months to grasp that he was talking about how magic our time together was. Lew's personality responded strongly to love and kindness. It brought out the best in him.

Janey is my ex-husband Jonathon's cousin; she is married to Paul. They came to Lew's and my wedding, and we've always kept in touch. I regard them as precious family. They sent me a large cheque with a note saying they wanted to buy a painting and knew that now wasn't a good time to choose it. They would decide later. Neither Lew nor I were working so it was a magnificent kindness. We couldn't control the blows, but the thoughtfulness of friends was also unruly.

EMAIL to Tim: Lew had a great night last night, really good sleep!! He's/we are much better for that. He's just dozing in bed behind me now.

My kids and Jess came over for a relaxed low-key dinner. They were sooo lovely to Lew. It was such a nice night. Hugh is particularly fond of Lew and has been quite distressed, so it was good for him and Nick to hang out. Claudie comes up on the 28th ...

Last Requests

Eric was the father of a childhood friend of Lew's. He'd lived in the street next to where Lew had grown up, but was now in care. He'd been a Lancaster Bomber pilot during the Second World War and had been shot down over France and saved by the French Resistance. He'd never lost touch with the French people who'd helped him. Lew admired Eric, and he was Lew's witness at our wedding. Lew wanted to visit Eric one last time. He also wanted to see his Mum's elderly brother, Les.

Lewy had been told he was conceived in a cottage over fifty-three years ago at Chinamans Beach in Sydney. Ken Done, a well-known Australian painter, owned the house now and it was Lew's wish to go and have a look inside. They were unable to oblige at that time and told Lew they'd call him the following week.

But Lew wasn't well enough to do even these small things. He was exhausted from poor sleep and his painkillers also made him tired. His night sweats had extended into day sweats. He'd developed a new pain in his chest, but didn't want to go to hospital to have it checked.

I rang the hospital and they thought the new chest pain was part of his deterioration. We increased the Endone to combat it. They believed his night and day sweats were his body's response to cancer.

I realised I would have to chase up palliative care as Lew was getting worse. He was angry that he didn't have much time left, but not with me. I was so sorry for him. It was a lousy time.

Φ

From a caring friend, I received an article that had just been released by a well-respected hospital. It contained findings on alternatives to chemotherapy. This was my reply:

> *What a great article. Thanks for that. We don't have a microwave. We have been seeing a good naturopath and taking vitamins and compensatory things for chemo. Lewy eats a really healthy diet, except probably too much lean red meat and in the past definitely wine. He has cancer with an unknown primary, and these cancers are unfortunately sometimes very aggressive. We are so trying our best. The docs said whatever unknown cancer Lew has, it is rare and moving much faster than they expected …*

So many people meant well. We were given or lent many books, long handwritten screeds and audio tapes on cancer treatments, alternative therapies, recipes, philosophies, and special things to grow and eat. They were piled high in our living room. Certainly Lew dipped into them. And we'd both planted and grown things – although the damn cats kept weeing on the wheat grass, so we never managed to use it. Had we read them all, we would have had no time for living.

In Lew's advanced condition, thinking you have control over the outcome by your actions is not quite the right way to think. The only 'control' we had was that we adored each other and tried to make the most of every moment we had.

Φ

And then Lew had a good day. He went to see Eric, who was now in permanent care. Eric had been a father figure to Lew after his Dad had died and Lew was very pleased to see him again, although he was saddened that Eric was much frailer than when he'd last visited him. He also went to see his Uncle Les and talked to him about his Dad.

That night, Lew almost had a good sleep, just bad sweats from 4 am onwards.

It was our third wedding anniversary. We were aiming to go to Lew's favourite restaurant, The Malaya, for lunch, with our dear friends Pete and Kerry. We always celebrated two anniversaries within a week of each other. We'd hoped to be married on the same date as we met, but I was having an exhibition the month before, had organised our honeymoon, and was not on top of our wedding. Serendipitously, we ingeniously ended up with two anniversaries.

Lance, the owner of The Malaya, who'd known Lew since he was seventeen, generously gave us a bottle of delicious French champagne because it was our anniversary. Lew told him he wouldn't be here for Christmas.

We had a scrumptious lunch, as always with eggplant Szechuan and The Malaya's famous beef curry, with a backdrop of Sydney's Darling Harbour. Lew paid for everyone before I had a chance, so I bought him a ravishing bunch of flowers – large softly scented pink carnations, deep pink tulips and long reeds. What do you give someone who won't be around for much longer?

I'd bought him the loveliest card, a heart-shaped island on a coral reef, but I was so busy with making sure he was happy and comfortable that I never wrote in it.

This is what I would inscribe to you now: I love you with the openest of heart. My life since the day I met you has been the most tremendous joy and magical delight. Your love heats me with happiness. It is more than enough to just be with you.

We also had a gem of a night with Lewy's dearest friend, Paul. He'd spent much of the year living in Queensland, looking after his father who'd been unwell. Prior to this, when I worked on a Sunday, Lew would go out on Paul's boat on Pittwater for the day, loaded up with foreign foods. Whenever we travelled, Lew always took the time to choose a present that would be hopefully spot-on for Paul.

Paul has two adult children, and the love and respect they show him and the way they include him in their lives is endearing. He has the added charm of looking like a pirate.

Φ

EMAIL to Barbara: Really bad night, crappy day. On a whim Lew said, let's go out to lunch, so we did. I'm sort of hovering, doing what Lew wants. SORRY I'm SO UNRELIABLE. I really don't know what's going on from the point of view of planning ahead. Hospital gave great advice for pain relief, but it makes him very tired. All four medications cause drowsiness so you can imagine … Lew is feeling good tonight. Need good sleep for two. Love Fabeszzzzzzz

At night I would gently and softly wrap myself around Lew. When he was asleep, his breathing rattled and whistled. You could tell something was breaking down, beyond repair.

I was achingly happy to be holding him. This was my precious, secret time. But in the stillness of the night, the truth would slink in. One day, close by, he would not be here to do this.

Hospital

EMAIL to Tim and Lew's Mum: Hi, Friday was really gruelling, seeing the chemo professor and Lew deciding not to try again. Professor and I think it's the right choice. Obviously it's Lew's call. There's a five percent chance of success for second-try chemo for cancer with an unknown primary. His lungs are not in good shape and it's taken about two weeks plus to clear the chemo out of his system. So more, different chemo is likely to ruin whatever time he has with little chance of success.

We both were in shutdown when we arrived home. Lew exhausted, had a long sleep. We also spent a lot of time with docs trying to find effective treatment for bloody awful/exhausting night sweats. Have another drug to try (third). Quite tense here for 24 hrs, but then today was a good day by midday, almost normal. Lew went down to see his block, as there was an auction of land next door. I had intended to go with him, but I think he needed some space. Hugh is going to drop in also, so Lew should be really cheered.

Lew's been so brave and positive, but I can see him beaten by things lately. I just have to let Lew call the tune. Let's hope the anti-sweat medicine works …

I was so tired tonight and Lew said let's go out and have Thai at a restaurant that a nurse recommended. It was really delicious. Boy, sometimes that man has more stamina than me!

My heart's desire for Lew was simple: a sleep full of sweet dreams, and health, and quiet breathing. The anti-sweat medicine did work and he had a great sleep. We were thrilled that morning when he woke.

This was now where we went wrong. The palliative care people came to see us and cheerfully made a few suggestions. They must have seen Lew at a time when he was feeling okay. We had an appointment to see the doctor at their clinic at a different hospital in less than two weeks' time. We should have called that clinic and said Lew was really in trouble and could the doctor come to our place now. We were used to seeing the doctors at the other hospital and were drawn to them for help. Such bad timing and inexperience and no doubt denial.

Φ

Lew adored Claudie. She was twenty-four and had been living in Melbourne since the end of January. He was proud of her, and always told others of her achievements. He loved her full-on, joyful, enthusiastic and oh-so-kind manner.

She was far away and I was worried she wouldn't see Lew again. So near the end of June we flew her up to stay a few days and see us, her Dad and family. This was such a tonic, and Lew was extra cruisey and happy to have Claudie staying here. She's a beaut combination of a deliciously wicked sense of humour and gentle empathy. I had told Claudie not long before that she was such a breath of fresh air that whenever I hung out with her I felt terrific. She replied, 'Right back at ya, Mum!'

Mum and Dad dropped in that afternoon and we had Haberfield ricotta cake. That night, all the kids came over and dear Prim came too, bringing a huge luscious dinner for all. It was such a wonderful night, and Prim's dinner meant I could just enjoy my family.

Φ

Kitchen happiness

Our world was shrinking, but Lewy was not to be put off by being seriously ill and unable to travel. He decided that it would be grand if Prue came to us. So I emailed her asking if she could possibly come, and to come sooner rather than later. Lew wanted to shout her the tickets. Our dear friend dropped everything and came within the week. Lewy was looking forward to her great company.

On the last day of June, Claudie and I woke at some horrible hour and went out to the airport to pick Prue up. It was so joyful to see her again. 'Where are we, Fabe?' 'SYDNEY!' Which is what we have said in amazement over the years in Rome, Venice, the Cinque Terre, Barcelona, Pamplona, London, Old Government House Parramatta and even … Wahroonga.

The circumstances may have been awful, but the three of us drove home from the airport in hysterical fits of laughter. I had to beg them to stop as I was trying to drive. Claudie could come down to our level at the drop of a hat.

Prue can make you laugh until you are choking and spluttering. She can be serious and thoughtful and so in tune with a situation. Her cooking is adventurous and generous, and she has a passion for books and words.

This is Prue: fairly regularly she'd earn a big-time compliment. When it was given, her dismissive response would be, 'Don't be ridiculous' or, 'I don't think so'. So one day I told her *The Story of Nick When He Was a Little Boy*. He did the most beautiful drawings and I'd say to him, 'Well done, that's a great picture!' He'd respond in an absorbed-with-his-work, matter-of fact voice, 'I know'. I helpfully suggested he say 'Thank you' instead. I passed this little homily on to Prue, thinking she'd take it on board. She did. Ever after, when I gave her a compliment, she'd say, 'I KNOW!'

Why did I like her? How could you not!

We exited the car giggling, almost falling into the gutter with hilarity and carryings on, and into the house, where Lew was still in his dressing gown.

Prue rushed up to Lew, hugged him and said, 'How are you?'

He replied, 'I'm not good, mate, I feel terrible. I need to go to hospital.'

And just like that, I drove Lew straight to the hospital in terrible pain, further and further away from our blissful home.

Φ

The traffic was still heavy but not impossible, and we finally arrived at the hospital. I dropped Lew off and went and found a place to park. Returning to Emergency, where quite a few people were waiting, I told the admissions people that my husband had secondary cancer in his lungs and a broken separated rib and was in so much pain I was worried the rib had pierced his lung. They saw him straight away in triage and admitted him into Emergency.

Thank God! I thought, but all they had actually done was admit Lew into the section, where he sat on a chair with others while in terrible pain (despite the Endone and OxyContin painkillers he had taken at home that morning) and waited to see a doctor. Lewy always underplayed his illness, but I could tell he was really in trouble. *Shit, I thought, this is awful. We should have called an ambulance.* I asked one of the staff if Lew would have been treated faster if he'd come in an ambulance. They said no, it would have been the same amount of waiting.

At last, after some time, he was given a bed in Emergency, but the whole reason we'd come to hospital was still not being dealt with. I believe it was at least four hours after he was admitted, and only after I had pestered the doctor again, that they gave him some morphine. That doctor looked at me like I was such a nuisance. What did we do wrong? Should Lew have been bellowing? Why would no one treat his pain? All Lew's records were at this hospital and yet they had NO CONCEPT of dealing with serious pain for a very ill cancer patient.

I spoke to one of the cancer doctors and asked her how sick Lew was. She took me over to the computers and showed me a picture of his most recent chest X-ray. She didn't say anything, just walked away. My medical experience is limited to bringing up three children, but I think she believed that by looking at Lew's X-ray I would know how sick he was, which was ridiculous because I didn't know how many tumours in a lung meant you were really in trouble. Obviously I know now. For the second time that day I wondered why a doctor had chosen their career; both were devoid of empathy and common sense.

Later, another doctor told me the separated broken rib was not visible in the X-rays now because there were so many tumours.

Finally, they found a vacant bed for Lew in a ward and he was moved up there. I believe this was a mistake, because Lew should have gone to the cancer ward where the treatment was specific to cancer and geared more towards pain management.

Φ

EMAIL to all (1st July): Lewy has been admitted to … hospital yesterday with an infection in both lungs. His white blood count is also very high. The docs think that means the cancer has spread to his bones. He's a very sick boy at present. He doesn't want any visitors today, but things could improve? He's in a huge amount of pain and discomfort, despite morphine, etc. I'm so sorry to have to pass on such bad news. We have a very dear friend who has come all the way from Rome and he's not up to seeing her yet in hospital …

Barbara advised me to keep an eye on Lew's morphine levels if he was in pain, as she'd experienced a hospital's conservative approach to morphine with two people in similar situations.

EMAIL to Barbara: Thanks so much, dear Barbs, your advice was invaluable. Lew was admitted 11 am, given morphine 3 pm … Today I noticed the dose was cut in half and he was in such pain. Went straight to doc, wouldn't accept her response that she was on her way to conference. Lew also has to communicate better with hospital …

Φ

Claudie was able to visit Lew in hospital before she returned to Melbourne. He was so warm towards her and grateful for her company.

When Claudie said goodbye to Lewy, her eyes met mine. It was unspoken that this would be the last time she would see him.

Family Business

Lew had some issues with his family and lacked the skills to resolve these conflicts. Attempts in the past, for whatever reason, had been unsuccessful. Like his lung tumours, these concerns were now snowballing him. I quietly suggested that he let them go, but the doctors and nurses who were experienced in such matters said, no, at this time it was most important for Lewis to be able to say what was burdening him.

On the few occasions when I'd had something really bothering me (which were nothing to do with Lew), he'd sat down facing me, taken both my hands and looked at me ready to listen. *Oh*, I'd thought, *what a treasure*.

We'd been trying to pin down the psychologist again for some time. She was hard to catch, but luckily Lew was able to see her once more. She encouraged him to speak his mind. So, very late in his days, he was able to make his phone call.

When I returned, he was strikingly calmed. And relieved that he'd been able to express himself. Finally, at peace with the subject.

I understood now that it was crucial for Lew to do this. I just heartily regret that for his Mum and himself it hadn't happened sooner. A lot sooner.

Φ

Lew and I were in our belated forties when we fell in love. My youngest child was twenty-one. Not only was I basking in the freedom of no longer being responsible for my children, I was positively revelling. And yet within a couple of months I had a ridiculously sturdy longing to have a baby with Lewy. Due to a health caper some years before, along with my age and the fact that I didn't live in Hollywood, this was not possible.

I told Lew of my feelings and he was much moved. He said because of his background he'd never wanted to have children, but he would have loved for us to be able to have had a child.

Four years later, I was sitting next to Lew in hospital, holding his hand, leaning close. A kindly nurse came in. She knew how ill he was. Trying to be positive, she asked him if we had children. Without warning and for the first time, he burst into tears.

Silence hung in the air. I wish I'd said, 'No, but he has a wife and friends who adore him.'

Wrong Place

It took several days to sort out Lew's pain so that he was comfortable. Our great hope was to bring him home, with oxygen, palliative care, good pain relief and the people he loved around him. Lew didn't like hospitals and at last I could see why. I really wanted to cuddle up to him in our own bed. He loved cuddles.

Finally the intravenous pain management was sorted. The doctors then tried to put Lew back on to tablets so he could be treated at home. This was a disaster because trying to adjust the tablet levels put him right back into terrible pain again.

Lew was in a room with three other men. I joked with him that you had to be careful where you looked or you'd accidentally come face to face with someone's scrotum. Lew was always a sociable being, but now he was sensitive to noise and all the comings and goings and beeping of equipment were irritating.

I said to him, 'You know, we could afford to pay for a room with just you in it. I'm sure you would be more comfortable.'

Lewy's face lit up and he said, 'Yes, let's do it.'

Not ten minutes after we decided that, the doctors came in and said, 'We've decided to move you into your own room, we think you'll be more comfortable there. Your wife could sleep near you on a mattress on the floor.'

'Wow! How about that!' I said.

Lew's room was as close as you can be to the nurses' station.

The first night there he spent a lot of time getting in and out of bed, so uncomfortable and in pain. I spent a lot of time trying to help settle him down. I had stupidly stayed up the night before way past midnight with Liz and Prue, talking into the small hours. I was desperate for sleep.

The next day, I helped Lew to shower. He was exhausted, so he just stood in the shower and I washed him with a soft soapy cloth. I washed his silver curly hair again because of all the sweating, and he was so gently happy. It was the tenderest experience of my being.

I was extremely grateful I gave Lew that beautiful gentle wash. I'd helped him shower the day before, but he was less independent now. There's something about being in love and water, and again, despite all the pain, Lew could find something to enjoy.

Φ

Lewy was deteriorating quickly. His liver was enlarged. That hospital, so miserly with its pain medication, had made the magnificent gesture of giving him his very own staph infection. He had an antibiotic drip in his arm.

I wanted to bring him some of his favourite food, but he said the hospital had warned him he could catch an infection from outside food. He hardly touched their food and still he caught a staph infection. I had forgotten my thought: *when Lew loses his appetite he'll really be in difficulty.*

With dread, I called my son Hugh and asked him to come and see Lew as he was very poorly. Ellie was already on her way. Lew said to me, please bring Prue, as he wanted to have his money's worth.

We were sitting around chatting when tall, strapping, 28-year-old cheeky Hugh arrived with a single large red rose and walked up to Lew and said, 'This is for you, Lew, 'cause I love ya.'

Ellie had brought a beautiful box of yellow lilies. The dark crimson roses I'd brought had gone limp after two days and now mirrored my quiet despair. Why didn't I buy more?

Lew, always the party boy, had asked me to buy a bottle of Veuve Clicquot, and we all had a glass, although Lew didn't drink much of his. The room was dark as the blinds were almost closed and I went to open them a bit.

Lew said, 'Don't! My eyes hurt.'

Later, Prue told me that the strong painkilling opiates would have made Lew's eyes particularly sensitive.

At one stage, he thought the black radio behind him on the bedside table was my black cat Louie. The radio had been such a comfort to Lew. He'd often listened to it at home with an earplug when he couldn't sleep at night, but in the hospital there was no reception.

After the visitors had left, I went home to have a shower and change. I came back to the hospital with some oranges, as Lew had said he felt like them. A sympathetic and gentle doctor was sitting with Lew, and said to me, 'Has he been like this for a while?'

I told her I'd only been gone for around an hour and he had definitely deteriorated.

A second doctor walked into the room saying, 'His lungs are rubbish.'

I jumped up and said, 'Let's continue this outside.' Lew wasn't well, but he was quite conscious. 'What's happening?' I asked. 'Is this serious?'

The doctor said, as Professor Bleak had, that because Lew was in lots of pain he could have a heart attack at any time when the pain broke through his medication. They had noticed on his file it said, *Not to be revived.*

This was news to me, so I went back into Lew's room and gently asked him, did he want to be revived if he had a heart attack?

'Yes!' he said, in a voice that clearly said, *we've already discussed this.* He didn't go into any detail or say anything else. Saying yes was all he could manage.

I even asked him a second time in front of the doctors, because there was such a discrepancy between his file and his wishes. He managed a second, irritated, 'Yes.'

Back outside Lew's room, the doctor said that if they resuscitated him after a heart attack, it would only be to more pain. And he would continue to deteriorate. He had a broken rib, and the doctor reviving him could break others, as they had to be quite rough.

I understood clearly what she was saying, but hell, Lewy didn't know any of this. How could I talk to him about this at this stage, when I was so tender towards my boy who was so ill? I believed the doctor to be a fool. She talked about Lew as if he were already dead. She proudly said she was specialising in palliative care, and I thought how pathetic was her manner with terminally ill patients and their family; incomparable to our home nurse, Gake, who had a deep respect for her patients and a great sense of humour.

I told the doctors what Lew had said to Professor Bleak all those weeks ago, when he'd asked Lew about wanting to be revived. They said they would check with the professor on Monday and let me know, then they left. Would there be a Monday for Lew?

I couldn't understand how the professor had written the opposite on Lew's file when Lew had been so proud to say what he wanted. I remembered how Dr Kindheart had been conscious that one of us should know the true situation way back in March. I started to cry quietly and couldn't stop.

A beautiful, tall, nurse with a deep voice said to me, 'You must stop crying, you are distressing the patient.' Immediately I stopped. *Not crying means everything's going to be okay, doesn't it?*

A Life Ends

When I look back, I don't think Lew had eaten anything that day, or much the day before. I forgot to give him the oranges. His tummy was distended, his liver was enlarged and in trouble. He was coughing up blood and phlegm. His veins were collapsing where the cannula was. His urine was a strange colour and cloudy, and had been sent twice for testing because they'd lost the first lot. His hands and feet were cold.

All of these things those doctors were aware of. They knew he was in trouble.

I presume the two doctors then finished their shift.

Between 6 and 8 pm Lew started to be in more pain than the prescribed drugs could relieve. I asked the nurse for more painkillers.

Referring to the doctor whose station was only four metres away from Lew's bed, she said, 'The doctor on duty isn't qualified to increase Lew's painkillers so he will have to wait until after 6 am for higher doses, but he can have extra 5 ml top-ups of morphine.'

She wasn't the only person who told us that.

I rang Lew's brother and told him that Lew really wasn't well and to let his Mum know. I rang Ellie and asked her to call Kerry and tell her the same, and I also called Prue. Then I started to panic about leaving Lew alone so I went back to his room.

He wasn't getting enough oxygen because of the tumours in his lungs so he had one of those two-pronged tubes delivering oxygen through his nose. He had a deviated septum, which pushed his nose lightly to one side and caused the oxygen tube to keep slipping out of place, which was really bothering him. When I came back, he was wearing an oxygen mask, which was more comfortable.

Despite his pain, he would take off his mask and we would kiss, lots of soft gentle kisses, as if they were as essential to Lew as the oxygen. And then I'd worry he wasn't getting enough oxygen and put the mask back on.

We went to sleep fairly early, but Lew spent the night up and down, in the chair, sitting on his bed and leaning forward to grip the rails at its foot, bracing himself against the terrible pain over and over again. He said he wanted to lie on the floor to try and be comfortable.

Do you know what it's like to be in hospital because someone is in great pain from secondary cancer in the lungs and know you have six and a half hours before anyone can do anything about it?

I called the nurse and said, 'He needs some more morphine.'

She gave him 5 mls.

Ten minutes later I called the nurse again and she gave him another 5 mls; and ten minutes later another 5 mls.

Lewy wasn't settling and was in terrible pain. It was appalling.

Lew had asked one of the cancer doctors we had seen a few days before, 'How close am I to the limit of painkillers you can give me?'

This dear man with a straggly beard and reassuring smile had said, 'We've only just scratched the surface in what we can give you in pain management.'

'I think I'm dying,' Lew said to me.

I helped him out of the chair and sat him on the bed and gave him the biggest gentlest cuddles and kisses and said, 'It's okay, Lewy, you can go. I'll be all right, it's okay and I've been so very, very happy with you and I'll be okay. I love you so much, and it's okay, you can let go.'

Then I called the nurse again and asked her to bring the (non-prescribing) doctor, but what the hell he could do, I had no idea.

The doctor walked in and said to Lew, 'I'm sorry I've been ignoring you all night, but I'm here now and I've read all of your file.'

His words made me furious. I started crying and said, 'As soon as it's morning we're getting out of this pathetic hospital and going somewhere else that will alleviate Lewy's pain. Lew is the age of your father and how could you let him suffer like this?'

He was quite short with me.

And then Lew fell back onto the bed, not in slow motion like normally when something really terrible happens, but instantly, as though a bang had gone off inside him. Two short puffs of air came out of his 'rubbish' lungs and he was so still.

'Lewy, oh Lewy,' I softly said. 'Oh Lewy darling.'

Somehow, lots of nurses materialised.

The doctor said, 'The patient has had a reaction to too much morphine.' To the nurses he said, 'No revival.' Then he added in a loud voice, 'There was no indication by the way Lewis spoke that he had been in terrible pain.'

Now was not the time to contradict him. I was utterly bewildered.

The doctor said to me, 'I'm so sorry,' but it was as if he and everybody else weren't there, only Lewy and me, and Lewy wasn't there either.

And so ended the four years of the happiest time of our lives, at 2.35 am on Sunday 5th July.

Φ

I had thought that if Lewy died, I would snuggle into bed with him and just wrap him in my arms and cling so softly to him, but he didn't look like my boy any more. He was so awfully silent. He'd been sweating and moving non-stop for days, and now I was scared of my darling, oh so still boy. Where were his crinkly smiling eyes?

Some time later, I called Nick, who lived nearby, and he came immediately. When he came in he said, 'Oh Lew' several times, and calmed me down with his beautiful gentle manner and helped in all the practical ways. What a dear, dear person Nick is. How lucky I was to have him with me.

He quietly took Lew's and my belongings to his car, making numerous trips. And then he left me alone with Lew to say goodbye to him for a few more hours, and I put my head on Lew's warm shoulder and I told him I was so sorry for letting him down in the hospital and not getting him better care, and for not making them revive him as he had wanted.

And later, I took his beloved golden wedding ring off his fine worker's hand and put it on my middle right-hand finger, where it is now.

And then I cut a small lock of his glorious silver curly hair to keep.

And I took one last look at his darling feet.

And I kissed him again and again, even though I was fearful. He appeared so still. I thought he was suddenly going to take an almighty breath, maybe make a LOUD choking sound. AND NOT BE DEAD …

It never happened. It would never happen.

Finally, I joined Nick outside Lew's room and a strange thing occurred. There was a great angry rush of wind through the corridor and all the sets of big heavy doors swooshed shut as if the fire alarm had gone off. I so hoped it was Lewy leaving that crap hospital.

And Nick drove me back to our home without Lulu.

Φ

Dear dead women, with such hair, too – what's become of all the gold
Used to hang and brush their bosoms? I feel chilly and grown old.

Robert Browning
A Toccata of Galuppi's

Drawing of Lew

If Only...

If only we could live those last five months over again, knowing what we knew now. Lew would have had the first operation to remove the tumour, and then we'd have gone to the south of France – Lew's dream – for four weeks. To have given him just one more desire. No other treatments. Just bloody good painkillers, lots of fresh sheets and palliative care. None of the therapies Lew had slowed down his cancer. They just gave him foul side effects, which he endured with great courage and optimism.

Would we have hated ourselves for not grasping at all the straws available? Would the guilt of ignoring the treatments have eaten away at my peace of mind? No doubt about it. Every cancer situation is different. How easy it is to know in hindsight.

Some years ago I read Nancy Mitford's book *The Sun King: Louis XIV at Versailles*. I have since been struck by how similarly inhumane the treatments Lew received were to those in seventeenth-century France. You were much more likely to die if you saw a court doctor than if you let the illness or childbirth run its course.

Seventeenth-century courtly France: blood-letting, leeches, enemas, purges, laxatives, blood baths, toxic medicines – the treatments for ailments were often more deadly and painful than the sickness itself.

Twenty-first-century Australia's cancer treatments: high-dosage radiotherapy resulting in tiredness, nasty burns and crumbling teeth; toxic chemicals resulting in nausea, vomiting, mouth ulcers, distorted sense of taste, headaches, sensitivity to cold, tiredness and a vulnerable immune system. The treatments are sometimes more deadly and often more painful than the sickness itself.

Naturally, if these 21st-century treatments had been successful, I would have a completely different point of view.

Φ

Nicky dropped me home and I went into the house. I asked Prue if she would call my parents and some other people. I had called Tim from the hospital, and he'd said he would go and see his Mum.

I was numb and shocked and overwhelmed and tired. I just wanted to sleep, to escape the awfulness.

How could you be with us yesterday and not here today? How could I be washing you in the soapy shower and you be so delighted, and now you're g o n e? Today was going to be special. Your three favourite people were coming to see you – Paul, Pete and Kerry.

I told Prue I didn't want to see ANYONE. I could not understand what had happened to Lew.

Barbara was not deterred. She brushed past Prue and sat with me in our bedroom while I sobbed and rubbed my back and spoke so gently to me, and it helped so much. And then I went to sleep.

Φ

The next day, the palliative care woman turned up to organise Lew's care at home. I was completely beside myself, sobbing and sobbing about all the things that had gone wrong in the hospital. And that we hadn't been able to get Lew home.

A few hours before he died, my beautiful Lew had been tormented by a hallucination. Why … why did that have to happen to him?

She believed that his pain medication would have caused this. Her gentle common sense calmed my anguish.

Φ

Prue was convinced that Lew had brought her here to look after me when he died. And she was so unforgettably perfect: wonderful, caring and empathetic. She really is the grandest buddy.

It rained and rained flowers; our house was filled with the most glorious flowers you have ever seen. I don't understand when people say, 'No flowers'; the soft scents and the riotous colours so touched my heart.

Tall, bearded, laconic Tim came down from the country, bursting into tears at the front door. He never said it, but we knew. He was fifty-one and the only one left from three brothers.

Nick and Hugh took time off work, Claudie returned from Melbourne, and two days after Lewy died the family rallied for my inappropriate birthday without him. With Tim, we toasted Lew with the beautiful bottle of wine that Prue's friend, Monica the wine critic in Rome, had sent for him. The one we had saved for his return from hospital.

Then Amanda came up from Tasmania. And every time one of Lew's friends came over I offered them much of the Glenfiddich whisky that his Mum had given him.

And good grief, there was a food downpour. Kristen sent over some great dinners; Prue made loving meals for us all; and Prim dropped in, bringing more meals and a huge hamper of food from herself, Megs and Jan. For over a week, with family and friends and flowers and food, life was unreal and awful and very, very kind. Lewy would have loved it, and he would have cried.

In a state of panic, bamboozled by grief and with Tim's help, I organised for Lew's body to be donated to science. For me, the irrational thought of an insensitive, career-driven student-fool learning from Lew's body was unbearable. I had to pull myself together. I wanted to do something right for Lew. Both Tim and Lew believed a body was much more useful to science than to the funeral industry, and seeing Lew's opinions plainly reflected in his brother's helped me to be strong. Maybe something really good would come from this action?

For various sound reasons, Tim thought Lew should go to the University of New South Wales, but I thought he should be nearer me at Sydney University. Tim was such a trooper, and as I buckled he delivered all the right papers to Sydney Uni.

I tell you all now: if you want to leave your body to science, do your own paperwork – before you become ill. It's far too grim to let those who love you do it at such a time. But I knew that when Lew and I were married – paperwork wasn't his specialty.

Lew's fragmented body would be returned to us in twenty months for cremation and tear down my heart all over again.

Φ

Our cat Ozzie had been unwell for some time and had to be put to sleep the day after Lew died. Prim, who has a great respect for the ideas of the Buddhists, said that it was significant for a family pet to travel with a person who had recently died.

Oh dear, Lewy didn't really like cats, I thought.

Prim believes that when someone dies, they stay around you for three days and that I should talk to Lew. If there was anything I wanted to say to him, now was the time.

So when I went to bed that night, I talked to 'Lew up in the ceiling':

I'm so sorry I didn't look after you better in that hospital. That I forgot to give you the oranges ... I'm utterly sorry for not making them revive you. You were in such pain. I know I let you down. Everything was ghastly. It would have only been worse. I'm so sorry that I couldn't cuddle you after you died. How could I have been so scared, when you have been so brave? Dr Kindheart thought you had six months left to live, but you only lived just under two and a half months more. What happened to those three and a half months you were supposed to have? I want them for you. NOW! I love you big-time, Lewy. You are the finest of husbands, with your magical kindness and gentleness. Being with you has been the Best of Happiest Times. I miss you ... I miss you ... It's lousy, lousy, LOUSY that you didn't have longer here. That we didn't have longer together. I love you, Lulu. I'm so sorry ...

As I finished talking to him, there was a beautiful soft oval glowing light in the ceiling, and inside my chest, around my heart, it felt like there were two warm hands melting, oh so softly into my heart, to stay with me forever.

Poster for Lew's wake by Gwyn Perkins

Alone

It's so raw what has to be done immediately after someone dies. I had to draw strength from deep inside myself that was oh so heavy to haul out.

You were such a party boy. I was determined to celebrate your life and give you a joyful and loving farewell. We gave you such a great send-off that Saturday after you died. You would have loved it! Did you come? Did you see how many people cared and cried for you? The sunset over the water was exquisite. I heard someone say, 'Look! Sparky's putting on a great show for us!' How strange I felt so high.

Prue stayed for two weeks and then returned to Rome and her job. She would have stayed longer, but I needed to find my way. Even so, it was terrible saying goodbye. Her compassion had been boundless. And she knew exactly how to hold the fort.

I had to keep walking Molly, but sometimes I could barely get out the door. I would be desolate, my jaw clenched tight.

I bumped into my dear dog-walking Italian friend, Frank. He was struggling to find his words. 'Oh Fabia, I just don't know what to say … I'm very sorry.'

'It's okay, Frank. It's okay. Let's just walk …' Then I blurted out, 'He was a really lovely man, that Lewy!'

'Yes,' said Frank. 'He was.'

Other people I normally had a chat with I could hardly bring myself to say hello to. A dear little girl asked me if she could walk with me and appealing Molly. 'No,' I said. Her kindly grandpa looked startled.

For the first time in my life I developed Road Rage – a wicked presence that jumped into my hapless heart. I, who had been polite and patient behind the wheel, shamefully told a jay-walking pedestrian to fuck off. I gesticulated like a mime artist and honked my horn more times than in my whole life. I needed to stop driving so this nasty-tempered phantom would retreat.

So many gentle and caring people rang, wrote or dropped in. So many distractions engulfed me in the six weeks after Lewis died. But I wanted to run away from everything and everyone. To go away. To be left ALONE.

Everybody leave me alone, but you. I only want you. There's so little space in my brain. I want to hold on, hold on to you for longer with all those precious memories we have. But the passing of time is thieving you away, further and further.

Now, instead of being caught sobbing in public as I did when your illness was greedily progressing, I feel a horrible strangling chill. Are you watching me? Do you think me cold and indifferent? I'm not! I'm not! There was that day when people kept dropping in to help, your cousin's husband came to talk about your service, and I pushed past him out the door and ran into the rain, sobbing and sobbing. I didn't want to organise your service. I only wanted you. There's nothing anyone can do.

I'd go to bed at 1.30 am and be up by 4 am. Not that I couldn't sleep; just that I was wide awake. Traumatised. Afloat on the silence around me. A silence that gave me a chance to think about my buddy. But drowning in sorrow. No one could help me. I had to help myself.

I cracked a tooth from clenching my jaw. At the dentist, as I lay horizontal in her chair, tears rolled out of the sides of my eyes and filled up my ears. My saliva filled up the back of my throat. I felt like I was going under. I didn't fight it.

I wrote over a hundred healing thank-you letters for all the kindnesses that blanketed your death. You could not have found the words to speak of all the goodness that was engendered for you.

I let you down in that hospital. I didn't know how to deal with them. I didn't expect that a hospital we had gone to for help could be so inept. Your cousin warned me four months before: be careful of hospitals, they make huge mistakes. I should have been the hawk that watched over you, but I was so tired and worn. But mostly, I just couldn't realise that you would die.

Why Did It Have To Be Like That?

In his last moments, how conscious was Lew? How much was he frozenly fighting why we weren't helping him? And why did he have to be in such ghastly pain? He wasn't in a bus station; he was in a hospital.

For months, these haunting questions went around and around and around and around in my skull. It was so dreadfully hard to live with.

Nick had friends who were doctors. Why didn't I ring them and ask them to prescribe Lew something? When I was told no one was available to increase Lew's pain medication, why didn't I say, 'You bring someone here who can. Now!' Why was I short with the doctor who was there? No doubt that added to the terrible stress Lew was under.

I played these last hours in Lew's life over and over in my head. After Lew died, another doctor appeared at the work station. Why couldn't we have seen that doctor during the night?

I sent a long letter to the two professors who had been in charge of Lewy's radiation and chemotherapy treatments at the same hospital where Lewy had died.

I am writing to you both because several things happened to Lewis in your hospital in the last hours of his life that I did not understand and would like some help with, explanations from you or change of practice for my peace of mind …

Professor Bleak agreed to see me at the hospital and talk about the things I had written of in my letter to him. I didn't hear from Professor Hopeful, but I was relieved to be able to talk to at least one of these specialists.

I was seeing a compassionate grief counsellor and she suggested I take a friend with me, to keep me on track and also to listen, as it would be hard to remember everything under the circumstances. So I asked dear Helen to come with me.

Professor Bleak said that the 'system' had let us down. He didn't mention his hospital, his nurses, or his doctors.

I said to him that we always seemed to be in the wrong place. Lew's doctors came from the cancer section, and when the doctors in the ward did their rounds they didn't talk to Lew.

He said that was because Lew was admitted through Emergency and there was no room in the cancer ward for him.

I said, he was there for six days and he should have been moved to the right place. I told the professor that I wanted the doctor who had said, 'His lungs are rubbish,' to be told that was a really crappy thing to say in front of a patient and that a relative had complained.

He said that what the nurses had told us about the doctor not being able to increase the pain medication until the next shift at 6 am was not true. We had been given the wrong information.

I know I'd been given this wrong information more than once.

Professor Bleak said that the quantities of pain relievers Lew was being given at the time of his death were not the maximum available dosage to alleviate intense pain.

I had spoken to Dr Kindheart after Lew had died and told him how much pain relief Lew was getting, and he said it was pretty high, and that after the cancer has ravaged the lungs it can attack the nerves and there is not a lot they can do for that sort of pain. But according to Professor Bleak, Lew's medication had not reached this point.

When I talked to him about Lew getting in and out of bed, bracing himself against the pain by holding on to the end of the bed, and wanting to lie on the floor, he nodded and said, 'He was restless.'

He may have been restless, but more importantly he was in terrible, terrible pain.

I asked him, 'Shouldn't a nurse who was constantly running backwards and forwards trying to alleviate Lew's pain have told the doctor on duty that Lew was in trouble?'

He said, 'Yes, she should have.'

When I questioned him why he had written, *Do not revive* on Lew's file, he said, 'These things are very hard to discuss with a patient in that condition.'

I had certainly found it impossible to speak this truth to Lewy nine hours before he died, and it had caused me constant anguish for a long time, but I would have thought the professor would have had more skills in this area. Maybe he could have warned me and talked to me about it several weeks prior to Lew's death, when he first asked Lew. Just like Dr Kindheart had taken the time to do after Lew's first operation, when he felt we weren't understanding the position Lew was in.

I talked about Lew's death with Professor Bleak. He believed it was instantaneous, maybe due to a clot and not a reaction to morphine. He didn't mention a heart attack from being in too much pain, as the doctors had warned us about several times.

By the time we finished talking, I was crying uncontrollably. I wasn't able to say to the professor, who looked about my age, that if it had been his wife or child in Lew's condition for those last eight hours of his life, he wouldn't have stood it for one minute let alone all those hours.

I have no idea if my seeing the professor made any difference, if there was a change of practice at the hospital. I was relieved to have seen him, it was important to have written down the interview, and I was thankful to have had a witness.

That night, my long-since-retired family doctor rang me. She'd been away when Lew died and had only just heard. She said she'd been told of several people dying in public hospitals in severe pain on weekends.

Φ

The next thing I did was definitely odd: I did Lewy's tax. My beloved dead and I spend several weeks doing his tax.

This time I was going to do things right, and Lew's Abandoned Tax Affairs were not for sissies. My old friends Barbara and Beth came over and helped me sort out all the boxes, bags and bundles of papers that I found. I can't bear to say how many years they covered.

When I had finished and given them to the accountant in Massive Expertly Filed Order, I found another two stashed-away bags which had to be sorted and passed on. And later, another. And, of course, just one more.

Goodness knows why, but at the time it seemed to be something crucial to face, deal with and then forget about.

But I could not feel calm about Lewy. How could I go on? Desolate, inconsolable thoughts floated in and out of my consciousness.

I am not staying here without you.

It seemed miserable to throw away my life when Lew had wanted very much to live.

In the past, I'd been stalled or broken by several doses of despair when I'd been unable to deal with the intractability of life. Travelling had picked me up and set me on my way again. At varying lousy stretches, and during some of the most joyful, I recognised that hurling yourself out there and placing step after step, particularly in the loveliest of places, could clear the head and restore the soul.

In 2008, Helen had lent us a television series called *The Naked Pilgrim* by Brian Sewell. We were enthralled, and somehow it had struck in my mind. Sewell drove the Camino Santiago in an old brown Mercedes, starting from Paris, and was a most amusing speaker.

Earlier in that same year, Lew and I had travelled enchantedly around Spain and Morocco, missing the far north of Spain. We had wanted to return and explore that part. The idea of walking across the north of Spain, sometimes to the point of exhaustion, seemed hopeful. I decided I would walk the Camino Santiago, 750 kilometres across the top of Spain. Prue would be with me for the first eight days, then she'd return to Rome.

Did we speak Spanish? No, although Prue spoke Italian.

Was I up to huge daily distances? No idea.

Was I fit? Not really.

Was I desperate? Yes, and determined.

My Mum is a worrier ('How long has she been like that?' a friend once asked. 'Just since the Second World War.') so I let her believe that Prue and I would be together for the whole walk. I didn't actually lie, just omitted the truth. Dad, who is not a worrier and who also saw *The Naked Pilgrim*, thought we were starting our walk from Paris.

A few people were concerned about my safety on the trek, but I felt oddly fortified against anyone causing me mischief. I was, unconsciously, carrying deep inside me an unresolved anger at the hand that Lew was dealt.

I was an atheist, but some of my friends seemed worried that I might join a convent somewhere along the way. 'You're going on a pilgrimage?' they said.

I liked colourful clothes too much for that, and have always been sceptical of the things one cannot prove. Quietly disdainful of astrology and psychics, and not impressed by organised religion. Brought up in the Church of England, I couldn't relate to a God who 'tested' Abraham by asking him to sacrifice his son to him – a foretaste of how he treated his only child.

I've never wanted more life than the one we have here and now; and perhaps because I've always welcomed sleep, I've not been afraid of dying. But I COULD NOT ACCEPT the concept of 'That's It' for Lewy. I desperately wanted something or someone to be with him.

Φ

I'd always organised my trips with stacks of research, and that was part of the fun. This time, I read pretty much nothing. My concentration was shot. I booked flights, hoping my escape would fall into place.

Had to get away. Say goodbye to my darling. Find some answers. The absence of Lewy was unbearable.

No more of us being squashed together on the comfy red couch, where each time you left your seat, Molly-Dog would jump into your cosy spot. No more at our kitchen table, where I would sit while you cooked and we would natter. I keep talking to you when I'm in the shower. For some reason that's the strongest place I need to talk to you. It's still our bathroom haven now. We idiotically renovated it in winter. You did everything that was heavy and tricky. I did all the easy work and painted it that lush lemonest of yellow. And no more squinting from the sun in our tiny back garden with you …

Just before I left Sydney, Nick and Jess told me their joyful news. They had just found out they were expecting a baby. What heavenly news. I was so happy for them. A new, tiny person would be coming to join us.

Rome

Sydney – Kuala Lumpur – Rome: 16,324 air kilometres

Deep-voiced, best-laugh Prim picked me up and dropped me at Sydney airport. When I was racing to be ready for her, the lights in the back half of the house and garden went out. I couldn't make them work. Perhaps a fuse had blown. It was the first time this had happened and I wondered if maybe Lew didn't want me to leave?

Hugh and his girlfriend, Aimee, were going to mind my animals and home some of the time I was away, then Beth for a little, and Ailsa most of the time. I was so rushed and scattered, my only idea was to send Hugh an email from Kuala Lumpur with the details of various skilled or unskilled neighbours who might be able to help. I don't know why I didn't call him from the airport. I had talked to him earlier in the day – I'd rung on a whim to double-check they knew where the key was, and they said, 'Oh, is that today? We thought it was next week.' Lucky for little Molly-Dog and Louie-The-Cat I made that call. My communications skills were crap.

I was flying to Rome to stay a few days with Prue, who lived off Campo de' Fiori. I'd been to Rome about six times, but drew a blank when trying to think of places to visit. Also drew a blank when trying just to think. I had to email Much Travelled Barbara: *Tell me some places to see?* I could've asked Prue. So discombobulated was I … Then we would fly to Pamplona in Spain, and catch a bus to Roncesvalles to begin our walk. I was really looking forward to seeing scribbly-haired Prue again. She's been a magnificent friend. I'm lucky to have her.

Northern Australia from the air was elemental and vastly spacious, but mostly I sat there hollow and stunned about my beautiful boy. Worn out. My spirit remote. An ideal Mafia witness: I saw nothing. My darling husband gone. Nothing more than a vacant space where life had been so rich and warm.

Φ

We descended into Rome at dawn, a tranquil time of day Lew's illness had well acquainted me with. Idly I waited for my baggage with my scrambled brain for company, then met Prue at the customs exit. I was overjoyed to see her again, looking gorgeous in green. Back at her place, I dumped my stuff. And then we had Italian coffees and pastries in a captivating outdoor café near Campo de' Fiori, before lovely, undamaged-by-Australian-sun Prue went on to work.

Do you remember when we had coffees on the terrace on top of the Pompidou Centre? We were entranced by that snooty waiter and by the extraordinary views of the myriads of chimney pots on the rooftops of Paris. The coffees were twelve dollars each – our most expensive coffees in Europe. I thought it would make a great T-shirt.

Oh Lewy, I wanted so much more for you.

I went back to Prue's place for a little sleep; so good to be horizontal. One living room wall was full of gutsy masks. The huge beams and joists of her ceiling looked wonderful. Lew and I had slept in this bed for several nights on our honeymoon. Lew's closest friend Paul made a very moving and hilarious speech at Lew's Service. He said he'd had dinner with Lew around the time of our third wedding anniversary and that Lew had told him he'd been on a three-year honeymoon …

And then my brain moved out of idle, straight into top gear.

Lew's Dad had also died at fifty-three. I think this was why Lew believed life was to be enjoyed – because you never knew how long you had. 'Here for a good time, not a long time,' he used to say, and as he said he did. When Lewy turned fifty, I remember him saying several times, 'I never thought I'd reach fifty.' I didn't understand that at all. I should have stopped him and said, 'What do you mean? Why do you think you'll only live that long?' But I didn't. We were so happy and, I thought, invincible.

Lew was in his element being a most loving husband and having a fine time. He was such a big-hearted host. He adored cooking, food shopping, and being open to new experiences. You could see him melt when people were kind to him. I don't believe he ever took kindness for granted. He grabbed that kindness and held on to it always. How often do we do the opposite – only remember the slights? How lucky he had that outlook and that I was able to value these qualities. I was his Chatterbox and he was my Have-a-Chat. Life had been light, buoyant and beautifully uncomplicated ...

I had to learn to pace this brain of mine that wanted to race.

Ф

I slept from 10 am to 4 pm. Old Fabia would never have wasted six hours in Rome asleep. *Be kind to self, be kind to self. I'm alive, half alive. And feeling safer ...*

In the late afternoon, Prue returned. Fantastic Photographer Prue had a photo of Lew and me kissing that I hadn't seen before. How sad and glad I was to see this unseen photo. I could glimpse the lovely curling hairs on his chest peeping out of his white shirt so he looked like some Opera Hero.

Prue laminated a little photo for my wallet, with a photo on the back of an animated Lew looking like an enthusiastic voyeur coming down the tower of the Sagrada Família in Barcelona. Prue, Lew and I had, the previous year, gone up the tower like three aging, no-own-life spinster aunts to see where my son Nick had proposed to Jess in 2006. Nick had to be quick to pop the question before the Japanese tour group that was making its way up the winding stairs swamped the moment.

I want to kiss you, Lewy, kiss, kiss, kiss you. Wrap myself around you.

Ф

The next day, Prue went to work and I walked to the Vatican Museum via St Peter's. What a beautiful square and colonnade. The gardens of the Vatican were beautiful too, with those wacky Roman trees. I enjoyed the collection, but the heat of *agosto* had lots of gusto and I was tired, despite playing Sleeping Beauty the day before. Travel-Light Pilgrim couldn't resist buying the guide to the Gallery of Maps: glorious blue-green frescoes and a Vatican favourite for me. What is it about the dusty colours in frescoes?

I longed for you at the Vatican. We'd tried to go there together, but it was closed for the Saint Peter and Saint Paul Festival. Today the Sistine Chapel was crowded. I wanted to show your photograph the Sistine Ceiling, especially the Hand of God, it's so very beautiful, but I was too inhibited.

NOW, I had no trouble crying. Pinch, slow pinch.

Ф

Prue made the best dinner of pesto on pasta, tomato and basil on top, crowned with pan-fried marinated chicken finely sliced. At this time my cooking skills were about as useful to society as a dose of herpes.

Credit Card Wrangle

Well, this day was a stuff-up of my own making.

I think if you fly to another country it's good to have your first night's accommodation organised. Because I couldn't find a place for us to stay in Roncesvalles, Spain, I'd emailed a hotel in the nearby village of Burguete, but hadn't heard back from them. So I emailed Jane in Granada and asked her to ring them for me and speak her fluent Spanish to see if we could have a room. I sent her my credit card details, but accidentally sent them to the Jaén tourist bureau instead. My time on the internet was running out and I didn't realise I'd brought up the wrong address. I felt sick about this, and even now it's hard to write about.

Incapable of dealing with the problem, I walked, in the searing sun, to the Basilica of Santa Maria in Trastevere, one of the oldest churches in Rome, and found it closed. I was supposed to be meeting Never-Late Prue and her friend for lunch, but I became completely lost. I just made it in time for a delicious lunch, with falling-apart lamb and crunchy potatoes, while falling apart myself.

We went back to Prue's and called eight different numbers on her mobile phone, all the while demolishing her phone credit, to get a new credit card issued and cancel the old one. In the end I was crying on the floor of the bathroom, missing Lew and wanting to go home. I can't believe how badly I coped.

Calm Prue was so capable. We went to her work and phoned from a landline there, only to discover that the various numbers they'd given us didn't work from mobile phones.

We caught a bus back to Prue's, drained a few glasses, plus some headache tablets for me (don't do this at home). And Prue created a bursting-with-flavour pasta with olives, prosciutto and bacon.

We went to bed early. Fucking awful day! Except for the last bit.

Φ

I had to wait at Prue's for my credit card replacement, which I needed in case my cash card died. I did my washing, which I strangely always enjoy, organised my backpack, wrote some postcards and generally got my head together. It was tragic to be stuck at Prue's while seductive Roman attractions were so near, but my brain was less than ordinary, so time out may have helped or at least saved me from more mini-mishaps.

Prue's black cat, Henry, was sitting next to me at the table, swishing his tail. He was quite a scary cutie. You had to be careful you didn't collect a scratch or a bite – a bit like living with a difficult family member. Best Roman cat nose ever. He was dark, and with those short legs I think he had Sicilian blood.

I read a bit more about the Camino, although it was hard to take in any new information. Irritatingly, I'd no problem taking in food. I feared I'd have to change my surname to Winterbottom.

Prue returned from work early because she said she'd rung the follow-up line on my credit card. They claimed they weren't delivering it because I hadn't contacted them on a particular number – which I had! How else could I have all the other numbers?

A whole day wasted in Rome. Eeek! So at 4 pm I gave Lucky Prue a break from me and rushed out the door and had a look at the Pantheon, Piazza Navona and saw the outside of the closed Galleria Doria Pamphilj. The sights of Rome looked wonderful, and for the first time there was something outside my sorrow.

I also picked up an email from home, which said the lights came back on of their own accord when they touched the switch in the bathroom. Aimee had thought the same thing – that Lewy didn't want me to go. I also wondered if he'd been saying goodbye?

Spain

Rome – Madrid – Pamplona – Burguete: 1720 kilometres

We woke early and finished packing for the flight to Pamplona. Keep light. Keep light. My heart was heavy, too heavy. Prue bought me some soft shorts-like undies as she reckoned chafing would be a problem with my skirts. I'm not a pants person at all. I love the patterned fabric of skirts. They're generous and they swish as you move.

We flew to Madrid and then Pamplona. I saw *WANTED* signs up around the airport, portraits of twelve Basque terrorist suspects. Most looked quite nice. *I must remember on the Camino that perhaps I'm not a good judge of character.*

We couldn't stay at Roncesvalles because it was all booked up. Jane had found us a great hotel in tiny Burguete. The hotelier was a kindly man and told her no need for a credit card, he'd hold the room for us. So my self-inflicted credit-card-stuff-up drama had been entirely unnecessary.

We caught a taxi to Burguete as the once-a-Sunday bus had already gone. Prue started to ask the driver for a fixed price. I said no, let's use the metre, as the information person at the airport suggested – no doubt the cousin/brother of the taxi driver. The trip cost waaay too many euros, which I thought was a rip-off. In vain I argued with the driver, who I believed deserved a massive Chinese Burn. Patient Prue said nothing about my too many shabby slip-ups.

Unlike me, Burguete was charming. Not really like Spain as I knew it. It looked more like a Swiss mountain town, or maybe a French mountain town (if I knew what that looked like), with steep roofs, colourful shutters, window boxes and flower pots full of brilliant red, pink, orange and purple flowers, and, like Switzerland, scrupulously clean. Skilfully constructed stone channels of icy mountain water ran down either side of the main street. Reflections of light made repetitive shadow patterns in the water, which reminded me of the fine rippling sand contours in the shallows of the seashore in mid-coast New South Wales. Funnily enough the colour of the water there always reminds me of Spanish glass.

My delectable dinner was all white – white bean soup, chook in Roquefort sauce and crispy roasted potatoes, rice pudding, and a bottle of white wine to share.

Φ

Burguete – Roncesvalles – Burguete – Espinal: 9 kilometres

We walked east to Roncesvalles from Burguete, leaving our backpacks at the hotel, as we knew how to plan ahead. What guide books did we take, you well may ask? Prue printed out from the internet a SINGLE most precious page, printed on both sides, which listed the various towns along the way with distances between and their altitude levels (just to scare us). I'd also brought my *Lonely Planet Guide to Spain*, which was ridiculously heavy and only gave fairly general information on the Camino. It did say no need for maps, just follow the yellow arrows – I hoped that was correct. I planned to use it for finding places to stay, sights to see, and on my travels later with Jane. It had been invaluable when Lew and I were in Spain last year. I'd also brought a small Spanish phrase book.

We walked along a quiet tree-overhung road with few cars. We enjoyed looking around Roncesvalles, a harmonious and pretty medieval town with a big church, cloisters (Spanish – *claustros*), a museum, the tiny twelfth-century church of St James and the oldest building, La Capilla de Sancti Spiritus, also known as Charlemagne's Silo. Charlemagne's Silo was a strikingly sculptural building, but underneath it had a burial ground where you could see many human bones. These were haunting to see as they reminded me of the reality of Lew's death. Perceptive Prue said, 'Don't look, Fabe.'

We picked up our pilgrim credentials from a large room near the church, which was full of long tables and chairs with pens on strings. They must be hammered from time to time by pilgrims; luckily not that day, or maybe that day but much earlier? A woman stamped and dated our credentials with the most beautiful large blue leaf-shaped stamp of the trip. There were places in the credential for forty-one stamps. I decided to only stamp mine where I stayed the night, and immediately stuffed that up as I forgot to get it stamped at Burguete. Saintly Prue said, 'Don't worry, you didn't stay the night at Roncesvalles so it's quite balanced.'

We had coffee with a Spanish ham and cheese baguette for brekkie. Beautiful incomparable Spanish coffee – it's soft, nutty and milky. And from Colombia, not like those Ethiopian beans they have in Italy (unless it's the other way around?). I tried to tell the barista how perfect my coffee was when I ordered a second, which he mistook for me wanting an extra strong coffee. So, loaded with rocket fuel, we realised that observant pilgrims could walk on a beautiful track through the dappled sunlit woods and not on the road. Oh dear – so far, not so smart. We headed west back to Burguete via an exquisite beech forest and collected our packs.

We walked from Burguete to Espinal. We couldn't find the pilgrim path, so we walked a lot of this distance on the not-completely-soulless road, until we found the track. Prue made me swear I wouldn't tell anyone about this mistake and I haven't.

In Espinal, we rested in an open grassy space sprouted with ancient circular gravestones that were carved with Celtic patterns. It was tricky to become vertical again after sitting. We'd only walked 9 kilometres and we were hoping to do 15 the next day. Walking certainly softened my tenseness, and Prue distracted my sorrow.

The buildings in Espinal also looked Swiss. We found a great cheap hotel (Spanish – *hostal*) that was clean and charming, with golden squeaky pine floorboards and a pretty *hostal* owner. Outside our upstairs window was a lovely flappy view of long lines of pilgrim garments billowing in the sunny breeze.

You were always helpful hanging out our laundry – I never had to ask, you'd just appear. You always brought the washing in at the end of the day. I wasn't used to such thoughtfulness.

Our dinner at Espinal was terrible. My pork, which was in batter, had no meat, just all fat and bones. I couldn't eat it. The restaurant still charged me for it, despite my huge and unlike-me protests. Lew would have been cranky at such a rip-off. I left the restaurant in a huff.

Thoughtful Prue said, 'Maybe it's a traditional dish here?' Nevertheless, she followed up our rip-off by ripping the menu off the wall outside the restaurant when we left.

Later in bed, and for the first time since Lew had died, Prue and I laughed and laughed. I have no idea about what. Such a release, especially after my restaurant rattiness.

We met when we were giggling teenagers. For twenty years she had lived in New York, and for the last nine in Rome, so somehow we'd bypassed learning how to behave maturely together. It was uncannily easy to slip back into those days of carefree laughter. Choking on our own nonsense felt heavenly.

Looking Forward To Sleeping Tonight

Espinal – Zubiri: 15 kilometres

As we were leaving Espinal, we noticed beguiling mustard-coloured lichens growing on their fruit trees. We walked through undulating hilly countryside and several picturesque towns.

I'd ambled off by myself and into my own headspace when I saw two enormous bulls in a low-roofed barn. In an adjoining part of the barn I saw two more giant bulls and no door. I watched my back for about 400 metres, checking out any trees that I could climb. But maybe these terrifying bulls were only cows …?

It was when I was walking separately from Prue that my thoughts about Lew's last days haunted me – the ineptitude of the hospital to deal with his pain, his staph infection, cannulas failing, and the insensitive doctor who spoke so heartlessly in front of him. The heaviest barrage was made up of Lew's suffering, his death, and my frozen ability to make the doctors do as Lew had wanted – to be revived. I desperately needed time to think about all this and to find a way to process the loop that had overtaken the inside of my head.

The landscape and Prue's company brought some relief.

The last 4 kilometres of this walk were steep. Puerto de Erro is 800 metres above sea level, and Zubiri is 525 metres above. Walking down steep slopes with a backpack was tough, and I was hot and bushed when I arrived at Zubiri.

Strained Prue, arriving soon after, looked at me as if to say, what the hell did we do that for? I had been thinking that you can love someone very much for what they don't say. Lewy's courage was like that: manifest because of his silence. A darling courage that silently shimmered.

How did you manage to be so intrepid, Lewy? I've had a few hiccups and my response has outshone any five year old's. Please help me to calm down. I'm ashamed of myself.

Φ

I knew so few Spanish words, but I'm okay at charades and was getting better at lisping. In my diary I used Spanish words for accommodation, which was confusing because their word for a cheap hotel is like our word for a youth hostel. *Albergue* – youth hostel; *hostal* – cheap hotel; *hotel* – nice hotel.

In Zubiri, there was no *hostal* accommodation available. The available *hotel* was too expensive, so we stayed in a private *albergue* for ten euros. Towel and sheets were an extra four euros. There were eight in our room on four double bunks. Prue slept up top, as I'd had some trouble sleepwalking and I was worried I'd break a leg or something.

The place was conscientiously clean, but too cramped and with no privacy. It was hard to shut the toilet door, the shower floor was mega slippery, our beds were awkwardly narrow, and you had to lean to the left out the window to hang out your washing between the Spanish bars. On the upside, we found a luscious late lunch of white bean soup and salad and shared a bottle of rosé.

That afternoon, Intelligent Prue chose to rest and I walked around the town in the blazing heat like an idiot, no doubt trying to make up for Rome. The whole town was sensibly closed for a siesta. Only myself and I presume mad dogs were out and about.

When Previously Exhausted Prue woke up, we went and sat on

the riverbank, near the ancient two-arched Rabia Bridge, with our feet in icy-from-the-Pyrenees water for ages. It was deliriously fabulous and my equilibrium returned.

We had a cool drink at a little outdoor café with many, many flies buzzing around. A man in jeans and a white apron splattered with blood walked past with a perfect lamb minus its skin slung over his shoulder. He continued to go backwards and forwards with large bits and pieces of freshly killed animals. I must have looked disturbed, as again Prue said to me, 'Just don't look.'

A little later, various friends of this attractive man walked up to him and happily chatted despite his by-this-time-blood-drenched clothes. It's odd that there's only one letter's difference between *laughter* and *slaughter*. Death. It's just too cruel.

The shock of Lew's death had produced an alertness I was unfamiliar with. Could I be alert and befuddled at the same time? It seemed I could. My senses were raw, so any breathtaking moments were vividly felt. I was so bloody grateful for anything good in my life, and the kindness of others gave me an aching appreciation. Tricky incidents could be a freezing strain because I had no resilience. But personal discomfort was nothing compared to what Lew had to put up with, and underlining everything was the black hollowness known as *Lewy Is No Longer Alive*. And sometimes I couldn't quite believe it – *surely not, surely not …?*

We gratefully watched, in a large field nearby, several lively caramel-coloured horses with shaggy blonde manes and tails cantering around their domain. Eventually these irresistible creatures came over to talk to us.

Φ

Normally when I travel I don't bother with the internet; but this time it was a lifeline. It was so good to hear from home.

I was worried my parents might be concerned about me (contagious, isn't it?), and because I didn't have a phone I emailed

Barbara and asked if she would kindly call them to let them know we were safe.

Although in Rome I'd managed to botch my credit card using the internet, I was also able to use it to unscramble the problems I'd created. And slowly I began to be able to express my thoughts.

> *EMAIL to Barbara: I am so glad to be walking. It's therapeutic, strenuous and meditative and it's very magical here. We are lucky to have been in an alpine area where it's much cooler, with beautiful forests, lichens, shade and wonderful Basque villages, although this afternoon is stinking hot. I love it and have lots of time and no pressure. Although I dissolve at the most trivial things … Poor Prue – who has been terrific … Feeling very sad about Lewy and really don't understand how it all went so terrible for him …*

I had forgotten to bring my address book and couldn't remember my own children's addresses.

> *EMAIL to Jonathon (their father): Thanks for the addresses very much … will just have to be patient and kind to myself. There's a great sense of freedom with my little world on my back. We're staying in Zubiri tonight, north of Pamplona. Please say hi to kids …*

> *EMAIL from Beth: I can't imagine your grief, my friend, but we're all there in spirit with you. I'm in Dee Why at the mo. I just remembered in the street that the last time I was here I ran into gorgeous Lewy and he offered to drive me home to Mona Vale. He'd probably been to his favourite deli buying olives or some such taste sensation for you, and the darling was quite willing to detour all the way to MV on his way home to your place …*

That was a side trip that would have added an extra 20 kilometres to Lew's journey. Beth had also lived on Scotland Island, and was the friend who'd bumped into Lew and me on our first date. She's a singer with a glorious voice and a thoughtful and upbeat writer.

Zubiri – Villava: 16 kilometres

We were glad to decamp the cramped *albergue*. We eventually stopped for breakfast in a pretty town called Larrasoaña. Over 16 kilometres we walked through quite a few small likable villages. We were nearly knocked off a narrow track whose lower side dropped away steeply by eight, roaring-out-of-nowhere, hornet-impersonating cyclists. I really didn't like the cyclists, but that could've been envy.

Some of the time, blackberry and blueberry bushes lined our trail. They were covered in ripe fruits at ideal eating height. I didn't eat any blackberries because I was worried they may spray them like we do in Australia, where they're classified as a noxious weed, but Fearless Prue was happy to partake.

After hard walking up hills I loved the expansive views that unfolded before us. We saw quinces and fruits we didn't recognise, cows, bulls, horses, sheep, goats, very thin cats, dogs, giant slugs, haystacks, icy cold rivers and pilgrims from all over the world.

As I walked ahead on my own, I was sorely troubled by a little dead frog on the road. I needed to push myself, to try to blunt that awful rawness and emptiness that rattled around in my heart and spongy brain and all the steadfast bones of my body. I could not make any sense of what had happened to Lewy. Doctors. Hospital. Helpless. Death. Around and around in my head. So awful. So awful. So Final.

This day was the first day of spring in Sydney. The jacaranda tree that I so treasured would contrarily start to lose its airy-fairy leaves sometime during this season. It would be as undefended as my raw heart.

Ф

We'd had it by the time we found an *hotel* just outside Arre at Villava.

But our alluring bathroom cheered us. We did our hand washing and hung it around our room in a colourful artistic display. From our beds, out a huge window, there was a terrific expansive view of the sky fringed by the town.

When I was going through my too-heavy backpack to see what I could throw out I found two weighty 1.5-litre bottles of water. Three times the amount I needed to carry. I could only throw out a few receipts and a sock with a hole. I bet that hole weighed a lot.

Our lunch/dinner of veggie soup from a big pot and a large platter of salad with white asparagus and a shared bottle of wine recharged us. That night I was so grateful that we fell asleep choking with laughter again. Grief was an erratic creature.

It's Worth Noting That I Never Saw A Spaniard Having A Tantrum

I've always kept a diary when travelling. The excitement of what I see has to bubble over into somewhere, but this time I found it difficult to write. My brain was conspicuously lame and my diary entries at first were jumbled and inconsequential.

But I found myself checking my emails if the internet was available where I stayed. I wanted to hear from my friends.

> *EMAIL to Ellie: Hi, how was your trip? Am a bit wobbly, would love to hear from you!*

My island friend was always supportive. I remember talking to her one day about Lewy, long before he became ill. I said we were so deliciously happy that I was uneasy that it could be taken from us.

> *EMAIL from Ellie: Well, my dearest friend … I miss you very much and think of you every day … a few wobbles are perfectly human. Do you know I often think of Lewy … every time I have a glass of wine or anything else, I toast him. This morning I was making the bed and said out loud, 'What a bugger Lewy's not with us to have a bit of fun with' – but he's sitting on your shoulder taking the easy walk with you …*
>
> *Hey, how's Prue? Sorting all those Spanish out? Has she some stout*

walking shoes?

My trip to the Centre was fantastic … it's so dramatic and harsh; makes Pittwater look so tame (and a bit boring really). You're going to see some fantastic scenery too … starting in the Pyrenees …

EMAIL *to Ellie: Thanks so much for your email. I think it's crap that Lewy's not here too, but he did try his very best, and was so positive to me right to the end. I have brought his photo along and am showing him lots of lovely things. When I lose the plot, Prue says I'm having a few junior moments. Have had a couple of near tantrums in public – so not me, who always wants to do the right thing.*

It's so good to think about my buddy while I walk. And every time I see something wonderful I wish Lew could see it, and any electrical whatever I think of him … (Work was the last thing on his mind when we travelled.) He was so alive and happy; sometimes it's hard to believe he's gone.

… My throat and chest are still tightening up, and my teeth clenching, but I'm sleeping much better at night because I'm completely exhausted. Brain is still questionable, but that may have been always the case. Looking forward to more improvements.

We are down from the Pyrenees now … Each day we are trying to walk a little more and are heading towards 25 km. I fancy dropping my backpack off a cliff …

So glad your trip was good. It is the best place, Central Australia. Love You.

EMAIL *from Ellie: Dearest Fabes, junior moments keep you sane, I think … Tantrums in public in such a Latin country are probably ignored … although what the hell, have them more often – I think they are healthy. Dear darling Lew will be laughing and sooooooooo understanding … It seems that you are describing heaven, but you are going so fast, 25 km in a day! Make sure you can absorb and remember it all – although the walking/exhaustion is probably the BEST, BEST thing you could do at this time. You're such a wise woman, Fabes –*

knowing that this was so essential at this time in your life. My darling girl.

Villava – Pamplona: 6 kilometres

We were woken at 12.30 am by my credit card service. I didn't know where I was, so I asked them to call again at 9 am. They called at eight, so I hadn't had a chance to work out where we'd be in a few days' time and if there was a *hostal* that could take us and hold my credit card. My plan for the trip was to have no plan.

With much help from the kind hotelier and Prue, a plan was made. They called back at nine, and after much talking said my card would be delivered to a *hostal* we had chosen at Estella on Friday. We'd arrive there on Saturday.

We leisurely packed all our clean dry clothes and set off for Pamplona. At the entrance to the city we crossed the sculptural thirteenth-century Magdalena Bridge. It was steep with pointed arches and its scale and proportions were warmly human.

We found a *hostal* from the *Lonely Planet* guide, up four flights of stairs with appallingly rickety railings but oodles of charm. The floors creaked and squeaked cheerfully. Our bathroom was tiny and its windows gave all the close neighbours a high-class sideshow.

We set out to look at Pamplona, but were sidetracked by what we call the Meal of the Day, which is a set menu. This *menú del día* was everywhere and a great cheap way to eat well. It's made up of three courses and costs usually around nine or ten euros. You could have a fresh healthy salad or perhaps soup as a first course, then a meat or chicken dish for seconds, and a tiny dessert to finish, plus half to a full bottle of local wine. Because the Spaniards have lunch so late you can make it a combination of lunch and dinner.

Afterwards, we walked around Pamplona. From the outside, their Baroque town hall was splendid. It was bedecked with colourful flags, gilded lions and crowns, red geraniums and curly carved details. On the top of this building was a trumpeter with a golden trumpet, giant bells, more crowns and lions, and they were flanked by a couple of bare-chested muscly types carrying spiked clubs. Sadly, sightseers weren't allowed past the foyer.

Pamplona's Santa María Cathedral, fourteenth to fifteenth-century Gothic, and the Church (*Iglesia*) of San Nicolás, thirteenth-century Romanesque and fourteenth-century Gothic, were WONDERFUL. They housed poignant, painted Gothic wooden statues of long-faced Madonnas and child, which were minimal and pure.

I lit two candles for Lew in San Nicolás and in the cathedral, but I found San Lorenzo bland and San Saturnino uninspired, so I didn't light candles there. Lew had taste.

We walked to the huge bullring. Rory, who had shown Lew and me around Madrid the year before, had recommended they were worth seeing when the show wasn't on, but it was shut tight. I had images of a powerful, bloody, bewildered bull stomping around in my brain.

I hope that's not how you are, wherever you are …?

Beauty

Pamplona – Uterga: 17 kilometres

This day our walk was the most beautiful so far. We saw lots of little bleached snails attached to plants. They looked dead and dried from the summer heat, but magically they were still alive. We walked through fields of sunflowers almost ready to harvest for their seeds. The repetitive pattern of the bowed heads of the browned flowers looked like mourners at an interment.

Bowed heads of sunflowers

In Zariquiegui we found the lovely Romanesque church of St Andrew, which looked ancient and had a great sense of place. It overlooked a huge plain fringed by mountains called the Sierra del Perdón. I looked up the definition of *sierra*: a chain of hills or mountains, the peaks of which suggest the teeth of a saw. How much I wanted to go inside the church, but it was locked, as many disappointingly were.

We walked through dry fields being ploughed into perfectly spaced furrows, with occasional haystacks. The distant hills had wind-power generators in long lines along their ridges. They looked tremendous. As we rose higher and got closer, the hum of the giant fans was quite loud, but not unpleasant.

We finally arrived at the top of the blowy ridge. There was a marvellous larger-than-life-sized pilgrim sculpture by Vincent Galbete of many animals and people in two-dimensional silhouettes made of rusty patina sheet metal. It looked pioneering and adventurous and was both inspired and inspiring. The sculpture seemed to lean into the wind. A lot of what I was doing felt like I was leaning into the wind.

We then walked down, down, down to Uterga. We had a late lunch at an *albergue* of artichoke with vegetable soup and salad and shared a bottle of rosé.

We met some fun New Zealanders, smiling Mark and elfin Tracy, who had on her heel the biggest, bloodiest, rawest blister I'd ever seen in my life. I showed them the stray blisters on my elbows, of unknown origin. We were diligently unstinting with the quantities of wine we guzzled with them and a young Belgian guy, although Mark drank little.

Prue was putting empty pistachio shells over her teeth and looking very swamp. One of the jokes she told was: 'Can you believe all these drinking illnesses? First there was Evian Flu and now it'S Wine Flu.'

Thank goodness for Prue is all I can say. It was irresistible that we had those body-shaking, choking laughs together. It was comfortable being with her; there was much we didn't need to say.

I can't remember going to bed … But we didn't lose anything.

Uterga – Cirauqui: 15 kilometres

We set off a tad late because we had to wait for the *albergue* person to arrive to see if we'd paid. Our room was up several flights of stairs; God knows how we made it the night before. The girl's eyes flickered with amusement when she told us we had.

The weather was overcast and cool and we had a great walk to Cirauqui, through fields of asparagus, olives, grapes, rich red peppers, and pretty little villages with closed churches; and we saw some huge crazy sunflowers.

Many towns were entered by crossing an ancient bridge that looked like it had always been and would always be there. Puente la Reina had a striking eleventh-century bridge built on the orders of Queen Mayor, the wife of Sancho III of Navarre. It also had appealing early churches and narrow streets. We saw unusual old houses with huge doorways that could have taken a carriage through them, and within the giant wooden doors were smaller doors for people only.

We arrived at Cirauqui around 2 pm and found an *albergue* with a room for just the two of us with a bathroom and an expansive countryside view. This was the nicest sleeping place yet. I sat on my bed with my feet up and haphazardly wrote in my diary.

After our showers, we walked around the town. It was amazingly hilly and so steep, up and down everywhere, like a giant lumpy mattress. Our up-high veranda overlooked the church, which glowed amiably in the afternoon sunlight.

On the veranda, I did my hand washing in a sink with a chunky bar of soap. Outside our window, three storeys up, was a metal multi-line to hang our washing.

Prue and I were using the word 'cupcake' if one of us was peeved, so the other knew to back off. Mind you, just saying it caused heaps of laughter, as did her capricious facial expressions.

We had an inexhaustible dinner with copious red wine in an

arched ancient stone basement with all the other travellers. Tracy took a picture of Unkeen Prue and myself. I woke in the middle of the night to find Pissed-off Prue was sleeping on the bathroom floor because of my red-wine snoring. I was mortified.

Φ

Cirauqui – Estella: 12 kilometres

We were up at 6.30 am. Our clothes were dry and we were on the road within the hour. The walk was steep and difficult from the start – usually it became worse as the day progressed. Despite this, I still felt the high I experienced when we set off each morning. A welcomed feeling of freedom and happiness, which was such a relief. These highs lasted about two hours and then the quest for a rest set in.

We stopped at a café/bar/restaurant in Lorca. I felt much better – it had been a mistake to walk on an empty tummy.

Inside the café, an Australian woman was crying. I asked her two friends if we could help. No, they said. I insisted that I'd love to help. 'Well, you could carry her backpack, that would help,' her friend said. *Cripes!* I thought, *I'm only just managing mine.*

Out in the fields surrounded by olive trees, we found a solitary, almost windowless medieval church. It was built in 1062 and called St Michael the Archangel. It was unlocked, so in we went. Inside was cool and minimal. People had touchingly left mementos on the simple altar table that stood in front of the austere eastern wall.

I wished I had a spare set of Lewy pictures from his service to leave there. I couldn't bear to part with the only one I had, but I was so torn. It was now two months since beloved Lew had died, but it felt far further-off since he had been alive.

Φ

We arrived at Estella around 1 pm, having walked through Villatuerta. Estella is a pretty medieval city that thrived in the twelfth century, so there are lots of narrow streets, churches, former monasteries, palaces and a big plaza (pronounced *platha* in Spanish). The River Ega winds through the town so there are plenty of stone bridges to cross.

In Sydney I hate barred windows, but in Spain many windows have fantastic curly ironwork, especially the ground and first floors, which over the centuries have protected people's lives, not their televisions and computers.

In a side street off the plaza, we had lunch in a little upstairs restaurant. I had a plate of cooked veggies and lamb stew to follow. My knife slipped and I threw gravy across the tablecloth and onto me. Does this happen to anyone else?

Prue had a siesta while I walked around the town. I kept going into churches, lighting candles and fervently praying to a God to look after Lewy. It seemed an essential thing to do and I was sure Lew would've liked it. There was a calming solace in many of the Romanesque and Gothic churches, with their beautiful painted timber Madonnas with their long Spanish nose. I didn't feel this same sensation in Baroque churches.

This was what I wanted the most for Lewy: to be cared for and to be at peace. He was in so much pain. He was wrenched out of this world. *Fuck that hospital ... Calming peace ... Fuck those doctors ... Calming peace ...* It was a contradictory time.

Later that night, Prue and I laughed ourselves to sleep. Again, it was a very contradictory time.

Φ

Of course my credit card never arrived. It was not only me being a fool; they were also quite talented in that department.

I phoned my Credit Card Replacers and, incorporating some choice swear words, told them not to bother replacing it. This would be the last time I behaved like a ratbag.

> EMAIL: *Hola! Darling Nick and Jess, hope you are OK? I am, and getting a few muscles. Can you please ring Granny and tell her I'm at Estella. She worries ...*

Last Day With Prue

Prue talked me into staying in Estella another day. It was easier for her to catch a bus from there to Pamplona for her flight home to Rome. So we had plenty of time to walk around and discover more of the city. It was nice to fluff around. We had the wickedest pastries with coffees at a *pastelería* for brekkie.

A little later, and with little notice, I had to race, and I mean *RACE*, into the closest building, which was a former Dominican monastery and now an old folks' home, and ask if I could use their toilet as I was *d e s p e r a t e*. I was well on my way to mastering a lack of pride.

On the side of a hill, nearby to my closest of shaves, we explored another minimalist Romanesque church, Santa María Jus del Castillo, which had been built over the site of a Jewish synagogue in the twelfth century. Inside we found a good exhibition of the history of the area.

The Spanish really know how to light their churches. In this church, and in some others, they'd suspended several large copper-coloured rings from the ceiling. Set in each ring were twelve downlights. This gave the church an ethereal quality.

Lewy, you would have loved the lighting!

Later, we did a steep, steep walk further up the hill to the almost disappeared ruins of the Castle of Zalatambor, built in 1026, which gave us a terrific view of Estella. It was fun being alone together

Courtyard at Estella

sitting way above the town. Prue sat at the highest point, between what I think was the flag of Navarre and the beautiful ornate ironwork Cross of Los Castillos.

The Spanish government had voted for shops to be closed on Sundays. I thought this was an excellent idea. Good on them for having a day off, not like us little Sydney consumerists. But it was disappointing that some of the cultural places I'd discovered and wanted Prue to see, and a couple of spots I hadn't visited, were also shut. The day before I'd seen an exhibition of paintings by Julio Romero de Torres, whose museum Lew and I had visited in Córdoba. I found his work in dubious taste; a bit like the Australian painter Norman Lindsay, but on a grander scale.

On the edge of Estella, we were checking out the façade of an intricately carved ancient church with a faded slate-blue door, when a huge hot-air balloon came drifting above our heads. The bright blue sky, the vivid orange balloon and the whoosh of the gas keeping the balloon afloat were quite magical.

I don't know why, but the prospect or occurrence of death repeatedly turns my face to the sky. The more I search it, the more I feel a tiny part of the infinite. And the beauty of the sky can be astonishing.

We saw some desirable ceramics, including a beaut huge jug about fifty centimetres tall, but I didn't buy it as it was way too heavy and I wasn't completely brainless. I was desperate to travel lighter, so I threw out my slightly broken sandals and found a few things that Kindly Prue would send home from Rome.

> *EMAIL to Laraine, a workmate: WOW! Have actually run with my pack on my back. Just showing off, of course!*

Φ

Estella – Los Arcos: 22 kilometres

Prue walked me to the edge of town and stood in an archway that went over the street, and like children we waved and waved and waved goodbye. I ingeniously took advantage of the distance between I Hate My Photo Being Taken Prue and me and took several of her as she became smaller and smaller as I walked up the hill, from now on, on my own.

It was miserable leaving Darling Prue, who I could only see when one of us travelled halfway around the world. I knew for sure that she had saved me from myself quite a few times; and not only had she not said, 'You are a nitwit!' but she'd masked all evidence of her thinking it.

But being by myself would give me more headspace to think about Lew, which was what I needed more than anything. His death was unbelievable, and I kept ransacking my mind to work out how I could have done better for him. Maybe I would be able to make some sense of things. At the very least, if I could walk harder I believed the tormenting images might subside.

Φ

I was walking through a grape-growing area and came to a tiny place, Irache, that Lew and Prue would've adored. There was a little courtyard off the track, and mounted on a wall were two stainless-steel taps for pilgrims, one with water and the other dispensing red wine. Uncharacteristically wine was the last thing I wanted, but a generous German pilgrim offered me her cup and insisted I had a taste.

The wine poured slowly from the tap and, grateful for her thoughtfulness, I had a little sip. It was light and delicious. Lew always drank sparkling wine with me. It was several years before I discovered he preferred red. Poor Lewy.

After a 9-kilometre walk I had an early lunch of chorizo and cheese (*queso*), crunchy/soft baguette and lemon juice. Spanish ham, cheese and chorizo are sliced finely and loaded with an intense and transporting flavour. Then I met up with a pleasant English couple, Jack and Mary, who were a bit older than me. Mary looked like Alice from *The Vicar of Dibley*. I enjoyed walking quite fast with them for an hour or so, but I wanted time to be on my own so I fell back. They were such nice people; I hoped they weren't on the terrorist poster at Pamplona airport.

The after-lunch walk was maybe 13 kilometres. I walked steadily and managed a total of 22 kilometres, which was my best so far. A fairly easy walk, but the weather was blazing hot, so I was horribly thirsty and mighty thankful when I reached Los Arcos. Previously it had been pretty perfectly overcast.

I found a bohemian-looking *albergue* in Los Arcos run by Austrians, but decided not to take the last bed in a dormitory of nineteen, as that seemed waaay too many. I ended up in another *albergue*: four euros for the last bed in a room of thirty-six!

I avoided drinking as I wanted to be fitter and lose weight. I hoped being on my own would be better for that. Without grog to block out the pain, there was more space to think clearishly about Lulu.

I was like Alice in love in The Vicar of Dibley when I first started going out with you – quite deliriously, joyfully, idiotically happy. Just over three years ago I wrote a speech for our wedding and spoke of the ridiculous, blissful joy I felt when we were together. I warned you and our friends that according to psychological studies, a besotted fool in love can take up to eighteen months to return to normal, so there were still six more months to go of my happy, scatty brain in its present state …

Walking alone had gifted me more time for Lew and I welcomed the sweet memories as they joined me.

Consolation

Late in the afternoon I slept for two hours and my spirits revived. That night I was going to the Pilgrim Mass at the local church and hoped it would be worthwhile. The things you do without a good book …

I was sorry I was glib because the Spanish Mass, where I hardly understood a word, was beautiful. I had Lew's picture with me, and sat next to Mark and Tracy. St Mary's Church was big, impressive, full of gilding and, with the lights on, bedazzling. The congregation's singing was stirring: they sang a deep and haunting unaccompanied song as they waited in line to take communion. This singing hummed through my body and moved me mightily.

The Sign of Peace was so friendly. At the end of the Mass, the priest had a special blessing for the pilgrims. He asked us to come to the front and he handed each nationality a prayer card in their own language. He had a great sense of humour, putting his finger to his lips to think and choose which nationality to call up next – Portuguese, French, German, Danish, English, Spanish, and more. He was quite theatrical, his colourful vestments were richly embroidered, and he had a twinkle in his eye.

I guess in the old days when the Mass was in Latin, the congregation would have understood about as much as I did – well, apart from the sermon. I was so glad I went. It was nothing like the colourless, dreary, grey and desiccated Church of England events of my childhood.

Φ

Music was an important part of my life with Lew. The last Christmas present I gave him was tickets to Mozart's *The Magic Flute*. He'd never been to the opera before. How lucky that his gift was an experience rather than an object. And Mozart's music is so lush. Lew had loved the film *Amadeus*.

Every year we went to a Gilbert and Sullivan operetta at the Sydney Opera House. I knew little of these delicious works until Lew told me how much he'd enjoyed performing in them at school, and it was a great joy for me to discover this heavenly music. Lew always sat transfixed and I loved how much he relished each performance. *The Gondoliers* was a knockout: witty, tuneful, exquisite, full of the joy of life and bouncing with colour and energy.

Every specialist appointment, every grim test, every awful treatment (sometimes twice a day), the fractured rib, the broken rib, the horrible burns — everything you suffered in the five months of your illness we drove to with boisterous Gilbert and Sullivan blaring at us. Mum had given us her CD, and we couldn't help but smile or laugh at this magical nonsense, despite your situation.

Φ

Los Arcos – Logroño: 28 kilometres

I slept well in that room of thirty-six, managing not to fall or walk off the top bunk. I slept with my wallet – normally inside my pack – as it was my only source of funds. Lew was much more enveloping.

Everyone was up before the dawn, but I didn't leave until daybreak as I didn't want to walk in the dark. The early morning walk was just marvellous. The air was cool, there was mist in the hills, and I watched the huge moon disappear and the sun rise. The softest pale blue and pink pastels were in the sky. Lew would have LOVED the light. All sorts of plants growing by the side of the road were glowing with illumination. I took heaps of photos with some pilgrims ahead and some in the distance behind. It was the best morning walk yet.

I wasn't sure how far I'd walk that day. I could try for Logroño, but it was 28 kilometres. Prue and I had been averaging 12.6 kilometres a day, as she'd found it hard going, but I loved the walking and was hoping to do more each day, up to 25 or 30 kilometres. Otherwise I wouldn't be home until Christmas. I'd see. Viana was 19 kilometres away and I didn't want to wreck myself.

Which was exactly what I did.

I walked and walked until I came to a gorgeous little twelfth-century Romanesque (*románico*) church with an octagonal floor and domed ceiling: the Church of the Holy Sepulchre in Torres del Río. It was clean, minimal and awe-inspiring.

Church of the Holy Sepulchre, Torres del Río

I stayed for some time. There were no chairs, but you could rest on a stone ledge around the walls. No candles to light for Lewy, but still captivating. I put my camera in the middle of the floor and photographed inside the dome, where fabulous stone ribs crisscrossed to form a star. I was deeply moved by the early thirteenth-century crucifix with a carved and painted wooden Christ about a metre high. I was cheered in this peaceful and simple church. I love the idea of people handing down to unknown future generations such a gift.

I walked to Viana, a lovely town 9 kilometres along from Torres del Río. This part of the walk was quite steep and known as the 'donkey killer'. I was hot and hungry, so to sever the baguette shackles, I sat down to a satisfying *menú del día* – mixed salad, thin crispy pork chops with chips, then ice cream and all the *vino tinto* you could drink. It appeared I could sustain my grog consumption all by myself … I drank over half the bottle, and after an hour my feet were better and I toddled off, in a burst of wine-infused enthusiasm, to Logroño.

This was a Big Mistake as my feet and whole body were exhausted when I entered Logroño around 4.45 pm. There was no relief from the sizzling sun anywhere and the purple road was radiating heat big-time. I felt awful. Who drinks more than half a bottle of wine during a 28-kilometre walk?

Are you laughing at me, Lewy?

Ф

Logroño is a big town with lots to see, but my feet were wretched. Before I found a place to stay I was quite scrambled from dehydration. Luckily I bumped into Tracy and Mark who were happily eating ice creams and they kindly stayed with me until I sorted myself out.

I found a *pensión* (which seemed just like a small *hostal*) up six excruciating flights of stairs. In my teeniest bathroom I only just managed to squeeze into the shower.

Out and about again, I drank a giant fake fizzy orange juice, which helped not at all. I had a look around Logroño's cathedral, Santa María de la Redonda. It was rebuilt in the sixteenth century in a Gothic style on the remains of a twelfth-century Roman church. It has two later-addition Baroque towers, known locally as the Twin

Towers. Despite it being an affecting space I couldn't even make the effort to light candles for Lew, so I straggled back to the *pensión*.

Walking 28 kilometres in the heat and with wine was a crackpot combination. But longer walking was effective: the tormenting loop in my skull was petering out. Still, I found it hard to sleep that night as I was sooo stuffed.

I was too tired to miss you, Lewy. I don't want to not miss you; I just want it to not hurt so much.

Little Things

Logroño – Navarette: 13 kilometres

Usually I research with gusto the attractions of the cities or towns I plan to visit, and I did half-heartedly dip into my *Guide to Spain*. But this trip was for Lewy. Whatever else was revealed by chance along the way was a bonus.

In this finest-wine-producing province of La Rioja, there's a Frank Gehry building in Elciego worth making a detour for. Gehry is a wonderful modern architect. I heard about it after I'd left the area, and no doubt there were other artistic treasures I didn't even know I'd overlooked. And yet this living in the moment, in a minimal lifestyle, valuing the simplest of things, was very fulfilling for my shaky soul. It was also very Lewy. He loved having a coffee out, but it wasn't about being on the way to somewhere or needing a pep-up because we had so much to do. It was about stopping, chit-chatting and enjoying each other's company. The same with going for a walk, or showering together, or sharing a simple lunch with bubbling laughter in the back garden. His relaxed personality was highly infectious. So much so that simply being together made each moment special.

Φ

My left foot was quite peeved from a blister. This was how you achieved injuries on the Camino – by overdoing it. When I was walking with Prue, sometimes I wanted to go faster and further, but to build up our fitness gradually was much better. It was also harder to keep an eye out for those occasional drippy yellow direction arrows when there was only one of you.

Four kilometres out of town I stopped and belatedly put on band-aids times two. I could hear my foot calling to me: 'Oi! Get off me. Let's go horse riding!' Remembering that Lew never complained helped me a lot.

Leaving this town was the opposite of entering it: a long walk through a most beautiful huge shady park, which also had a lake. Stopping in the park, I saw a tiny long thin chestnut squirrel. It dashed down a tree, along the grass and up another. It was so ethereal, delicate and pretty, it seemed to barely touch any surfaces as it scampered. The appearances of little creatures also helped to defuse the grim images that were in my mind.

There were many almond trees flanking the road. The fruit had ripened and split and the nuts were ready to eat. I didn't try them as I wasn't sure how resilient my teeth were after so much clenching. I wanted the anguish to go, but the teeth could stay.

Prue and I had passed several cairns along our way. Fantastical piles of flat stones, created by pilgrims whimsically adding to them as they passed. I came upon an alternative type of cairn: a cyclone wire fence stretching along the track into which imaginative pilgrims had woven crucifixes using wheat, grass, sticks, wood, rope and even a bike tyre's inner tube.

I walked 13 kilometres to Navarrete, an attractive town. My feet could have done 5 kilometres more, but the next town was another 13 kilometres and I didn't want to go further in the heat after the previous day. Preferring to be alone, I found another *pensión*. I often saw familiar faces of pilgrims on the road or in restaurants. It was so good to wave to or greet them, but then to stay on my own if I wanted to and be able to think my Lewy thoughts.

Navarrete cathedral was beautiful. It was grandiose like Los Arcos, with a massive gilded reredos, (a decorative facing on the wall at the back of the altar) but also quiet and peaceful. I lit six candles for Lewy and prayed full-heartedly that a God would look after him. I prayed to a fatherly God figure who had big shoulders and arms to put around Lew. He'd often said how much he missed his Dad, and it had distressed him that he'd not been hugged as a child. I was more than happy to oblige. One day I smugly asked him, 'Do you have enough hugs now?' 'Not yet,' he said. He was right: there's no such thing as enough. How lucky that I was with him before he died to wrap myself around him.

Did it help, Lewy? There was so little I could do.

I needed to punctuate this trip with fervent prayers and lighting candles and tears, sometimes not so gentle, for Lew. And it did help. I loved this quiet time; it gave me comfort and calmness.

We gave each other so many kisses through the day. I missed my beautiful boy wrapped around me at night. We snuggled together perfectly. It was unfair! I know that life's not fair; if you don't know it, you're in trouble. But it was still so not bloody fair!

Φ

Outside the cathedral was a shaded-with-plane-trees plaza with a fountain of four griffin heads spouting water and a life-sized bronze statue of a serene woman carrying a large water jug on her head. This place was tenderly beautiful.

I returned to the *pensión* and went up to my room to do some washing and put the feet up for an hour or so. How easy to do the washing in the basin of my room and then lean out the window and hang the clothes on the little line in the sun. I used soap or shampoo or bubble bath, whatever was going. All seemed to work, except my little white socks never looked clean. Who brings white socks on the Camino? Only me? I was grateful that life was uncomplicated.

Navarette fountain

I wandered about the town for some time. Apart from food and clothing markets, I couldn't find much more to see other than the cathedral. I found an internet café/beguiling sweets shop and answered and wrote emails. Then I strolled back to a pleasant bar in a shady plaza and drank *vino blanco* and nibbled on flavourful fat green olives with Hamish the Canadian.

He'd been walking huge distances daily and would almost be finished before he'd started. He was used to hiking with a heavy pack at steep high altitudes in the cold of the Canadian mountains. The Camino to him must have seemed like a stroll in the park. Relativity – that was a whole new issue. Also representing relativity was Swiss Pascal, who I believe had walked all the way from Switzerland.

They reminded me of what a friend had said to me – that losing Lewis was the second-worst thing that could happen to me. Did that mean relatively speaking it wasn't so bad? I know tragedy can occur on an appallingly huge scale, but this was our own heart-shredding tragedy and Lewy had lost everything.

I left these inspiring folk for a last visit to the cathedral. In the silence of the nave I remembered the piercing sorrows of my friends. I thought about a young woman who died aged twenty-six from depression, via Sydney Harbour's infamous The Gap. When she was well, you couldn't have met a more animated and delightful person. And of a young man who was only twenty-one when he was run over by a drug-and-alcohol-fuelled woman in a fit of road rage. A dear bloke who was just finding his way, with the hard stuff behind him. Or a beautiful healthy babe who died hours before he was born, strangled by his treacherous umbilical cord. At forty-two, his mum had had a difficult, asthma-troubled, final pregnancy. And now Lewy, who so relished life, dying of an unknown avaricious cancer at fifty-three when he was so bloody happy.

Such tangled passions of grief at their deaths. Life starts and life finishes; when it finishes we have no idea. Dive in, have fun, be kind, cherish those you love.

When I'm missing you it's worse if I'm standing up, surrounded by hollow and empty air. Much better to miss you lying in bed and snuggle my face into the pillow with at least one side of my body against the soft mattress. The enormity of what has happened affects me more when I'm still and alone.

Φ

Navarette – Azofra: 22 kilometres

I woke refreshed from a long, sound sleep. After a brekkie of just-out-of-the-oven baguette, I set off feeling brighter and expectant for whatever the 'road' may throw up at me.

On the edge of the town was an extraordinary columned and carved stone Romanesque gateway to the sadly locked cemetery. Peering through the iron gates I saw an unusual building in which they bury people in tiers above the ground.

I walked through a vineyard which had vines bulging with mostly red and some white grapes. The ground was extra dry, but the grapes were velvety and lush. I didn't pick any. They would have been someone's livelihood.

Along my way, I'd seen a number of seriously undernourished young cats. I'd bought a few tins of sardines for them, but when I saw the most starved ones I had no food on me. Country life has so much beauty, but also a harsh reality.

I had lunch with boyish East Berliner Alex in the unattractive outskirts of Nájera. He had a sweet but earnest disposition. He was about thirty, spoke perfect English, absolutely hated making English mistakes and social blunders, was full of hormones, would have loved to meet a cute girl and was endearingly charming. He was deeply questioning his way of life, so I wasn't the only one full of angst. Nevertheless, he was easy to hang out with, a lot because he was close in age to Nick.

As we headed into the busy town, we went our separate ways. I tried to go into the unusual, castle-like, Gothic monastery St Mary the Royal, which looked fantastic and had three storks' nests on the tower, but the door was locked. Later I was disappointed to find out that I could've entered through an obscure side door.

I decided to do a longer walk that day and not stay at Nájera, but trek on to Azofra. I walked out of the town up a quiet, steep, long, long hill. I met tall and becoming 25-year-old German Anke. Luckily for me she spoke English. She had a marvellous deep voice, her hair was curly flaxen and she was the only pilgrim I'd met who wore mascara. She needed it not at all. We talked and walked so the hill wasn't so bad. This often happened on the Camino, and of course in life.

Anke strode off ahead and I was happy at my own pace. Eventually I heard behind me a woman *singing* beautifully, and I met up with Singing Beatrice soon after. She was around thirty and Basque. She loved my Red Lewy Skirt as much as I did. It was a generous skirt with big red flowers and splodges of green on it. Of all my clothes Lewy liked it the best and I wanted to wear it for him. Beatrice took off into the distance and I walked happily alone again. Meeting these interesting people out in the sunshine, however briefly, gave me more positive living pictures for my brain.

Further on I met up with faded-red-haired Luke, tall, slim, from California, wearing a white woven hat. He looked about sixty, and was resting at a stop sign and drinking some water. I couldn't resist saying I was glad he was obeying the traffic signs. Sometimes I'm tragically like Dad, who makes cleverer flinching-wincing puns, but as Mum says, you always have to listen just in case he makes a really good one.

Luke and I walked on together, enjoying each other's company. He'd recently turned seventy, was an improvisational actor and teacher, and great fun. He'd just come from Russia, where he'd been teaching, and was finding the going tough because he'd already done much walking there. We talked happily the rest of the way to Azofra, where we found a terrific *albergue*. When we went to check in we found that all the sleeping rooms were small with only – *bravo!* – two to a room. The *hostelera* told us we could have the last two rooms, but I would have to share with a man.

Luke piped up and said his male friend would share with the bloke and he was happy to share with me, as at least we knew each other. I tartly blurted out my husband had just died and I didn't want to share with any bloke whether I knew him or not. Luke exclaimed that he was gay and I would be quite safe with him. Then the *hostelera* said she'd made a mistake and that there was a woman in my room not a man.

Later I told Luke I was so sorry; it was just a hard time for me at present. He was fine about it, and I was grateful that people forgive you a lot when you have lost someone close to you. I could hear Lewy laughing at me.

And when I walked into my room, who should be there but superhealthy, large-eyed, short-haired, suntanned Beatrice, who spoke English and was so very nice in a great bolshie way. This was her second year on the Camino. She had started last year, and hopefully next year would do more.

The *albergue* had a large square fountain with dazzling blue icy-cold water that you could dangle your legs and feet in. Just the best experience. I sat there for over an hour on that hot day, talking with dear Anke, my emotional feet in the water. Bliss.

Beatrice was excited to share a room with me because she'd been sleeping with a lot of snorers and was tired and she could just tell that I wasn't one. *Oh dear*, I thought. *Keep off the red wine, Fabes.* I said casually, 'Actually I am a deep sleeper and if I do by some chance snore just tell me to stop.' She only woke me once.

Φ

Azofra – Santo Domingo de la Calzada: 15.5 kilometres

Time was sprinting by. At 7 am I was having breakfast with Beatrice at a café. Whenever she talked about food she put the fingers and thumb of one hand together and kissed them. Her large eyes looked directly at you when she spoke.

Lots of pilgrims were having breakfast there, and all our weighty backpacks were lined up in the street outside the café. If only mine could've been stolen. We had toast, orange juice, coffee and rockmelon. The waiter offered me some rockmelon to eat on the way.

It was Beatrice's last day on the Camino so off she went by herself. Basque Beatrice was definitely a Separatist. She liked to walk alone. When I went to pay for my breakfast she had already paid for me.

Sometime later I caught up with Luke. We talked all the way to Santo Domingo and I could feel myself smiling. Strangely, Luke did not look like a Luke. Later he mentioned that his name had been Terry and he'd changed it.

The scenery was a little dull, but the conversation was fun. I decided to travel only 15 kilometres, as I wanted to see Santo Domingo and I still regretted not staying at Viana.

We went through a disquieting new town called Cirueña. It was fascinatingly clean and neat and we saw no one there at all. It may have been a show place for new homes with manicured minimal-vegetation gardens. We were keen for coffee and feared that the golf club we'd seen at the beginning of the town was the only place that sold it, but we weren't prepared to go backwards, even for coffee. Then, rising out of a rampantly overgrown field, we saw several amazingly schmicko houses. This place looked like a Tim Burton film set. Finally, at the other end of town, we found the original town, where the houses and overgrown gardens were in harmony. Which way was the disease spreading, I wondered.

In the old section of town we savoured our snack of Spanish omelette, lemon juice and coffee. Eggs are popular in Spain and the Spaniards are skilled with them.

We arrived at Santo Domingo in no time. Our cheap *pensión* was unusually disheartening – a nasty stain on my bedspread, dingy furniture, the shared bathroom door wouldn't quite shut, and no shower curtain so there was water all over the floor. But I was glad to have my own room with its welcome air of peace.

We set out to explore. The town was celebrating its foundation nine hundred years ago. Luke and I went up the bell tower and had a ranging view of the town's terracotta-tiled roofs. I loved being up high. There were giant bells near our heads, which scarily struck twice: *LOUDLY! LOUDLY!* From up there we could see the pilgrims' entry and exit to the city. I wondered if anyone sees our entry and exit into this world.

Together we went up the Eiffel Tower Lewy. I was frightened in that mega-steep-angled lift. We stopped on the second level and only you went right to the top. From that elegantly engineered iron construction the views were wonderful. I walked down from the second level. No way was I going back into that lift. You were really disappointed I wouldn't go to the top with you. I would be brave now! We had a better experience from the top of the Arc de Triomphe one cool evening after a stinking hot day, looking back down the Champs-Élysées, seeing the lights of Paris and the twinkling Eiffel Tower light show.

Luke and I visited the restored Convent of San Francisco, which is now a swish *parador* hotel. The Spanish government has taken over run-down historical architectural gems, restored them and turned them into fine hotels full of antique Spanish furniture and oodles of charm.

We also went to see the cathedral, which was delightful. I was being extravagant with candles – I suddenly realised, *why not?* The great big, bold, gold Spanish Baroque behind-the-altarpiece (reredos) had been moved to a side chapel, and so now the reredos was simple, with beautiful original Romanesque stone carvings. A live hen and rooster were kept up high behind barred glass to illustrate a miracle that had happened there in the Middle Ages.

The story was that a German pilgrim travelling with his parents refused the advances of the innkeeper's daughter. Spitefully she hid a silver cup in his haversack. He was accused of the theft and dismally hanged the next day. (No clogged courts there, I guess.) His parents, before continuing on their journey, went to say goodbye to their dead son, but found him alive thanks to the intervention of Santo Domingo. When they told the judge what had happened, he said it was as likely that their son was alive as if the roasted rooster and hen he was about to eat should live and breathe. Suddenly the birds stood up and started crowing and clucking. I recalled hearing of an almost identical miracle in Barcelos, a city in Portugal.

This cathedral was a light, airy and sparkling place to be in. I really liked it. And it was so visitor-hospitable, it even had toilets. There was a big didactic exhibition about Heaven and Hell and the Seven Deadly Sins in the museum section of the cathedral. It was interesting and weird, and gluttony and sloth looked quite appealing. Overall, the depiction of Hell gave Luke and me the creeps. To think of someone you loved in a place like that …

I answered all of the Hell quiz questions incorrectly – always talented at denial, especially of the concept of Hell. Heaven was fun: you went up to the roof and into a giant plastic dome where you watched an artistic video light show. It was curious that the Hell part was a lot more complex.

Like the Heaven Dome, the love and happiness Lew and I shared was so easy that I find it difficult to describe without making it sound insubstantial. A talented haiku poet could do it.

Up Hill And Down Dale

Santo Domingo de la Calzada – Belorado: 23 kilometres

I enjoyed walking mostly on my own this day. Luke was tired so he was going to stay an extra day in Santo Domingo. Watching the sun come up as I walked was fabulous. The sky was deep grey with a pink hue near the horizon and the sun was a ball of red gold. Close up, giant sunflowers, their heads dipped in sleep, would soon wake and turn towards the light. The sky became a smoky pink and mauve and the red glow in the sun vanished as it eventually faded the moon. Again I saw pilgrims ahead and behind as the countryside rolled out before me. We were buzzed early from above by two separate guys with curved parachutes and fans behind them. A vision of freedom. Beautiful dry rolling landscapes of sunflowers and shorn hayfields were the backdrop of this day. My breakfast of cake and coffee in Grañón tasted like ambrosia. They should have offered it in the Heaven Dome.

I joined Tracy, Mark and Freddy the German for the last kilometres into Belorado. I found the going full on; my foot was upset and I was trying not to be. Always happy Mark was showing off his energy levels by jumping and kicking up his heels with his backpack on. His debonair good-natured joy reminded me of Fred Astaire.

At the beginnings of the town we found a pleasant *albergue* with a pool, but as usual the water was way too cold to swim. I was surprised at the water temperature; it must have been well below eighteen degrees, which is when I chicken out of swimming.

Fields before Belorado

In a large dining room I had my favourite lunch/dinner of bean soup, salad and yoghurt while I watched a film on a big screen. It was about the Camino and made up from many poignant photographs interspersed with text. The text and sometimes the music were irritating, but the photos were excellent. I decided to buy the DVD. This was an unfamiliar decision – to carry anything extra in my pack.

I went into the attractive town centre to have a look around. Behind a large banner a touching procession had started from one church. All the men were at the front in their devotional best, carrying candles and singing; next came the priest and a dear little altar boy; and the women followed. They walked around the town and ended up at another small church, where I joined them for a Mass with singing that was full of life.

I saw fantastic, enormous, out-of-scale nests on the tops of bell towers, probably built and used by storks. If it were up to me, I would also put storks' nests on bell towers in the Heaven Dome.

EMAIL from Hugh: All your messages were great to read but full of struggle and you miss Lewy. I know it's really hard and you have been through hell but now things seem to be working out. You sound like you are enjoying it more as the rhythm builds. Aimee says 'Walk, walk, walk and you will find it,' and I agree ... Watch those junior moments. I'm sorry you lost the mighty Prue. She must have lots of boring responsibilities in Rome.

Travel safe and endure all the physical struggle with Fabo style. I send you all my support ... I don't know what else to say other than try to be happy and enjoy Spain and the Spanish etc. Talk to you soon.

Hughie was right: the rhythm of the walk was building and I was feeling better.

Φ

Belorado – San Juan de Ortega: 24.3 kilometres

When leaving Belorado for San Juan de Ortega I crossed the lovely Bridge of Song, whose arches are low and stretched. I was walking along gently, thinking my own thoughts, when suddenly I was bombarded by the clack-clack-clacking of lightweight aluminium sticks. A party of tightly organised, fast-walking pilgrims came up behind me, clacking their sticks like giant praying mantises. Maybe I've seen too much *Doctor Who*? I had to step aside as they swept past, looking more like a workout than a walkout.

After a while I met up with David, a Catalan from Barcelona, who was a boyish dark-haired forty-one and just starting the walk. He worked for the emergency services and only had ten days' holiday at a time, so he had to walk the Camino in stages and this was his third. He was warm, friendly and good to chat with. He spoke Catalan, Spanish, French and English. His English was spot-on.

Lots of pilgrims had said the walk from Belorado to San Juan de Ortega was terrible – 24.3 kilometres and the second half was uphill and mighty steep. Some were having their packs delivered to the next town. I didn't want to do that, but I admit that by the end of the day, the arches of my feet had typed up a list of complaints.

We walked up to a slightly chilly 1100 metres, passing young conifers and delicate alpine flowering shrubs. We came to a moody conifer forest. I hadn't seen wooded areas for some time. David thought this forest had been used in filming some of *Doctor Zhivago*, so you can imagine how atmospheric it was. The fine metal-grey trunks were covered in circles from branches no longer there, and crowded so densely that their shadowy green foliage could only exist at a lofty height. The tall leaning grasses by the side of the track were bleached from summer.

On the way to San Juan de Ortega

We met up briefly with Anke and ate our packed lunches under the trees by the side of the dusty dirt road. Then we staunchly trekked up and down the steepest of hills, passed several gigantic haystacks and continued down to tiny historic San Juan de Ortega. David went on to the next town. I was happy to stay put.

The notable *albergue* was a fabulous old building with sixteen bunk beds to a room. Despite the place being quite grubby, I was glad of a bed. The two-storey structure was built around a small courtyard. On the second level were verandas all around, with lines and railings festooned with pilgrims' washing drying in the afternoon sun. At the bottom of the stairwell were many, many rows of walking shoes and a huge pile of walking sticks. Thoughtful *alberguistas* required you to leave your walking shoes or boots outside your room so that no one asphyxiated while sleeping. After that hill, I guessed out the room and down the stairs was a better idea.

I tried to walk around the tiny community, but my feet told me otherwise. I hadn't realised they were so highly strung. I managed to have a quick look at the lovely Romanesque Chapel of St Nicholas, which was thankfully just about next-door. It had an exquisitely proportioned bell tower with three bells.

I had a drink of beeno blanco (Spanish pronunciation of 'white wine') at the nearby bar; and later attended a Pilgrim Mass at St Nicholas's. I'd seen an attractive swarthy man of about forty-eight earlier in the *albergue* who looked a bit shifty, so I thought I'd best keep an eye on my stuff. He turned out to be an Italian priest who assisted in the Mass. In a fit of Camino zeal he'd gone too fast and for too long at the beginning and now his feet were wrecked, hence the expression on his face. A pilgrim later told me that he'd had to return to Italy because of his feet. I don't know how correct that was.

After the Mass, the *alberguistas* served us, in glazed terracotta bowls, a traditional meal of thin watery garlic soup with small pieces of feathery bread drifting in it. It wasn't enough to sustain us after a long day's walk, but it was gratefully received.

Chapel of St Nicholas, San Juan de Ortega

I met up again with Jack and Mary in the bar and we had giant Spanish omelette baguettes. They were great to talk with. Mary said she felt bad when she saw me because they were so happy and I'd lost Lew. I said I was always glad to see people happy together and it was actually not that common. They told me that when they were young and wanted to marry, Mary's father had said absolutely not and that if they did marry he'd write her out of his will. When Mary's father died, even though she'd been content with Jack for forty years and they'd had a family, she found he had cut her out of his will.

I wished Lewy were there. He could have said something about families. He'd found it insufferable hearing members of his family speaking with disdain about his deceased Dad for almost thirty years.

After my shower, I shook myself dry. I needed to buy a tiny towel. That night two girls left because they thought the place was too dirty, but I fell into my very comfy bunk exhausted.

Φ

San Juan de Ortega – Burgos: 26 kilometres

I took off at 6.30 am believing the dawn was looming. Certainly it was cooler at that hour, but it was irrational to leave before it was light. I had no torch; I could fall over or go in the wrong direction. Where the hell had my dreary common sense gone?

As it was too dark to read the signpost for directions, I tried to follow some pilgrims' torches way ahead in the black distance. Several tiny pinpricks of light. Such an allegory for how my mind was that morning: black and lost, with little jewels of relief.

Oddly enough, walking sightless through the quiet woods was welcome. The softness of the silence and concentrating where to place my feet overtook my dark thoughts. I walked for forty minutes through a forest before the dawn started to break straight ahead – which, as I was supposed to be heading west, was a worry. I would not do that again.

I stopped at Agés for breakfast, which tasted fresh and wonderful. And the bathroom was sooo clean. It was such a blast when toilets had paper and then *soap* and a towel.

Leaving Agés I bumped into David again and companionably walked with him. He was extra nice and I was grateful to be walking with a Spaniard. Most of the people I met were particularly heart-warming. Along the way we saw more giant golden haystacks as tall as a three-storey building. Two pilgrims overtook us on a hill and were giggling as they passed. I realised I'd accidentally tucked the back of my skirt into my knickers in my bathroom bewitchment … yikes! David hadn't said a word.

The last 10 or so kilometres were difficult. They were along a main highway through a characterless industrial area of Burgos, which was a lot like Sydney's dismal Parramatta Road. The footpaths were hard on my feet; my arches were about to complain to their union. I dared not tell them their fees were unpaid. Some pilgrims had said they were going to catch a bus along this stretch. *Why?* I'd thought. Now I knew. It went on forever. David and I joked about it, but it wasn't funny. We rested about 2 kilometres from the city centre and had a cup of coffee as I was the worse for wear.

When we arrived in the historic centre of Burgos, I stopped at the first hotel I came to. I couldn't walk another centimetre. I needed to empty my pack out all over a *w i d e* bed, drop my clothes on the floor, walk around in my underwear and not hear pilgrims rustling their poxy plastic bags at 6 am. I had a shower in my fresh bathroom with TOWELS and a bathmat. I had my clothes washed by a laundry as I couldn't be bothered.

Just before 4 pm I had a fantastic veggie stew for lunch at a restaurant. The waiter was grumpy – I think because I was eating late – but there were plenty of people still in the restaurant. I like to smile, but I didn't give him one. That showed him.

Afterwards, I set off to look at Burgos's famous cathedral and streets. The ancient centre was lovely. Many of its five-storey buildings had unusual decorative multistoreyed timber and glass verandas attached to their fronts. St Mary's Cathedral, built during the thirteenth to fifteenth century, had quite a lot of external filigree stonework, which gave it a lacy look. Inside, there were beautiful painted patterns at the sections where the ribbed vaulting met. Not a fabulous cathedral, but pretty good with several lovely old frescoes.

I hated being too tired and jumbled to enjoy Burgos. The town and its cathedral were probably a lot better than my skewed perceptions recognised. I kept seeing things that Lew would have loved, such as moody lighting, an extravagant chandelier, a funny little fruit and vegetable shop with unfamiliar produce; or I met people that he would have clicked with. We'd both loved Barcelona and I knew he would have relished talking with David and hearing his opinions of his hometown. Sociable Lew enjoyed the random company of others. When they were kind or extra helpful he was much moved. I so wished he was with me. He was missing out on so much.

Φ

EMAIL from Megs (It Doesn't Pay to Omit the Truth): Hi Fabes … guess what, I had your Mum and Dad at the surgery the other day! The new doctors who have moved into our surgery are theirs. So we had a good chat and I told them that I had received an email from you … and that you were having a very therapeutic time. I told them of your candle lighting and the beautiful time with Prue. Unfortunately I told them that Prue was leaving and your Mum said she didn't realise that and then I felt terrible. But she came back and said she was not worried and was so pleased that she had run into me and that you were going really well and that you had met many other people … Sorry, Fabes, but I hope that was OK. They said next time I'm writing to you to wish you well and that they were happy with the info. Things are just the same here, still have Lewy on my shelf and tell him what you are doing …

Tall, soft-voiced Megs is a dear and gentle friend and Lew responded warmly to her kindly personality. She invited us over several times for terrific dinners when he was quite ill.

EMAIL from Helen: Fabe, last night I dreamt of Lewy. The three of us were together and we knew he wasn't well. It was a very peaceful and happy dream. Lew was calm and smiling and looked beautiful. I hope I'm not making you sad, but the feeling of it all was of a physical warmth and joy. I was lucky/blessed to have had this dream.

  Please keep the emails coming; we keep looking at the map.
  I picture you under the moon …

Φ

Since you died I've only had one tiny dream about you. I was standing on one side of an uncrossable busy four-lane road, you were on the other. You were wearing your soft yellow T-shirt and long cream work shorts. You were still, looked quite beautiful, your curly hair was a little longer and you were looking at me seriously. I felt you were saying, without words, that we could no longer be together and goodbye. Why don't you come to me in my dreams? I miss you so much. We could be carefree and tender.

By the evening I was thoroughly miserable. My good friend Tiredness enabled me to fall asleep fast.

The Delight Of The Unexpected

Burgos – Tardajos: 10 kilometres

I slept dreamless. After a breakfast with eggs in the swishhhh-for-me hotel, I went across town to the post office to send home receipts and pamphlets to keep my bag light. Here was progress: I could now make a transaction at the post office.

I was pleased and cheered to find a good raincoat, cheap sunnies (I'd broken mine) and a mini chamois towel at last. Old Burgos is a very pretty city to hunt in. I saw a large, black, full of life and fearless sculpture of a man on a horse with a sword: El Cid, who was born in 1043.

I planned to walk only 10 kilometres. My feet had informed me they'd resign if I kept treating them like I had the day before. If you do this walk, start off slowly with short distances wearing shoes you are completely used to. The former is harder than you think; because it's so beautiful you feel you can go on indefinitely. Also, perhaps catch a bus the last 10 kilometres into Burgos and then you can really appreciate the old parts of the city.

Around noon, just before I was leaving, I saw Tracy and Mark lining up at an *albergue* near the cathedral. Tracy was planning to buy new boots in Burgos in case of another blister. They had to catch a train to León the next day as her ghastly blister (which was now much better) had slowed them down and put them behind schedule for

El Cid, Burgos

their return flights. She said it was a really difficult choice to make – to leave so many friends they'd made along the way and leap forward to León where they would have to become used to new people. It was like leaving family behind, not knowing when you would see them next. It was beaut to see them once more and I was really sorry that I wouldn't see them again on the Camino.

As I left Burgos, I was thrilled to see a stork sitting on one of those impressive, large nest-constructions I'd seen, particularly on bell towers. Are all storks deaf?

My walk today wasn't that good. I was comfortable by myself, but I didn't experience much joy. It was more of a Tramp, Tramp, Tramp

– too much the previous day, I guessed. My spirits were down and I was glad to stop in a little town called Tardajos. I walked 300 metres past the *albergue* as I couldn't find it. A local gem of a woman took me all the way back and showed me where it was. From the outside, it was a most hideous-looking place.

It was run by volunteers – an Italian woman and her Bostonian husband – and payment was voluntary. There were eight in our room and they were all fun. Three Italians, one French, three Germans and me, all laughing. We spoke French to understand each other (mine was minimal) and arranged to go to dinner together at 8 pm. The kind Bostonian brought backgammon upstairs to see if we'd like to play. His dear wife lent me a little sewing kit to repair my T-shirt and insisted I keep it.

In the afternoon I walked around the town. The church was quite lovely with lots of character; I 'lit' about twelve white electric candles for Lewy.

The best buildings were honest, indomitable and reflected the character of the people who lived there. I saw an ancient house with huge stone lintels set within roughly dressed stone. The main doors were made from massive pieces of timber and the roof was earthy handmade clay tiles. A primitive wooden gutter poked out the front of the building, directing water back to the ground in a waterfall; and contrasted with two delicate urns cemented above on the roofline. Had there been more trees in this tiny town it would've been perfect.

We had to walk through a bar to go to dinner. Such a picture: it was chockers with local men smoking and playing dominos or cards, and the floor was littered with empty sugar packets, cigarette butts, matches and all sorts of rubbish. I would have loved to take a photo but it seemed crass. Outside, sitting on a bench, were four elderly men with hand-hewn walking sticks watching the world go by. I sneaked a shot of them when they were looking the other way. Sometimes the most charming of photos I didn't take because it would have killed the moment, or, especially in a church, it seemed inappropriate.

Dinner with all the people from the *albergue* was fun. We sat at a long table in a large dining room and ate either noodle soup or salad, then fish or steak, and finally ice cream, melon or choc pudding with *vino tinto* or *blanco*. The evening was extra friendly and lifted my spirits mightily.

We were all in bed by 10.15 pm. The Italians were chat-chat-chatting and laughing. The Germans were seriously trying to sleep so they could rise early.

More life lessons: the people had made the place.

Φ

Tardajos – Hontanas: 21 kilometres

I was woken early by those Germans: crackle, crackle, pack, pack. My views on their routine were: throttle, throttle, hack, hack. It was pitch dark and raining.

When I left an Italian woman called Olga asked if she could walk with me. I think she'd only started her Camino at Burgos. We walked for about an hour, but I wanted to be on my own, so I said *adios*, despite her being particularly warm and kind. I walked on by myself in light rain in my new prized raincoat.

Despite the rain, the countryside looked parched, and beautiful – yellow cut fields, grey tones, grey sky and rolling hills. This open and exposed area, for the next approximately 200 kilometres, is known as the Meseta. The infrequent villages lie in low valleys, which rise to elevated, austere and windswept plains. Here in the north, the grain crops had been harvested and replaced by a dusty dryness. Over this sparsely treed and unpopulated area the sky was all pervading, as it was when Lewy was ill. I was a tiny part of the infinite. Life choices, possessions and aggravations evaporated and I felt connected to the universe as the teeniest tiniest particle. I hoped that my buddy was out there somewhere.

Meseta sky

Gradually the rain eased and a striking 55-year-old Swedish woman caught up with me. She had also lost someone close to her. We talked for some time, but then she asked me about Lew and whether I blamed myself for his death. Perhaps she felt that way, but it was unbearable for me to hear. I had to get away. Fast. As soon as we stopped for lunch, I ate my fruit and then bolted with my own thoughts.

I was terribly upset to hear someone else say the words I had been berating myself with for the last ten weeks: I SHOULD HAVE DONE MORE IN THAT HOSPITAL. It didn't matter that I was out of my depth, or that there were signs in the hospital that warned *Aggression will not be tolerated*. Not for the first time had I confused assertion and aggression. I'd feared that asserting Lew's best interests would have been seen as aggressive. When he was suffering and I was exhausted, my clear thinking was cloudy. I ached that I could have done better.

Eventually, by walking and because the landscape was so beautiful, my thoughts settled as I headed towards Hontanas. Was that running away, or was I trying to deal with the unbearable as best I could? Certainly I had talked considerably with a grief counsellor before I left Sydney, but there is something in my personality that also needs an all-encompassing physical response. When I said I blamed myself for Lew's death it sounded reasonable; but when someone else said it, it sounded wrong.

Φ

Before Hontanas, I saw huge motionless wind generators lined along the horizon like vacant crucifixes. The town wasn't visible where it should be and I started to worry. Then, abruptly, a small, enticing village appeared in a valley up ahead.

I was pleased to stay in an *hostal* with my own room. I had lunch/dinner around 2 pm with graceful Francine, a pleasant over-sixty Frenchwoman. Then I had a long sleep as I was teary from missing Lewy. Sleep was a blessed escape. I was trying to escape my sorrow, but sometimes I just couldn't. Landscape, beauty, walking and dear peoples could not always calm my overwhelming feelings.

Late in the afternoon, I explored the town. I saw a local man carefully carrying like a dish the head of a sunflower as big as a dinner plate. The petals had withered into crispy nothingness and it was bulging with seeds.

I peeped through a door and saw a courtyard that I imagined belonged to a sculptor. There were all sorts of bits and pieces of warmly rusting farming paraphernalia hanging on a stone wall and a couple of strange-faced objects sitting on the ground. An unexpected artistic oasis.

Nearby, I saw two Alsatian dogs and a Siamese cat. One dog was awfully aggressive to the other dog and cat. Life can be ruthless.

I enjoyed the walk, however, and the light and sky were lovely from the rain. Sitting out in the street I met up again with Olga and we had a coffee. She seemed to have forgiven me for bolting from her company.

I went into the local church when it opened at 6 pm. It was a depressing place, no candles to light, and I didn't want to anyway. No cheer here.

I was thinking about Lew. Despite our overseas and local adventures, it was really in the little things of our daily lives that Lewy and his kindness shone the most. The cup of tea in bed each morning and the fabulous breakfasts he made – often with strings attached. The beautiful bunches of colourful flowers. The phone call on his way home from work: 'Anything we need that I can pick up from the shops?' Sitting on the couch in the evenings holding hands or his hand on my thigh. The many gentle kisses that punctuated the day. Lewy loved sitting together in our sunny little back garden having lunch, and always with food mostly generously bought and lovingly prepared.

I hate the way people call death 'losing someone'. Yes, it is a loss, but if only I could find you!

I was silently crying when in walked Catalan David and young Alex. I was glad to see them again and managed to get a grip. We went and had a drink, and then they went on to dinner and I went back to my *hostal* for some peace and quiet. I wrote a postcard to Ellie and washed my clothes and me.

I had walked 293 kilometres, which wasn't bad. Only 462 kilometres to go. David said 2010 wasn't a good year to do the Camino because it was a Holy Year and would be crowded.

A Holy Year is when the Day of Saint James, 25th July, falls on a Sunday; and the Apostle Saint James is believed to be buried in the Cathedral of Santiago de Compostela. During a Holy Year, Catholics may obtain a Jubilee Indulgence (a pardon from the punishments they believe their sins have accumulated) by accomplishing the following:

- Visit the Cathedral of Santiago de Compostela on any day of the Holy Year.

- Recite a prayer for the objectives of the Pope (usually the Our Father or a Creed).
- Attend confession and communion on the same day as entering the Cathedral, or fifteen days before or after in another church.

(Information sourced from website: The Way of Saint James. The Voice of Galicia. caminodesantiago.lavozdegalicia.com)

Hontanas – Itero de la Vega: 21 kilometres

I had a lame breakfast: a pastiche of reheat-your-pre-made-coffee, a splash of long-life milk, a small factory-made croissant in a bag and chilly toast made the night before with a dab of oil. As Prue said, 'Maybe it's a traditional dish here?' I left happily by myself on a cold, no-rain morning, just misty and pretty. After half an hour I met up with Olga again who sang a Spanish song for me. I walked with her for twenty minutes and then took off. All morning I photographed the landscape that was bathed in the softest of colours despite being harsh late summer.

I stopped at wonderful Castrojeriz for a couple of hours, a hilltop town that was a highlight of the Camino. There were three outstanding churches, a convent and, on top of the hill overlooking the town, a ruined castle. Everywhere looked cared for and gently prosperous, with many ancient historical buildings. I was sorry Tracy and Mark would miss it. In the last church I entered were many tapestries from the school of Rubens, a fine painting of *The Deposition of Christ* and a great *claustro* (cloister) – a covered colonnade built around the quadrangle of a convent, monastery, college or cathedral. Usually there is a wall on one side and the colonnade is open to the courtyard. They are repetitive, quiet and contemplative havens. The one in this church was small, with large pieces of rough-cut stonework contrastingly topped with small elegant Gothic arches.

Castrojeriz

Leaving Castrojeriz

Castrojeriz seemed to sum up how I think about Spain – much inherent and sometimes sombre beauty, not showy and a large quantity of dignity. For what it's worth, I think dignity is a tremendous and elusive quality, perhaps because I have had many high-spirited lapses of it.

The views to and from the town were breathtaking, with magic light because of the weighty grey clouds and angled and angelic sun shafts peeping through.

Hey, Lewy! More great lighting!

Little Gems And Heart Stabs

I walked out of Castrojeriz through the harvested and patterned fields and diagonally climbed a huge bare hill. From the top were fabulous expansive views of where I'd been and where I was heading and again a marvellous light. Down I went, along a dry and dusty road curving and curling through the parched softest brown landscape.

Later I photographed some fields of leaning, completely spent sunflowers and wondered when they were gathered. I thought I could walk more kilometres, but I stopped at 21 as I was resembling the sunflowers.

Φ

EMAIL: Hello dear Friends, sorry about the sad last letter, all became a bit much. I think the hectic German pilgrims got to me, up mega early and kilometres the most important thing. Mimicking them I wore myself out, very unlike me. Have recovered my equilibrium and I'm happy with this magic walk. It's just me, hopefully Lew, walking highs, grief, radiant candles, shifting landscapes, captivating villages and delicious meals.

Some nights I stay at an albergue, which is a type of youth hostel. I found out about them by chance. There are from two up to thirty-six plus in a room and you meet all sorts of wonderful people. Recently I bought a tiny towel, as sometimes I had to shake myself dry – which made me feel like a hippy free spirit (not an idiot at all). I believe there are people who snore, but because I'm so exhausted by the time I go to sleep I don't hear anything. Some are up sooo early that the rustling will drive you mad! (Plastic bags are popular.) As it's essential to stay on my own sometimes, a pensión or hostal (cheap hotel) does the trick. They often have the most Spanish character – squeaky timber floors, old family furniture, charming lacy curtains and bedspreads, Spanish pottery and tiles, and a gracious local caretaker. And one time when my feet mutinied I wallowed in a stylish hotel.

I'm the only pilgrim who travels in skirts. Some people have photographed me for this reason when I am wearing Lew's favourite skirt (of mine) and looking more like I'm on a Hawaiian holiday than a pilgrimage. At present I'm up about 1100 metres so again my proficient planning is questionable. Yesterday it rained lightly and I loved it. My flappy skirt was dry in half an hour

The countryside is very, very beautiful here, rolling hills covered in pale faded hay stubble, crisp dying brown sunflowers, grey rocks occasionally with brilliant-coloured lichens and more huge haystacks. (Great to hide behind for a wee.) The light is wonderful and does great things to the landscape.

I have recurringly met some really heart-warming people and some have done sections of the Camino over the years. I also LOVE to walk by myself and talk to Lew or rage against the medical profession or just suck up the glorious scenery, bridges or churches.

Ellie, could you please ring my Mum and say you heard from me?

I LOVE HEARING from you all and read every word carefully!

EMAIL: Hola! Dearest Jessie and Nick, thinking of you heaps. Let me know when I can open my big fat mouth?

I wanted to tell my friends about their baby-to-be, but waited until Jess had passed the three-month stage.

Φ

I walked around Itero de la Vega and became completely lost. There were few people out and about because it was siesta time. The church finally opened and I had a look inside. It was quiet and contemplative and I lit some candles for Lew; so good to be by myself.

The Meseta section of the Camino is short on trees, and the ones they do have are sometimes pruned so ruthlessly they look violated. The big beautiful plane trees outside the church had been completely shorn for winter. The trunks looked like a forearm with a hand of severed fingers grasping at the sky. Huge, not-yet-wilted leafy branches were piled in hacked disarray on the ground. After seeing Lewy's rapacious deterioration, I found the trees harrowing.

I've always loved the change of seasons, but the ending of summer now filled me with darkness. It was quite cold and there was something inside of me that was black and chilled.

I finally found my way back to the *albergue* and didn't bother about dinner.

Φ

Itero de la Vega – Villalcázar de Sirga: 30.5 kilometres

I set off in the sprinkly misty rain, grateful for my raincoat. Motionless wind generators peered out of the fog. They looked at odds with the empty furrowed fields.

In Boadilla del Camino I happened upon a fantastic *albergue* surrounded by a tall inscrutable fence with a large set of old wooden doors. Through the doorway was a luxuriant garden, where I sat despite the light rain and had coffee with a *jamón* and *queso boccadillo* (sandwich) under an umbrella. Such a contrast to the late-summer baked-dry landscape all around me. I was encircled by the greenest of grass and lots of pots made from carved pale stone troughs or baptismal fonts full of brightly coloured flowers. The *albergue* was owned and run by a painter and her son. The son asked me if I would plait his long hair, which I happily did. As the place became busier, a squabble erupted in the kitchen when Mum realised he'd been having his hair plaited instead of serving their customers. This was the only time it was fortunate that I couldn't understand Spanish.

I walked on to Frómista, where I went into a rich caramel-coloured stone church, San Martin, a Romanesque masterpiece built in 1066. There was a sense of awe in this church and the thirteenth-century wooden painted Christ was beautiful. There were no candles to light, but it was so peaceful to be still in this outstanding jewel of the Camino.

There seemed plenty to see in Frómista, but after the church I kept going. I was low and wanted to exhaust myself.

Sadly locked, Población de Campos

When I arrived at Población de Campos, where I'd planned to stay, I saw an elderly local couple walking along together. He was casually resting a scythe on his shoulder but was too benign to be the grim reaper. His wife was carrying a large bunch of tiny white daisies. Lucky, lucky them to be old together.

Grow old along with me!
The best is yet to be.

I love these familiar lines by Robert Browning, and gave Nick and Jess a card with them on the front for their wedding in 2006. This was how I'd envisioned my life with Lewy. We were so close in age, I thought we'd have decades together.

I went into the otherworldly little Chapel of the Virgin of Succour, set way down below street level; I guessed at the original street level. In this completely silent place with its natural forlorn lighting I lit some candles for Lew.

I thought about something Ellie had said to me when Lewy's cancer was rampaging to other places in his body and I was so devastated: 'Well, at least you're able to say goodbye.' At the time I wasn't able to see this at all and just crumpled at her words. But if you lose someone in an accident or a stroke or any of the awful ways that a person can die suddenly, you don't have that chance and that must be terrible. Lewy and I said our unspoken goodbyes in a blossoming abundance of ways during the progression of his illness. In some ways we were lucky.

Φ

I wasn't ready to stop for the day at Población de Campos. Walking, walking ... I sat on an old rendered wall at Villovieco to eat a lunch of a peach and nectarine and drink my water. Sitting with me was a grating older couple. Everything they did was better. Luckily they knew a far superior alternative route so off they went. I suspect if Mother Teresa had sat down next to me I would have felt just as ratty.

After walking through another village I finally stopped for the night at Villalcázar de Sirga. I'd walked a record for me of 30.5 kilometres. I'd just felt empty and decided to keep going.

Villalcázar de Sirga has a magnificent cathedral, St Mary the White, built in 1157 with an uneasy, eccentric LEAN to the left. I went inside at the special pilgrim price of two euros, which hopefully would go towards stabilising that lean. Such a beautiful Gothic/Romanesque church. Its gorgeous narrow stained-glass windows had been redone five or six years previously and looked kind of Kandinskyish.

In this peaceful space I lit a candle for Lewy. I'd been wearing his golden wedding ring on my right hand, where it fitted loosely, and I only had to look at it or give it a gentle kiss to start feeling wobbly. The yellow gold had looked beautiful on his large tanned hands. One time I asked if I could try his ring on. He said seriously that he'd not taken it off since we were married. He let me try it on and it looked much better on him than on me. I was very glad to have it now. I wanted to give it the life on my hand that it should have had on his.

I found a photo of you, the first I took of you on our honeymoon. We were in Florence. You were sitting on a stone wall and looking so tenderly happy and in love, your hand unconsciously near your face showing off your wedding ring.

Honeymoon bliss

Drearily Weary

I wasn't up to going to Mass in the impressive cathedral. At an outdoor bar in the plaza facing the church, I imbibed beeno blanco. Chilly inside and out, I returned to the *albergue*, which was run by two pleasant volunteers. Our room had only seven beds. You paid by donation, plus one euro for a hot shower.

An Australian woman and I were given the last two beds. She was very chatty. I wasn't. I'd met few Australians on the trip; Germans were the most common nationality by far. Their organised pragmatism contrasted somewhat with my bamboozled despair.

At dinner, the restaurant was full of pilgrims and the good-natured motherly waitress had them all in stitches with her histrionics. Now I was sorry that I couldn't understand Spanish. My German painter friend who was sitting next to me was exhausted. She'd secretly hitched a ride from the last town as her asthma was giving her problems. Two almost identical Spanish brothers sat next to us, my age and a bit older. They made it clear to us that they were both married, as if we were a couple of thinly-feathered vultures desperately waiting to launch an attack. I was amused. Somehow, hurling myself at a man just over ten weeks since my husband died wasn't on my Must-Do list of Spanish experiences.

That night it bucketed rain, outside and inside my head. I hoped I would be okay the next day. I had a horrible ache for everything that Lew had lost.

Villalcázar de Sirga – Calzadilla de la Cueza: 23.5 kilometres

Again, the pilgrims woke early, and with their rustle, rustle there wasn't much I could do but get, get going. In my scrambled state I'd slept with my nightie over my skirt. I had breakfast at the *albergue* of white bread and jam and coffee, which was a bit of a fairy-floss brekkie, but kind of the volunteers to supply it for free. I gave the wife a big kiss on her two cheeks before leaving; she was a tall, warm and charitable person and reminded me of Julie who owns the gallery where I show my work.

As I left her husband gave me directions and pointed out Orion's Belt and Sirius in the still dark and inky sky. I walked by myself for some time, feeling uncertain because of the lack of light, but I found my way. When I passed the two spoken-for Spanish brothers, again I managed to resist swooping on them.

Carrión de los Condes was 5 kilometres away. In keeping with that day's hyper-nutritional breakfast theme I had another coffee and a pastry snail there as there were no towns after that for 18 kilometres. I peeped into a monastery, but a Mass with nuns only was in progress so I quietly backed out.

I raced into an *albergue* to use the toilet, urgently asking a backpacker, 'TOILET?' 'End of hall,' he barked. It was a bit of a problem on the trek when Vesuvius was about to erupt and sometimes no Ladies' Powder Room was to be found.

Are you laughing at my hippity-hop bathroom alarm? Sometimes when you arrived home from work and we were kissing, you'd be hopping up and down busting for a wee from the strong coffee you'd had earlier.

I went into a beautiful Romanesque church, another St Mary's and enjoyed its structural simplicity. It had an exquisite three-spiral iron staircase. I gratefully lit twelve candles for Lew. It was such a poignant gesture in the dim quiet of the church; a small, warming symbol of hope and life.

I walked in a straight line for 18 kilometres through a landscape that was fairly flat and uninteresting, which was a bit demoralising. I tried to take photos but there wasn't a lot to capture. Maybe I should have tried to photograph inside my head where there was the dimmest of light, austerity and, despite the wind chill, a dampness, a greyed wooden floor and no Lewy.

I arrived at Calzadilla de la Cueza around 2 pm completely spent. Overrun, I suspected, by the kilometres of the day before. I found a hotel with my OWN ROOM. The hotelier carried my backpack up the long sweeping staircase. I was gushingly grateful.

I had a shower and really took pleasure in the Pilgrimless Silence. I lay on my bed and took a photo of my bare feet up in the air. They didn't look like they felt. They presented no visible signs of discomfort, swelling or wear and tear. At all. They became disgruntled because they'd hoped their photo would be more dramatic. I thought they'd become a couple of drama queens. I'd have to keep my socks on when I was back home watching telly.

In this quiet little town, I saw sheep in an indoor pen that looked like goats. They were snuggled together ready for the night and smelt of hay and warmth.

I lit candles for Lulu in the fairly ordinary local church. I hoped it made a difference for him. It made a huge difference for me.

On the internet at a nearby *albergue*, I composed a scholarly email about weeing on the Camino. Then I had drinks in a café outside the hotel in the still hot and glary weather with the grating couple I'd met back in Villovieco and gentle Alex. One half of the couple informed me that my feet were a problem because I wasn't wearing the correct boots like hers. Cripes, I hoped they hadn't heard her!

Φ

EMAIL: A Wee Walk. Hi all! Well, today I thought I'd talk about something that is a large part of this Camino experience. For about the second time in my life I regret being female. This is because if you're walking and, as happened today for example, there is a mere 18 kilometres to the next town, you may find yourself busting for a leak. The terrain here for the last 100 kilometres or more has been sunny gently rolling lands where shrubby trees are rare. There are some poplars, but of course they have no lower vegetation.

So when you hear the call of nature, you have to find a suitable spot where your illustrious backside (as mine is) will not be seen. Of course you can always find one if there are pilgrims 20 and 50 metres behind you. I've almost settled on a place only to be inundated by hornet impersonators also known as cyclists (where do they buy their clothes?). So finally when you find a place, no one around, you are sssooo busting that it is just excruciating (three children), because you don't just drop your knickers, you have to undo two backpack buckles, untangle the camera, put the pack on the ground, drop your knickers, don't wee on your skirt, shoes and camera, and where the hell are the tissues? I have met female pilgrims who say they can wee without taking their packs off, but I think it's too risky. I have visions of myself falling backwards, no knickers, completely stuck, legs in the air. I leave the rest to your imaginations.

BY THE WAY I AM HALFWAY THERE!

EMAIL from Hugh: The wee story was funny, but harden up and just take a leak. Sydney was covered by a dust storm yesterday that came from the desert and visibility was about 50 metres. It was red. Got to go …

Sounded like ideal outdoor weeing weather to me.

Calzadilla de la Cueza – Sahagún: 23 kilometres

I woke at eight after being sleepless between 1 and 2.30 am. Too much grog and not enough water – would I ever learn? After a flimsy brekkie I set off late, feeling slack for all of the above reasons. Fortunately I decided to leave my tiresome guilty thoughts behind.

The signs were confusing, but before long I found my way. The weight of my sadness was oppressive. Was it because this day's walk was uninteresting? Or was it uninteresting because of the weight of my sadness?

I don't like the word grief. Anguish is a more potent word. According to the dictionary, grief is more severe than sorrow, but to me sorrow *sounds* so much sadder. It's feminine with long dark hair, it doesn't wish to lie down, it wants to be doubled over and it's solitary and cold. So much to leave behind.

People say the Meseta part of the Camino is the least attractive and I had found it bleak in places. But I'd also seen some real jewels, and most of the little churches had been open so I could often be cool and still and pray for Lew which was very sustaining.

Out in the sunshined dry landscape I walked past a shepherd and his small flock with his working red dog. Not so far away were some underground houses, where all you could see were their front doors and their chimneys sprouting from a small hill. This inside–outside contrast was quite mysterious, not unlike being out in the wide open blazing landscape and then cool and enclosed in the churches.

After 8.5 kilometres I stopped for lunch and was joined by Alex. I told him how Lewy was talented about living in the moment and that when I was with him the most everyday things became fun. Alex said it was the same when he was walking with me, which was a bloody nice thing to say. I was quietly thinking that during the years I spent with Lew, I experienced the magical contentment I'd only known during pregnancy.

Alex was having trouble with his feet: they were blistered and sore. He wasn't walking as fast as some, which suited me. We walked and chatted together until San Nicolás, 6 kilometres away. He bought me an orange juice and I ate a peach while we shared a table with the prettiest girl. Hoping that a meaningful-relationship fairy was fluttering overhead, I left them to their own devices and walked on to Sahagún.

Tired and sad, I did much trudging with ill-tempered feet. I thought that maybe I'd stay two days in León. In the distance, on the other side of the divided expressway, I saw some huge, curly, thick wire, whimsical sculptures. And just like my dream about Lewy, it was impossible to cross over to see them close up.

Before Sahagún, I walked over an intimate stone bridge to make a small detour to the Chapel of the Virgin of the Bridge: a curious and enticing little building that would have been idyllic for hobbits. Frustratingly, even though it was Sunday, and also to make a liar of me, the church was closed. So, foot-sore, peeved and hot, I just kept going until I stopped. And found a bed where I could drop.

Φ

I was given a key to an upstairs room, 110. When I walked in, it was occupied by two people lying on their beds watching TV. Television seemed strangely out of place here. I painfully clambered back down the stairs and rearmed myself with the key to room 111. Then I lopsidedly scaled back up the stairs with my backpack and sore body parts.

I had a late lunch/early dinner at 4 pm of white asparagus salad, disgusting fatty no-meat pork and mini *flan*. I didn't complain. Prue would have been proud of me. Afterwards, I did some washing and hung it above my gloomy, roomy bath.

Shambling around Sahagún I was moved by its beautiful gateway, sombre churches and monasteries. The exceptional Mudéjar-style Church of San Tirso, particularly its apse and tower, was moody and sacred. Mudéjar is a twelfth- to sixteenth-century style of architecture and decoration strongly influenced by the taste and workmanship of the Muslims who were permitted to stay in Spain after the Christian reconquest. There's much variety in the styles of stonework of the public buildings here, and a tapestry of earthy colours. You see blocks of crisply cut stone, loose little or big chunky rocks set in concrete, skinny baked bricks, stucco, elegant bricked archways, mortarless circular stone window frames, towers, statues, carvings in relief, decorative ceiling vaults, and floors of plain stone or polished marble. Such assortment in the one building gives it a richness of detail that melds together to a marvellous sculptural whole.

I bumped into Alex who was roaring around the town with a look of unburdened joy on his face. At first I was tickled pink, thinking he'd hit it off with the pretty girl. But no, the *albergue* he was staying at supplied free bicycles. He looked different when his feet weren't a problem. Didn't we all.

I had a Plan for the next day: buy more fruit and pull myself together.

Φ

Sahagún – El Burgo Ranero: 18 kilometres

At breakfast I chatted minimally with some pleasant French men, my lazy schoolgirl French vaguely returning. I tried to see inside the Benedictine church once more, but again there was a service in progress with only nuns attending. Fearing I might be intruding, I backed out.

I walked over an ancient bridge above a sprouting-with-colourful-bounteous-plant-life river, then down a long tree-lined road and out of this wonderful town.

I found the directions confusing and started to worry that I wasn't on the right track. I realised all was well when the same French men from breakfast caught up and started chatting to me.

'Oh my goodness,' I said, 'I can't possibly speak French and walk at the same time.'

'But you must,' they said. 'It's good for your brain.'

I've never been good at multitasking; too many concussions as a child no doubt.

Along came Alex, walking fast. Dim me never considered he could've been on a mission and I dumped the brilliant French men, who could walk and speak English at the same time, and sped up to walk with Alex. I really didn't like it when someone invaded my solitude while walking, and I believe I unconsciously did just that to Alex.

After about 10 kilometres we stopped for a meal, then walked another 8 kilometres to El Burgo Ranero. Polite Alex and I had a pleasant day, but I still cringe at my thoughtlessness.

I would have preferred to walk more than 18 kilometres in a day, but the next town was another 13 kilometres away, which would mean 31 kilometres in total – way too far for my alarmed feet. I found a donation-based *albergue* built of a timber frame, mud brick and straw – an attractive adobe. There were quite a few buildings of that construction in the town.

I sat outside on a bench in the sun. When one of the volunteers asked me why I was walking, I blurted out that my husband had died two and a half months ago and I'd had to run away. That I couldn't bear to be at home without him. That I didn't understand his death. And that I felt this walk could and was saving me. It was strange to talk about Lew so frankly outside my own head on that sunny afternoon.

I walked around the town, which was fairly quiet and a little dull, despite a tranquil lake in one corner. I lit six candles in a sweet, light-filled church for Lew. A warm young Spanish woman was volunteering to keep the church open for pilgrims; again, a benefit of this hard-going Meseta section.

I had a couple of drinks sitting outdoors and wrote a postcard to my neighbours. I felt despondent – no exciting landscape to pull me out of myself, only walking, and that wasn't enough. Luckily there were only two more days to León, which apparently was a particularly beautiful medieval city.

I went to dinner with Canadian Tanya, 41-year-old Irish Ann, German Rene and Alex. It was a great night. Ann, a nurse, was hilarious and had a beguiling sing-song accent. She spoke of her exhausting experiences on the Camino with a splendidly loud snorer who woke, yawned and stretched in the morning, completely refreshed, while everyone else's night had been shattered. She was a marvellous comic and made our dinner a treat. One day, she said, she had walked 53 kilometres! She thought the Camino threw you back on your own mental resources when it was visually monotonous and you had to look inside yourself. If you were still bored, then your inner life was the problem, not the walk.

Certainly my inner life wasn't easy. Lewy's death and absence were hard to bear.

After this comradely dinner I seemed to have hardened up. I took my restored spirits to bed, concerned about my first step if sleepwalking from the upper bunk, but was fine.

Getting down for the bathroom at 4 am was tricky: wooden bunks creak horribly. I clambered down, rebounded off the bunk below and woke 76-year-old Spanish painter Juan who was sleeping there. My inability to bounce at this age meant I couldn't just drop to the floor.

I kept bumping into beaming Juan. He was an old benign rogue who slung dated controversial arrows at you to generate a rise. Like, how can you be a serious painter when you are a woman who has housework to do and a family? I told him he was just looking for a fight. He sketched happily along the way and took his time, but often ended up at the same place as me. I hoped I could walk the Camino at his age.

Φ

El Burgo Ranero – Puente de Villarente: 25 kilometres

Like many *albergues* you had to be out by 8 am. When I said goodbye to the volunteer *hostelera*, she gave me a gentle embrace and said a prayer for Lew and me.

Off I set, with the sun rising behind me and the sky in front a pinky blue. How much I loved this time of day and how grateful I was for the peace it gave.

The townspeople had planted untrimmed plane trees every 12

metres the whole distance to the next town, Reliegos, as shade for the pilgrims. The trees were not yet huge, but it was a big-hearted gesture and much appreciated as the day was hot. I walked parallel to the railway line and close to the road. Every time a bike rider passed me they shouted '*Buen Camino!*' So friendly!

After a couple of towns and some familiar faces, I stopped and had coffee with the classic fantastic baguette at a bohemian café and met up with Alex again. We chatted all the way to the next town, where we had yoghurt, an orange and grapes in the main square with Austrian Hildie and Swiss Clement. The town was historical and inviting, but silly me wanted to keep going as I was full of energy.

The afternoon was hot and I was soon sorry the four of us had continued walking as the white path reflected much heat and ran parallel to a charmless expressway. We passed shorn dry fields with many rolled bales of hay that looked like the abandoned fronts of steamrollers. After an unforgiving walk of 5.7 kilometres we finally arrived at Puente de Villarente. We had to cross an up high, narrow bridge with a tiny tight pedestrian way and big trucks were going past much too near. It was horrible and dangerous. I turned and pulled a face at Alex, and he said when I turned the passing trucks almost clipped my backpack. YIKES to that bridge and its terrible planning – my most dangerous experience of the Camino, apart from the availability of all that cheap and delicate local wine.

Alex's guide book recommended an *albergue* off the main road, which was rural and charming. There were sixteen in our room and I was on the bottom bunk! We went to find a drink at a local bar. I mistakenly bought a bottle of sickly sweet white wine, which was probably a dessert wine, and we shared it with Clement.

We ambled back to the *albergue* for dinner. There were three large tables. Ours included two Swiss, two Italians, an Austrian, a German, a Dane, a Spaniard and me. And no, they didn't say, 'I'm sorry you can't dine here without a Thai'. The vivacious Italians were showing off and entertaining. One was a barman who spoke many languages, particularly any phrases pertaining to alcohol, which would've been handy that afternoon at the bar.

It was a great night. I wanted to take pleasure in the time that Lew didn't have the chance to live; I was determined not to waste a good life. But sometimes when I stepped aside, I found it so strange that all continued on without him.

My feet were pretty shattered by the end of the meal and then my legs joined them, so I had a shower and went to bed. I couldn't afford to have hysterical body parts.

City Life

Puente de Villarente – León: 14.5 kilometres

I had a suntan like a 1950s' tennis player – white feet to the ankles, white legs above the knees and, the pièce de résistance, white tops of arms. Most fetching. I had to slather moisturiser on all sectors exposed to the elements, but otherwise I enjoyed having the contents of my bathroom cabinet out of my life. Older friends have had hip or knee replacements or shoulder reconstructions, but I'd thought because of my non-nimble lifestyle that would never happen to me. But I may need a right foot arch overhaul in the future. That should stop them complaining.

The 'short' walk to León seemed longer as the landscape wasn't beautiful and there was quite a lot of road walking. I walked with gentle, slight Hildie (Hildegard), an Austrian who lived in Switzerland. She had a faintly stunned air of someone who was bravely dealing with some of life's blows. Dear bubbly Spanish-speaking Lisa from Wales, aged nineteen, who had an imaginative bohemian clothes sense, walked with us too. There was lots of chatting on a beautiful, clear, hot, sunny day. I'd been lucky with the weather.

We walked past the biggest stork's nest yet, perched on a small church bell tower. The scale was completely out of whack. I just loved it.

You win!

The old part of León was a few kilometres into the city and reached by crossing yet another ancient stone bridge. I found a great little *hostal* from my Lonely Planet guide, right in the centre near the cathedral. My room was large with high ceilings and tall French doors. I decided to stay for two days as I was really buggered. My feet were melodramatic, my legs overwrought and my head was vacant. I couldn't think about Lew or anything much. Over the last few days, even though I'd encountered beaut people, my feelings of buoyancy from the natural world were scarce.

After dumping my pack, I found an atmospheric restaurant where I parked myself for some time. I bypassed the black pudding and tongue and instead ordered baked leek with mustard and honey sauce. Then I strolled off down the main street and saw the castle-like early-Gaudí building, Casa de los Botines. It wasn't as outrageous as his Barcelona architecture, but still intriguing. His buildings are so flamboyant and have such imaginative detail. This could have been a fantasy fortress designed by Cinderella for her nasty sisters: a six-storey stone building with fancy windows, flanked either side with tall turrets – one each to store her horrid sisters when they stepped out of line. And secure too. The castle was surrounded by impressively spiked, tall and twisted ironwork.

Inside was now a bank. You could only see the ground floor and much of that was partitioned off. The interior was unexciting and un-Gaudí and my disappointment was as strong as if I'd been a small child. However there was a bronze statue of Gaudí sitting on a park bench just outside the building. It blended into the square almost as if he were just another person sitting there. I loved it.

I had a look inside the Palacio de los Guzmanes in the same square. Like many Spanish buildings, it was built around a courtyard (*patio*), which is a beautiful way to live as every room has an outlook and light.

I went to see St Isidore's Basilica, a fine mostly Romanesque church built in 1063 with harmonious Gothic and Renaissance additions. The royal burial vault was exquisite. The ceilings were covered in some of Spain's finest Romanesque frescoes of plants, animals, angels, saints and a Christ. I loved the stylised animals and figures, especially their lively faces, which were naively drawn and yet had a powerful strength. The paint quality of the frescoes was gorgeous, and they were in great unrestored condition – a joy to see! I wanted to buy a book about the Basilica, but didn't dare add to the weight of my pack.

Then I went to León's Gothic cathedral, which was being noisily restored with machinery, workers, scaffolding and platforms. This stirring cathedral had countless glorious stained-glass windows, some of which depicted plants only, something I'd not seen before. It was a relief that taking photos was forbidden inside; a soundtrack of clicking was distracting.

I 'lit' some electric candles for Lew.

Swiss Clement, seventy and a hardened and jaded disparager, said, 'I can't believe you are putting coins in that box to light those tacky candles.'

Bite your bum, I thought. But I said, 'Lew was an electrician and would have loved the electric candles.'

Actually he might have been annoyed at me tossing all my money towards the God Botherers as he called them, but secretly I hoped he would be so very touched. *I'm coming back here without Clement*, I thought. The name 'Clement' means gentle and merciful and didn't quite seem to fit.

I went through an old double door to see the cloisters, which I always took pleasure in – such a contemplative space. I also saw the museum part of the cathedral, which was good not just for the collection, but because of the many different levels, stairways, alcoves and little rooms of display. I saw how a cathedral has many parts other than the main place of worship.

Some paintings of beatific Saint Sebastian full of arrows, or saints being disembowelled slowly over a turnpike or chopped into little bits, were really horrible and gave me the creeps. Why hadn't I noticed before that death was so apparent?

I went looking for a present for Alex who had a birthday the following day. I only found a large amount of tourist rubbish, crude mugs, etc. Who would buy and *carry* any of those, I wondered.

I didn't buy a Camino scallop shell to dangle on a piece of string from my backpack, because Lew and I had collected our own treasured colourful shells that were ravishingly abundant on Clifton Beach in Tasmania.

Φ

I'd been away from home for one month. I woke late on my second day in León to the joyful sound of no pilgrim bustling. While having brekkie I read the Lonely Planet's segment on the delights of León and met up with birthday boy Alex who was going back to East Berlin the following day. Today he was walking to the next town and then catching a taxi back to León. I would miss him as he was a warm and open being. He mentioned that he'd seen Prue and me waving our long goodbye to each other at Estella.

Shells, Clifton Beach, Tasmania by Amanda Thomson

It was such a rich time for meeting champion people and weaving in and out of each other's lives, and a new experience for me to be travelling overseas and bump into people I know. On previous trips I'd occasionally thought, *Wow, I'm in wherever and none of these faces I've ever seen before, and they look so different from the people back home.*

I walked what seemed like several kilometres within León to see the Convento de San Marcos, nowadays a *parador* for wealthy tourists. There was a beautiful, oddly empty-of-furniture church attached, with cloisters and a museum. It may have been a pilgrim myth, but I'd been told you had to pay to use the hotel's impressive toilets. I just had to swan in and try this toilet for myself, impersonating a well-to-do tourist. Possibly my no make-up, crushed clothes and girlish limp gave me away, but the invisibility of a woman of a certain age can work for you sometimes. The toilets were undeniably grand, the opposite of weeing behind a giant haystack, although each has its own charm, that's for sure. The minimalism of what you needed on this walk and how much joy it could bring to the most troubled soul could make grandness seem a little out of place.

I enjoyed being able to jump the centuries to visit the Museum of Contemporary Art, where time and disasters had not yet weeded out the inane. In a colourful modern building, with the usual hip gift/bookshop and café attached, they had four large exhibitions on display. The first three I didn't like, but the fourth was great and well worth seeing – big, loose and expressive paintings by Madrid artist Jorge Galindo. The exhibition was called 'The Paint and the Fury'.

I remembered being in Florence with Lew. We were in the Uffizi Gallery and I sat in front of Botticelli's *The Birth of Venus* for ages, gazing at it in wonderment. Lew came up behind me and placed his hands gently on my shoulders; I could feel his warmth behind me. He was letting me know he was moving on, but didn't want to interrupt my delight in this magical picture. Also in the Uffizi was a magnificent exhibition of Leonardo da Vinci's machines, which Lew found completely absorbing.

I took Lewy's photo back to the cathedral as I wanted him to see it. I was calm and peaceful by myself and I went into an exquisite chapel, away from the restoration, to pray. There was a woman sitting up the front wrapped tightly in her clothes and thoughts; such a singular person alone in her prayers. I wondered how many people had sat there for silent prayer over many, many centuries. How much comfort had this hushed chapel given?

I'm so grateful, Lulu, for all the radiant happiness you gave me.

I miss you and I wish you near.

This last sentence was the phrase that most often went around in my brain.

And So Forth

I took a little snooze in the afternoon as I was having dinner with Alex and his Camino friends for his thirty-first birthday. I gave him a box of handmade chocolates that you could select yourself. The chocolatier let me try a couple. His favourite, chocolate and rock salt, was heavenly.

Alex told me he'd read a popular German book, *I'm Off Then: Losing and Finding Myself on the Camino de Santiago* by Hape Kerkeling, which described how some friends each had a little silver bell and when they returned home they'd ring their bell and think of each other. Alex said when he was home, he'd think of me each day when he ate a chocolate. (I thought, *what restraint, they wouldn't last so long in my gobbler's hands.*)

He also told me that Kerkeling had trouble finding *albergues* that weren't full and that was why most of the German pilgrims raced out the door before it was light. That didn't make sense to me. I wasn't a fast walker, often started later than many (although to me it seemed commendably early), took lots of photographs or stopped for some time in places that moved me, and always found a place to stay. That writer had started a rather nasty contagious disease.

Other pilgrims gave Alex some kitschy tourist gifts which he loved, and they did have a likable charm or was that the wine? We had such a happy night and I met properly Carsten and Marianne from Denmark whom I'd seen before, and young German Danny, their adopted Camino son, all of whom I liked. My great-grandmother Charlotte Petersen was Danish. Apparently in Denmark, her name is as rampant as John Smith is in Australia. Marianne looked not so much like my Mum, but a lot like one of her twin sisters.

I was sad to see the last of Alex. My feet were still grumpy and puffed-up and my legs were slow to follow, but I was looking forward to being back on the Camino.

Φ

EMAIL: Hi all, sorry I haven't written for a while. I've been quite homesick and missing Lew, so words weren't flowing. Haven't been homesick since I was eighteen. It's nearly twelve weeks since Lewy died, but it seems like much, much more. Feels like I haven't seen him for about nine months. We always spent so much time together that it's quite unreal to be without him.

León was a wonderful city, so I stayed an extra day there. I thought maybe my homesickness, etc was related to tiredness, and although I rambled the city all day, with no backpack, it was a good rest and the beauty of the place was inspiring.

The huge Gothic cathedral was awesome and a heart-rending place to be in. I went with Lew's picture and showed him how lovely it was, trying not to look odd at the same time. There were over 1800 square metres of gorgeous glass ... Many of the colours were different to the colours I have known in my time as a painter.

And there was a beautiful quiet chapel to pray in, sealed off from the hustle and aggravation of renovations and tourists. At the rate I am going with lighting candles, praying and walking to Santiago, I just might have amassed Lew a place in heaven with a queen-size bed, an ensuite, a water view, a nice place to fish and a regular supply of vino tinto! I can't think what more he'd want?

... To end on a cheery note. One night I met at dinner a fabulous Irish nurse. I happened to comment on an American man who had asked me straight out why I was wearing a skirt. I was a bit nonplussed and of

course could only think of a vaguely smart answer after he'd gone. She said, tell them you have thrush and it's easier to scratch!

This same woman had decided to leave her watch at home as it dominated her life. So one morning she woke, had a shower, dressed and packed ready to set out, only to find that it was one o'clock in the morning.

Hope you are all well. Please write. I love hearing from you …

Φ

León – Villar de Mazarife: 24 kilometres

Unlike villages, the edges of cities don't just morph into countryside. It took an hour and a disheartening 4-kilometre walk through the dismal outskirts to exit the city.

I followed an alternative route as I'd had enough of walking next to the main highway. It was good to be in the landscape again, but not that interesting. I saw a few more underground houses built beneath a mound, and a defiant stork's nest on top of a lone Corinthian column. My legs were strong AND I managed to wee with my backpack on. I couldn't wait to tell my friends that earth-shattering news.

I arrived at Villar de Mazarife and found an *albergue* with character and the internet. I did my washing outside in a deep rectangular basin in their paved courtyard with a big bar of soap, and revelled in the simplicity of it. I hung my wet, washed-yesterday cotton jumper on the sunny clothesline and it was dry by nightfall as were my colourful skirts. It was so good to put on a clean jumper.

I walked around this small town in no time. Two local women tried to talk to me in the general store when I was buying fruit. I explained in Spanish that I didn't speak their language, but they just kept chatting to me. It was so endearing and had happened a few times. I could feel myself melting at the kindness of strangers.

The sculptural, wacky-scaled little church with an eccentric bell tower and three storks' nests had a warm and enthusiastic volunteer to show you around.

Church, Villar de Mazarife

I tried to avoid dinner as I was worried about my weight. Like many people who've lost someone close to them I was eating like a bird – annoyingly that bird was a vulture. I sat in the sunny courtyard and had a drink with two Australians. The husband had walked the Camino five times; it was his wife's first time. They were shickered from a fierce home-brewed lemon drink that three locals had been giving them. And a little panicked as they were running out of time. They'd used up their free days so had to walk 30 kilometres to Astorga the next day in order to catch their flight at the end.

I had plenty of time, but for some stupid reason took their panic on board and determined also to walk to Astorga the following day. It was fortunate that I didn't meet up with a bank robber, because I seemed much influenced by those around me.

I unexpectedly ran into Hildie and my no-dinner resolve dissolved when she asked me to join her. It was lovely having a meal with 65-year-old Hildie who had a sweet nature and was suffering from tendonitis.

There were 286 kilometres to go. I'd walked 469 kilometres! I remembered Hontanas, when almost the same numbers were reversed.

Roller Coaster

Villar de Mazarife – Astorga: 30 kilometres

The breakfast area wasn't open in the morning when they said it would be. I lazily sat on the stairs and waited. Outside, the bell tower loomed black in the glinting pre-dawn sky. The Australians were in a state. She was cranky because she wanted her breakfast and he was cross because they couldn't start early on their long day. As New Zealander Mark would have said, they were the 'meano' in Camino. Eventually they stormed off. I was thankful to be travelling on my own. I'd had so many ups and downs and it was a relief not to be carrying the burden that I was shredding a friend's nerves.

I set off for Astorga, which apparently was gorgeous. I walked by myself for some time and really enjoyed my morning thoughts. I met up with gentle Hildie at a village 5 kilometres away. She bought pastries fresh from a bakery and I bought heavenly coffees, which we happily consumed together in a café.

The café won the award for the Stinkiest, Worst Bathroom of the Trip. No seat, paper, soap or towel and it reeked! It was as if the local footy team had gone in there and weed all over the walls. Yeetchhh. The opposite was true – when you found a really great bathroom it was tragically, hugely exciting. Well, on the Camino, that is.

Likewise, when a person is seriously ill, it's the littlest things that give such joy. A caring phone call, a happy dog, a beautiful sky, some great piece of music, kisses and kisses.

Hildie and I set off again and a thoughtful man pushing a wheelbarrow full of just-picked tomatoes gave us each one. We ate them like apples and they were delicious.

After crossing a beautiful curved bridge, the Bridge of Honourable Passage, with nineteen unequal arches, we arrived at pretty Hospital de Órbigo. We shared a contemplative pause in St John's church and then a leisurely lunch in a pleasant restaurant, which didn't start to fill up until after three o'clock.

Hilde's mum had been afflicted with Alzheimer's and had died recently. It was so heartfelt talking with her about her mother. Her company was a balm of calm.

A Spanish family at a long table were particularly outgoing to us and all said warm goodbyes when we left, which made us float. Because of her tendonitis, Hildie could only walk another 5 kilometres to the next town. I went a different way as I wanted to walk the 15 kilometres to Astorga.

I found this walk difficult and felt low. Probably because much was via the highway and the cars roaring by were unnerving. Also the signage wasn't clear, so a few times I felt lost and kept crossing back and forth over the highway to find my way. I knew this would be a hard walk because there was only one town to stop at and that was 12 kilometres away. By the time I arrived there I was exhausted, but with only 3 kilometres to go to Astorga I made myself go on.

I passed a brimming pumpkin patch full of giant green, brown and orange pumpkins, some plain, some striped. A winter's worth of food.

Trudge, trudge, slow, slow, in glittering weather. I had to cross the railway line by going up four long, long, looong ramps, across the top and then down four more ramps. I had never been so exhausted, in my life. An elderly, tiny Spanish woman, all in black, ignored the ramps and just crossed the line. I could have kicked myself that I hadn't just followed her – and both my feet would have gleefully done it. Astuteness. You just can't rest it, even for five minutes.

As I walked, I thought, *what the hell am I doing?* I was hugely miserable. Endurance: it was possible, but horrid. Couldn't Lew have endured with his broken rib and lungs drowning in tumours? He'd been so happy. Wasn't that enough to keep him here?

Walking, walking, up, up, the hill, the hill, slowly, slowly. It was almost 7 pm by the time I arrived at Astorga.

I went into the first *albergue* I came to, which was big and run by two French men. I liked it. I shared a room with three young women: Orsula, an eighteen-year-old Hungarian; a Brazilian girl whose face and long curly hair could have emerged from a Botticelli painting; and a Japanese girl who had walked 40 kilometres the day before. These young women were lovely (you forget how glorious young people are). I had a shower and felt much better. Great idea when wrecked – to shove yourself under a shower straight away.

I set off to investigate the town. Wow! It was really, really outstanding. The plaza was booming with life, lots of churches, a cathedral, and the surprise of no research meant I unexpectedly encountered another highly original Gaudí building, the Bishop's Palace. I was so glad to be there, my mood entirely reversed. I explored the whole town despite having been so dilapidated.

I sat down for dinner in a lively restaurant and ordered a tip-top goat's cheese salad. I pulled out the anchovies, no worries. I was joined by a gentle journalist, Flavio, who worked in Italy for Rupert Murdoch. I unconsciously squirmed when he said RM's name and he asked me why. He told me that RM's was the only newspaper that criticised Berlusconi and was thought of highly in journalistic circles there. Luckily Prue had a few intelligent opinions on Berlusconi so I sprouted those. We had a great broken English chat. There's no doubt travel improves the mind, and of course I have no idea what he really thought of me. When I went to pay the bill, the dear charming man insisted on paying.

I'd had such a bad afternoon and then it turned around completely. I walked back down the hill to the *albergue* and gingerly up all the stairs like a cat with four sprained ankles. I fell asleep quickly despite pains in the legs and feet.

Φ

EMAIL: Hi guys, just wanted you to know that I have 260 kilometres to go and I have walked almost 500 kilometres. How cool is that? Does anyone know how far up the coast from Sydney that is?

… My deeply spiritual news is that I was talking to an Australian woman and she said the average amount of weight a man loses on the Camino is 6 kgs. The average for a woman is NIL! So I went and weighed myself just to prove her wrong, 'cause I know my knickers are loose. And how right was I! I have lost 1·3 kgs after walking almost 500 kilometres. Doesn't that give me the !*@!+#!%*!

But I have managed to perfect weeing with a backpack on, which should be a great skill when I'm back working at the RSL …

EMAIL from Florence and Leicester (who are in their eighties): Howdy Fabes, fortunately you are the woman with the loose knickers and not the other way about!

I can tell you that you have now walked as far up from Sydney as South West Rocks, just above Kempsey. When you have completed your walkathon, you will have reached the equivalent of Tweed Heads! This is becoming an epic walk and we follow it with a kind of burning fascination, which I suppose your feet do on occasions.

A strong sense of spirituality is coming from your really atmospheric prose. Does this mean that you are on a version of the Road to Damascus?

EMAIL to Florence and Leicester: Thank you, dear friends, for your calculations! I guess I'm on the Road to Damascus for dear Lewy, perhaps to hold on to him for as long as possible? I hope to write a letter based on my feet at some stage! That will be more down to earth.

Φ

Astorga – Santa Catalina de Somoza: 8.5 kilometres

The three tousled adorable girls awoke, packed and skedaddled. I decided to stay in astonishing Astorga until noon. I wanted to see inside the cathedral and the early Gaudí building, which had both been closed. I walked up the hill to have an evil breakfast of choc-filled croissants, SO GOOD with soft Spanish coffees.

The outside of Mr Gaudí's Bishop's Palace again conjured up fairy tales, but on a friendlier scale. Here would be where Cinderella and her fella would live happily ever after. Three larger-than-life, impartial bronze angels graced the garden. They looked as if they'd be intrepid in a crisis. Inside, the palace was enchanting and housed a collection of first-rate artworks. The details of doors, windows and vaults were fabulous, as were the arrangement of rooms, stairs and balconies. As you went up a shallow spiralling stone staircase, on each level you could look via a balcony over the rooms below, which gave the building a sense of space and the opportunity to see high building details up close.

Gaudi's Bishop's Palace, Astorga

The four-storey palace had an exquisite basement with a low vaulted ceiling. There were two floors in between, and finally an attic, which had an ideal top-storey feeling. I don't know of other architects who so delight in basement and roof spaces, using the most appropriate colours and materials for each. Such a shame you couldn't take photos inside as the pictures in the official sad book didn't do it justice, but I was able to buy a set of postcards.

I sauntered off to the cathedral, which was majestic with heavenly high ceilings. Inside I could hear some engaging choral singing, so I decided to stay for Sunday Mass, which was starting in a few minutes. I thought the service would have that haunting singing during the communion, but instead a talented visiting choir sang. I was sorry about it being left out; however, a priest's passion for the choir manifested itself each time the congregation had to sing a response. He made big encouraging gestures with his arms and his face was rapturous. His enthusiasm was contagious. It was a pleasure attending a Mass where the women beside me were whole-heartedly singing in Spanish. At the end of the service, the congregation clapped and clapped the choir and evening-suited choirmaster.

Afterwards I went to the museum next to the cathedral, but there were too many graphic depictions of dead people, which reminded me of darling Lewy. I couldn't stand it, so I left hastily. I walked down the hill to the *albergue* to pick up my backpack and then back up the hill and out of that magical town.

Ф

Today was Helen's birthday. When Lew and I were married, Helen and Fred gave us the best ever wedding present to take on our honeymoon: a map with directions to their favourite restaurant in Paris, a copy of the menu, and a crisp princely euro note to spend on our meal. We went there blissfully happy. The restaurant was full of polished brass Art Nouveau Parisian charm. I tried to explain in my halting French that it was our honeymoon and that some friends had given us this meal at their favourite restaurant. The air was rich with exotic fragrances – from the kitchen, the guests, the tiny flowers at our table and a nearby elderly woman smoking an intoxicating cigar. We ordered a delicious meal and Lew said, 'How would you feel if we ordered Veuve Clicquot!' At another table a waitress was making crêpe suzette in a copper frypan. She smothered it in Grand Marnier and then set it alight. There was also a birthday party and the whole restaurant sang 'Happy Birthday' to the birthday girl. After we'd finished our meal and champers, the waiter asked if we would like dessert? 'Oh, no, thank you!' we said. A few minutes later the head waiter and two others came out, black-aproned and with starched white shirts, carrying an elegant tray of cakes, biscuits and chocolates with sparklers ablazing and two glasses of champagne and they sang 'Happy Anniversary' to us.

You had tears rolling down your cheeks. Even later when we were back home, you couldn't retell the story of that perfect evening without tears.

When we arrived back at our hotel we rang Helen in Sydney. We had to share with her how glorious an evening we'd had because of her and Fred's generosity and thoughtfulness. How wonderful to give a couple a wedding present they remember joyfully for the rest of their lives.

Φ

The time was 2.15 pm and blazing hot. I'd planned to walk 12 kilometres but I just couldn't. After 8.5 kilometres I stopped at Santa Catalina de Somoza and thought, *stuff it*. I had trudged the last 3 kilometres. It's all very well to start in the cool of the morning and gradually acclimatise to the heat of the day, but dive into the baking heat when you first start to walk and it's hard to last. I felt like the little frog that had been put straight into boiling water.

This town had attractive and gutsy buildings constructed of stone with stucco fill in warm earth colours. The doors and windows were painted glossy bright green, blue or red. It was an elevated and cared-for town, with fine countryside views revealed between the buildings.

My two-storey *albergue* was built around a paved and potted-with-bright-flowers courtyard. For three euros I washed nearly all my clothes in their washing machine as I was over doing it by hand. Their too-strong powder left a light bleach mark on my vivid scarlet cotton jumper, just below where my heart was. I thought it quite poetic, especially as my heart felt so low. The afternoon turned cold. With most of my clothes damp on the line, I had little to wear.

I washed your white towelling dressing gown, the one I used to tease you about: 'You look like Bob Hawke with your thick curly white hair.' Never-before-seen yellow stains appeared around the neck and under the arms, despite the wash. That chemo poison was still there. I washed away the smell of you not knowing you wouldn't come back from hospital. I was trying to look after you.

(Bob Hawke, a former Australian prime minister, was tastelessly photographed with his second wife both wearing matching white dressing gowns. His first wife, Hazel, was much admired by Australians.)

After a brief walk around the tiny town, I sat outside in the sun in the silent, narrow main street eating a little dish of fat green olives and drinking *vino blanco*. A group of locals arrived and two began playing music while the others folk-danced in the street. One musician played a simplified recorder-like instrument with one hand, while beating a drum with a stick with the other. When he only beat the drum there was no dancing, but when he added the recorder everyone danced. The other musician was an elderly man playing castanets. Colourful ribbons flowed from his wrists.

There was a captivating woman around seventy who was barrel-shaped and a wonderful dancer. A heavy dancer who is light on her feet is one of the joys of life. Her front teeth were picturesque – some were okay, some were stumps and some just plain old spaces.

Also kicking up their feet were a stylish forty-year-old couple, a young girl of maybe ten, two older men full of vigour and joy, and a couple with two young children whose mild antics their anxious mum hadn't learnt to ignore. Lastly there were two carefree thirty- and forty-plus women whose eyes sparkled. A few others joined in later. According to what tune was playing they danced in different formations, all with colourful ribbons cascading down from their wrists and all horse-clopping away with castanets. The sound was loud, reverberating and intoxicating. Initially so peeved at first that I had no energy to go further, I was now entranced to have happened upon this local dancing.

Oh, Lewy, your eyes would have shone!

The Solaces Of Landscape

Santa Catalina de Samoza – El Acebo: 28 kilometres

From hereon the Camino became relentlessly and astonishingly beautiful. My days were stretched on frames which were hung alongside each other, generously saturated with fresh air, braced by panoramic backdrops and medieval stonework, sprinkled with farm animals, and peopled with sometimes familiar faces. Drifting through the skyscapes were my thoughts. The sequence, the single picture and the tiny details were similarly a delight. Walking brought both relief from the strangling symptoms of anguish and refreshment after the night's deep sleep.

Up by 7.30 am I peered into the bottom bunk at Sonia the Brazilian, who was lying there fully dressed and looking stunned. On only her second day on the Camino, she'd woken, seen her watch saying 7.30, quietly dressed and headed out. As soon as the front door to the courtyard closed behind her, she checked her watch again as it was pitch dark and realised it was just after one o'clock in the morning. She'd read her watch upside down. Unlike Irish Ann, she couldn't re-enter, as the door was self-locking. She spent four and a half hours huddled outside in the cold and dark, with nowhere to sit and unable to wake anyone to let her back in.

The previous day, her first on the Camino, she'd headed off with a group who'd gone in the wrong direction, so today she stuck to me like glue. It was surprising I didn't make more mistakes considering how little planning and information I had and how wobbly my brain was. I'd certainly been lost a few times but luckily I'd gone astray in the right direction. I do have a sense of self-preservation, and knowing any directional mistake you've made means it's compounded getting back to your starting point probably helped considerably. Of course, I was with Prue at the beginning.

With our coffee we ate large wedges of crunchy toast and jam for breakfast. The dawn was glorious. Stretched along the parched countryside was a dry-packed, speckled-with-lichen stone wall, with bleached white seeding grass between it and the side of the road. In a pinky-golden light all were luminous.

On a narrow track with lots of slim, lichen-covered trees, Portuguese-speaking Sonia and I walked past a dedication written in Spanish to a man who had died on the Camino. We thought the sign said he'd died after either walking 50-plus kilometres in one day at the age of seventy, or 70 kilometres in one day at the age of fifty! I had passed perhaps five memorials to people who had died on the walk. Each place was quite exceptional, and I would hope a better place to die than in an Australian hospital.

In the albergue last night was a sign saying 'goodnight' in various languages. English was 'sweet dreams', which is what you used to say to me each night as we fell asleep. I was a little sorry to have Sonia with me much of the day as I wanted to think about you wrapped around me, your resonant voice tenderly murmuring in my ear.

Sonia and I chatted briefly to an outgoing council worker as we walked. He wore strikingly effervescent deep blue trousers. He asked where we had started from and told us we were in for a treat as this area of the Camino was extremely beautiful, one of the loveliest parts. He wasn't wrong.

Really that day had been a highlight, slowly walking up and up and up. I found if I leaned into the hill it was okay. I was actually quite unfazed; I must have become fit without even knowing it. We walked through more feathery, lichen-encrusted oak trees and it was silent and beautiful, the light dappled and shimmering.

We walked together to a town 17 kilometres away in the right direction, where Sonia was stopping. After depositing her at her *albergue*, I had a mineral water and she was nowhere to be found. I guessed she was settling in, grateful she had progressed on her journey at last, perhaps asleep already after her previous night's fandango.

I continued on and had a good cry about Lew's gentle requests for my sweet dreams. It was truly an awe-inspiring walk and I was happy on my own after I'd disentangled the anguished sweet dreams from my system.

I was especially lucky to have had such fun with you. I just wanted so much more for and with you. And my brain is so stuck with how sweet you were to me and how heroically brave you were dealing with your illness.

I didn't think I could take another break-up or death; I wanted to live softly with my dog and cat.

I walked through the most beautiful high mountain areas, about 1500 metres in altitude, and it was as if I were in a divine parallel world at the beginning of creation. The landscape was massive all around me and lightly misty in the distance. I was a little speck with giant rolling hills all around! Somehow, feeling insignificant in the scheme of things was reassuring and healing. How lucky was I to be doing this.

I walked through grassy pastures that held giant cows with horns and just one electric fence wire between us. The last 3.5 kilometres were treacherously downhill and tiresome on my knees. Down was worse to me than up. I went slowly and gingerly, and suddenly and most welcomely a grey slate-roofed town appeared in view.

I found a large good-condition sandal on the way down this steepest hill. When I was almost at the town, endearing eighteen-year-old French Canadian Carl came up and said thank you so much for bringing his sandal down for him. Apparently many people had seen it and no one had bothered to pick it up. All those visits to the bus depot when my children were small to retrieve jumpers, jackets, school shoes, a shared school project and even a guitar, had taught me a thing or two.

I was glad to be in El Acebo, having walked 28 kilometres. I found an excellent *albergue* that supplied dinner and not-before-8 am breakfast (lots of *albergues* throw you out by eight), but it was full. Luckily there was another one just around the corner.

My funny little place had two floors. There were four horrible depressing beds downstairs, and a tiny bathroom where the shower curtain stuck to you in the shower. RREEEECK! You had to place your toiletries and clothes on the toilet and mop the floor before you started. But up the tiny spiral staircase – hard to negotiate with a pack – was a lovely stone room with three beds and a large square window. I slept there with two English backpackers, Tim and Jane, who'd recently joined the Camino. I think they had extra warm sleeping bags because they slept with the window open and it was chilly.

Before dinner I wrote in my diary in a bar with *vino blanco*, sometimes talking to dear Claudia, a vet, who was writing in hers too. Like those fanciful jacarandas, Claudia also was a native of Brazil.

A cyclist came in and we asked him to join us. He said no, but how about dinner at 7.30? I said yes, not realising Claudia would say no as her *albergue* supplied dinner. By the time he came back I was happy from three wines, no food and walking all day. I bought him a drink and avoided one for myself.

He was a bit of a wally, talking about himself all night. Unlike Flavio, the first thing he said to me was, 'Let's get this straight – who's paying for this dinner?' I told him I was happy to pay for myself and didn't offer to shout him, which I had loved doing on this trip motivated by generous Lew.

He told me he was retired from the public service and had been almost the equivalent of a deputy minister. *Hmmm*, I thought, *pomposity – my favourite trait*. I talked to him about Lew. He replied that he was glad his ex-wife had died of cancer (they had one son) because she had taken a lot of his money in the divorce settlement. When you talk with someone like that, there really isn't much to say.

He looked so regretful when my dinner came and it was bigger than his. I think he was the sort of person who if you were stranded on a desert island with him and no food, he'd eat you. I didn't consider him a true pilgrim because he was on a bicycle.

Such a big waste of an evening. After I'd clambered down from my high horse, I clambered up the tiny staircase to my bed. Hopefully the wine had worn off and didn't cause me to snore.

Ф

El Acebo – Cacabelos: 32.2 kilometres

I woke after a restful sleep, but had to wait for the English backpacker to go downstairs before I could put on my militarily engineered bra, etc. I felt daunted by the prospect of walking from almost 1200 metres down to 600, because downhill with a backpack was tough. (I was relieved to find the descent was stretched out over many kilometres, so it was fine. AGAIN, don't worry about things until they happen.)

Downhill walking

Along my trek I'd walked through or passed many vineyards with lush, ripe-looking-to-me, mostly red grapes and fields of ready-to-pick sunflowers. I'd kept wondering when they harvested. I didn't know if it was a tradition to start gathering in on the 29th, but it was as if a starter's gun had been fired and the grape harvest was on. Suddenly through all the villages there were tractors with big metal containers being filled with red or white grapes. Everyone was working in the vineyards and it was exciting to see.

In the seventies, when I was nineteen and a student, I worked as a grape picker in the Hunter Valley of New South Wales. It was hard, heavy work and I became as fit as a flea.

Did I ever tell you that, Lewy? I don't think I did.

Φ

I'd decided to stop in the town of Camponaraya, a walk of 26.5 kilometres. Camponaraya wasn't small, but I discovered it had no accommodation whatsoever. Not no accommodation available, but no accommodation at all, ever! I had to walk another 5.7 kilometres and seriously contemplated getting a taxi as I couldn't see how I could go on.

Finally a taxi went past but I didn't grab it as it seemed a bit unCamino to take it. I must have had rocks in my head! I hadn't made a particular strategy with myself of no buses, taxis or having my backpack carried by some service, but somehow I quietly seemed to want to do it without any help. Worn-out Fabia really had a go at independent-hippy-free-spirit Fabia.

Lewy had suffered so much without complaint; I'd found that so impressive and adored him for it. And his courage made it effortless to look after him; it was such a loving and special time for us. What I was doing by choice was not comparable with his experience.

I miss you and I wish you near …

Finally, 3 kilometres from Cacabelos, I was sitting on a bench thinking, *how can I do this?*

A Californian woman with a sing-song voice came bouncing along and said, 'Are you okay?'

And I said, 'NO. I've miscalculated where the accommodation is and I've had it.'

She sat down next to me and gave me a small chocolate-type bar and said it had all the right minerals, etc, for women (I actually needed something for my broken-down feet) and would set me going again. Then she chatted for a while. She was positive, patient and no-nonsense. She then asked if I was able to go on and was it okay to walk with me? My pace was much better and I was lucky to have met her and have her help me. Thank you, Lucinda.

At last we reached Cacabelos. At the first stayable place at the very beginning of town, we parted and in I teetered. And wow! Not only did the hotel fetchingly reek of the capsicums they were roasting, but it also reeked with Spanish character – up-high balconies built around a courtyard, dark timbers, ironwork and fresh white lace. The owner offered me a glass of red wine and an empanada, which she said they gave to all their pilgrim guests when they checked in.

The hotel was comfortable and I had the prettiest room ever and a sparkling clean bath, which I filled up and soaked my rigid limbs in for ages. It was difficult to clamber in and slippery difficult getting out. Then I did heaps of washing; the ground was dry and dusty so everything was grubby.

In Sydney I washed your beautiful pale grey woollen jumper, the one you looked so sexy in. Before I washed it I darned all the small unravellings on the cuffs and around the waist. And that tiny hole near the neck. Into the eucalyptus-scented frothy water it went and was gently pushed around, up and down, back and forth. Then rinsed in clear cold water. Lightly squeezed and put out in the soft winter sun on a clotheshorse to dry. I didn't know you would be so sweaty and unwell you would never wear it again.

Φ

I forgot to say when I was ruminating that morning over the silly cyclist, he came flying past on his bike and stopped. He said he'd been thinking about me and that I had to keep strong physically and be as creative as I could and one other thing that I've forgotten. (Maybe it was to embrace new things?) Then he was embarrassed he had spoken and said in ten minutes he'd be 10 kilometres away. Narky foot-travellers 'love' hearing that sort of thing.

Joy

Cacabelos – Trabadelo: 19 kilometres

Look at the song-like names of these towns, so appealing.

Lew would have loved the hotel's coffee-with-cake breakfast and been charmed all day from it. The elegant fare contradicted the outdoor life I led. I had to fluff around the hotel until I could find someone to settle my bill. But I do admire the way the Spaniards start their days late and impressively party on, only ceasing their day when the next one has started.

I left with the rain spitting pettily. Cacabelos looked interesting, but I was on a hunt. The day before I'd been unable to pray and light candles for Lew because all the churches had been locked. It was DISAPPOINTING! Again they were all locked. Why? It seemed you had to make a choice: either you walked in a staggeringly pretty area or the churches were open.

Only 2 kilometres down the road was Pieros, a magic little place. Everyone was participating in the harvest. A husband and wife sat on a stone ledge at the front of their home peeling charred capsicums out of blue buckets of cold water. A woman wearing a smock was carrying a big bucket of capsicums and tomatoes. There was so much to see and everyone was working hard. I passed a variety of fruit trees laden with ripe colourful fruits and there were vivacious flowers in people's gardens. I saw, and smelt as I brushed past, flourishing herbs growing in the street gardens. Everywhere looked vibrant and joyful, with much lush productive landscape up hill and down dale. Hello to a donkey in a field! A light shower flitted by.

I walked through a vineyard where they were harvesting and passed a strong man working amongst the laden vines. He was carrying on his shoulders a black tub full of white grapes with the name LUIS written in large white letters on it. It was hard work and he was struggling. I took a photo of him carrying the tub, which he was loading onto a trailer that held lots of other tubs with the same family name. He looked like a pilgrim with a heavy load. He looked like me carrying my sorrow for Lew.

Harvesting

My darling boy.

Ф

I arrived in the beautiful town of Villafranca del Bierzo, which had three wonderful churches ALL OPEN! In the first, a moving and simple church, I lit a giant scarlet candle for Lew and was thankful to find a place to pray for him at last. I enjoyed dawdling around the second church. The third basilica was sophisticated with elegant patterned stonework on the ceiling and walls and refined ribs. I enthusiastically lit more rows of candles for Lewy.

I left this lovely town over a high and fairly dry bridge. Somehow I missed the turn-off for the scenic over-the-hill-and steep-decline walk. My legs and feet chorused 'thank you' in brittle voices. I walked with the river on my left, and on my right, on the other side of a low concrete barrier, was a minor road. This way turned out a little shorter.

I walked through Pereje, which was surrounded by forests and had a mill. There were huge towers of wood made up like pallets, I guessed to stop the wood from warping. As I walked out of this town, a lovely woman aged about seventy gave me a big bunch of grapes that they were just about to press. I gave her two kisses on her lovely soft cheeks. She smelt so fresh, not like us poxy old pilgrims.

That day was one of the finest of the walk: such richness of outdoor life, the beauty and poignancy of the churches, the man in the vineyard, and again the kindness of strangers.

Finally I walked into Trabadelo, panicking because my piece of paper said no *albergue*. But there were two. It was a relief to stop.

I found a bar with the internet, which was free as long as you bought something. I answered emails and sent one big one. I was bursting with stories. I bought coffee, mineral water and then wine so I could keep writing. Eventually someone else arrived to use the internet and I felt pressured and found it hard to write. I felt like a five-year-old having trouble sharing.

EMAIL: Hello everyone! I have been so inspired and have more to write than time available! I will just tell you about the happiness of today.

It is now harvest time and it's like living in a Richard Scarry children's book because the scale is small and sooo charming. Everywhere all of a sudden there are people gathering grapes — just small family affairs, Papa, Mama, grown children and little trucks. Everyone's scurrying around with ladders, tractors and tubs, picking, picking. I was walking through a small village called Pieros and I could see ripe figs, apples, apricots, pears, grapes, chestnuts, capsicums, quinces and blossoming colourful roses and sunflowers in a garden. There's an abundance of rosemary, sage and thyme. I passed a man with his car boot full of pumpkins and asked if I could photograph him and he proudly said yes. It was joyful.

I see stacks of healthy young cats, so endearing and unlike the half-starved ones I saw earlier on the walk. This afternoon I saw a blind man in a shed curled up in the dim light with his own little cattie.

Quite a few weeks ago with Prue, I ate a strange fruit from a tree that I didn't recognise. It was utterly foul; I imagine the taste was like cyanide and arsenic rolled together and I was furiously spitting it out. No long-term effects, but today I saw the same fruit ripened and split open. I'd tried to eat the outer flesh of a walnut. Will let the Department of Primary Industries know that there's no future in cultivating the outer part of walnuts.

Distance signs in Spain are inventive. Yesterday, 2 kilometres from a village it said 195 kilometres to Santiago de Compostela. Three kilometres out of the same village, it said 220 kilometres. This is fairly typical.

I am bubbling over with things to tell you but will have to let someone else use this computer.

I slept in an *albergue* with eight in a room. Carsten, Marianne and Danny were there, but I felt shy to chat.

Trabadelo – O Cebreiro: 20 kilometres

I left with a carping back. The first 4 kilometres were grim. On one side of the track was a pristine stream bedecked with tall slim trees, stippled light and the babble of running water. On the other, a two-and-a-half-foot concrete wall and a two-lane fast road where huge trucks racing by gave me the creeps big-time. And so did the cars going by not too fast.

I arrived at a café and bought a coffee, really so I could use their toilet. And then continued on. Finally I came off the main road and savoured the quiet.

In another village I unexpectedly came across a pastry shop with an available toilet. Imagine my surprise when I found myself consuming a chocolate pastry and another coffee. The coffee and bathroom routine was a bit of a vicious cycle.

These verdant villages were full of charm, although this one had an immense concrete expressway hovering high directly above it, which would be unnerving for residents. You just had to look up and there it was suspended above you – worse than living with tax returns owing.

I walked through several communities with lounging cows and veggie patches growing what looked like cauliflowers gone to seed, but I think they were a spindly-looking vegetable called Galician cabbage or *col gallega*. It's popular in a delicious Galician soup called *caldo verde*. Red tomatoes were still around, as were regular cabbages and pussycats.

I loved being by myself. I was able to think of Lew, to rant at the unfairness and be teary.

I trekked up 700 metres in altitude very quickly and was hugely whacked. So much for the 'don't mind going uphill'. I stopped for lunch at a village called La Faba. I was disheartened by the look of this place whose name was similar to mine. Someone must have won the cement lottery. Everywhere were bland concreted lanes splashed with huge sloppy cowpats. La Faba was so vertical to get to, *and I went downhill* for a long way also. When you are travelling on foot with a backpack towards a very high altitude point, as my single piece of paper was telling me I was doing, you may start to sulk when some of that uphill includes some downhill. Such a bloody waste when the long-term aim is uphill. However, the La Fabans do make a brilliant baguette, with the rare added thrill of tomato.

Finally, after a tough walk, I arrived at O Cebreiro, which was divine and very cared for. All the buildings in this village were made from tan or grey stone with either grey slate or thatched roofs. Their shapes were sculptural, low-slung, harmonious and settled nestling into the hillside. Probably it would be bitter there in winter, but that day had been warm and smiling.

In their uplifting church, I lit a large red candle for Lew, only just managing to take it from the girl I bought it from and light it myself before she did. I placed it in a large sombre alcove full of expectant red lit candles. I was cheered by this simple church, an intimate and warming space.

The impressive *albergue* was made of stone and overlooked a vast expanse of countryside. There were fifty-six beds in the room (a record for me) and some, including mine, were pushed together. I asked the woman at the reception if I was sleeping next to a bloke. No, she said, absolutely not. I'd no sleeping bag and there were no blankets supplied. It was now chilly outside, so it would be an interesting night. I was able to buy a pair of warm socks in a nearby shop.

I accidentally almost walked into the men's shower room as I was too weary to take in the different-from-usual Spanish word for *men's* next to the entrance. A man I'd met previously said, 'You can't come in here.' I couldn't work out why – now that's tired.

The women's communal showers and dressing rooms had no privacy so I had to shower and change in front of others who'd not had children or stacked on the kilos through greed and menopause. I didn't grow up with sisters and luckily never went to boarding school, but I adapted frantically fast as there were no alternatives. Then I had to walk quite a few naked metres to grab my tiny can't-hide-behind chamois and fresh clothes. *Ay yi yi!*

Later I caught up with sweet Anke again and her Canadian friend Carl whose sandal I'd picked up. I also tried to apologise to the Spanish man for nearly walking into the men's showers, but I was so bushed that I couldn't explain properly. I was giving up when he said, 'It is okay, take your time, I want to understand what you're saying.'

I received such kindness and decency from these Spanish people whose characters were impressive and full of integrity.

Φ

EMAIL: *Hi guys, oh my, I am in the most wonderful place: 1300 metres up at O Cebreiro. I scrambled from 600 metres to 1300 over 8 kilometres. Hardest climb so far. Have been higher, but this was sheerer. Only 20 kilometres today, but totally stuffed! This village is sooo affectionately glorious. A painter must have picked its colours and a sculptor shaped the buildings. In their old and cherished church I stood contemplating a giant red candle that shone for Lew and felt so much peace.*

This walking in the mountains is utterly astonishing and I can't really do it credit via words, but it's like being in a William Robinson painting (I believe, the best living Australian painter). Up here you are on top of the world. The landscape sweeps out around you in all directions. You feel like a child who could roll down, down a huge hill. Fantastic lichens, blue mountains receding in the late afternoon light, shades of green, beauty everywhere, icy cold water, large cowbells JANGLING – those poor cows.

I have seen quite a few squirrels; they are airy and adorable. Also saw a rabbit. The cows are giant and soft and healthy. This area is bliss city for dogs and many, many cats that are quite young and small. Today I had lunch at La Faba and sadly the town wasn't much chop. I will write to the local council and see if they can swap the names for this town – much, much better!

I'm a happy tired pilgrim, having café con leche in a bar.

Have walked 600 kilometres. Approx 150 to go. Then I'm going to hang out with Jane in southern Spain who is lovely, so I just can't be sad.

Am missing kisses and cuddles from everyone …

I'd made a blunder by organising to meet Cousin Jane in Granada too early. Flying out of Santiago de Compostela on the date we'd chosen meant I had to keep my daily kilometres high.

Jane is blessed with a terrific personality, an impressive intelligence, a golden beauty, a treasure of a husband and adorable teenagers; and not so blessed by the ongoing side effects from her cancer treatment as a teenager. She has been on familiar terms with grief, being an only child who has lost both her parents.

Φ

O Cebreiro – Triacastela: 21.5 kilometres

I woke in the pitch dark, a moody swirling fog surrounding O Cebreiro. Below street level, in a full and bustling café, I bumped into a recently retired architect. He'd walked out of his front door in Switzerland and all the way to where the Camino starts in Spain. He then went along the northern Spanish coast to Santiago (Camino Primitivo) and was on his way back, just walking the best bits of the Camino Frances so he arrived home before the snow hit. We had a good chat and he gave me a big hug when I left, which hurt my neck, shoulders and back. Everything was tight from the tensions of grief.

The lightened landscape was bathed in clouds and exquisite. I took lots of photos, and a Korean man asked me if I would be in his photo because of my mostly red with splodges of green skirt. He said he hadn't seen anyone on the Camino in a skirt. I could have said he was the first Korean I'd met. Why was I so defensive?

I had trouble finding the way as the path directions weren't visible. It appeared that while I had been fluffing around everyone else had departed. A lot of the pine trees were twisted and broken as though strong hurricane-like winds had spun their tops off. I started to suspect that I was lost, but spied fragments of tissues and a small yellow paint daub on a rock. I laughed out loud at a red and white STOP sign to which someone had added 'Complaining!' A few people had injuries but I'd heard little to no complaining, apart from the cacophony coming from my feet.

O Cebreiro

I climbed even higher and came to a powerful 3-metre-tall pilgrim statue. A South American woman with three French bulldogs and two fluffy dogs she'd found on the Camino (one called Molly) was offering tea, coffee, water, orange juice and biscuits for a donation. I was glad to oblige.

I walked through beautiful countryside where the clouds still veiled the valleys. Here and there the trees were starting to turn and their colours were unrestrained. It was likely that in not-so-many weeks from that warm and gentle day, the quiet rolling hills would be covered in snow. Impossible to visualise; just like I couldn't picture life without Lew.

I arrived at the top of a hill and had the usual full-of-flavour lunch while absentmindedly watching several people repairing their bicycles. Again the bathroom of the café reeked. Perhaps they started off fresh and equipped each morning, but by the time many pilgrims had passed through they were pongy and lacking in supplies. Now that would be a valid reason for the German pilgrims to start early.

After I left the little hilltop stop, I was saddened to see rubbish lining the roads. However, it was a magnificent walk through lovely high countryside, churches and villages. I felt like I was out in the middle of nowhere, completely alone, utterly safe; but when I stopped for a rest, perhaps within fifteen minutes another walker would pass by.

I ended up at Triacastela and searched for a room on my own. I found a nice clean place with its OWN bathroom and an incongruous high-tech shower. I did my laundry in an outside soapy tub in a flower-filled, sunshined garden and hung my clothes on the line. They flapped happily in the sunny breeze. How much contentment I had with such things.

In a weathered-to-grey formidable church I had my credential stamped as where I was staying didn't do this. The inside of the church was warm and welcoming from the sun which shafted its way through the doors and windows and lit the white walls.

I bumped into Anke again, who was the same age as my Claudie. In an inviting street café bathed in sunlight we shared a bottle of wine. She told me she was walking to try to understand something that had happened to her as a child. When she was in primary school her parents split up. She chose to live with her mum, and her brother went with her dad. Her father never forgave her and said she was no longer his daughter. This really distressed her. She was very likable and it was a heart-rending story. What dad without rocks in his head wouldn't be thrilled to have Anke as a daughter?

She said she'd be sorry to finish the Camino. I wasn't surprised. A few people had said the same to me. She also said she'd been wearing a sarong as a skirt sometimes because she liked my skirts.

I asked her to join Brazilian Claudia and me for dinner, but she was already committed to her three friends. They'd each buy something and cook a cheap meal together in the *albergue* kitchen. It always smelt delicious. Their gentle camaraderie was quite inspiring.

Later, Claudia and I had a meal in the restaurant part of the same café. I had veggie soup and a luscious steak served on a wooden board with a serrated knife. I imagined this was how you'd eat steak in Argentina. We talked for ages and had a great night, but with more wine I gradually morphed into shickered and tired. I sashayed back to my room, where luckily I'd taken my dry clothes off the line and hung them around the walls. Without changing I fell into bed and asleep. It was silly and careless to be so plonkered. I'd been fairly good except for the hilarious night with Prue and the New Zealanders.

Φ

Triacastela – Barbadelo: 24.5 kilometres

The next morning I drank heaps of water and blissfully put on fresh, dry clothes with not a pilgrim in earshot. I had a brekkie of big slabs of crispy toast with jam and yoghurt, which really kept me going. I started walking in the cold with a mild hangover at 9 am. A lot of the path was uphill in a forested area, but it was okay and before long I took off my jumper.

I met an Austrian called Stephan who had an extraordinary amount of personal charm. He was the CEO of a bank and had just finished three years of juggling studying and full-time work. This was his big celebratory break. When he asked why I was walking, I spoke to him about Lew. He told me that when he was seventeen, he'd been badly injured in a fall and had drowned. After he was revived, he said that he'd seen a white light and felt great peace and was not afraid of death. We talked for some time and he was a most engaging person. It was the only time on the Camino that I stopped walking while listening so that I could grasp every skerrick of what he was saying. He asked me where I thought Lew was and I burst into tears. I just didn't know. He said he was sure Lew was with me.

We continued walking and later I was able to point out to him some Australian eucalyptus trees. He kindly said that when we'd talked the time had flown and then he took off. I was glad to digest his ideas. They were caring, calming and hopeful.

Next I met up with Sonia the physiotherapist. She was German and lived in France with her partner and her nineteen-year-old daughter. She was wearing various shades of blue, had a curtain of curly hair like my Lew, was perhaps forty and I liked her. She said her daughter's father had been an alcoholic and she now lived with someone she'd gone out with when she was seventeen. He was good with his hands and had made her the loveliest garden.

I treasured these fragments of the heart that strangers offered. It's extraordinary what a difference just a handful of sentences can make.

Again the scenery was beautiful, with undulating hills, forested walks, exuberant vegetation and little villages that looked fairly poor. There were stacks of cow poo in the main concreted thoroughfares. It's not rare to see the Spaniards be heavy-handed with featureless concrete in their tiny northern village centres. I guess it's a defence against all that mud propagated by the high rainfall. Along some of the old forest tracks I saw ancient massive tree trunks that had sprouted new branches. They looked like something out of Narnia or Tolkien's world.

Although the 24.5-kilometre walk was steep and hard, it seemed quick because it was beautiful and intermittently there were thoughtful people to talk to. I'd been walking by myself for a few days and was appreciative of a little company.

I arrived at Barbadelo, which was a tiny village with a church, two *albergues*, a restaurant and a few houses. I stayed at a private *albergue* in an old rural house with lots of character from its maze of rooms, furniture, lace, curios and many family photographs.

There were quite a few pilgrims sleeping there; in our room, three Germans and me. At first I thought I was in a room with three men. What's wrong with me that I hated that idea? The woman I'd dimly thought was a man was a woman, Gertruc. I raced over to her and said, 'I'm so glad you're a woman.'

After a shower I met a kindly older English couple who had lived in Canada for over forty years. Her foot had swollen up so they were going at a snail's pace. There was no shop here so I gave her my Voltaren, as Lew would have done, and hoped she would recover faster.

I remember telling you I gave each month to Médecins Sans Frontières. 'That's a great thing to do,' you said. And then after you died and I did your tax, I found those monthly commitments you'd never mentioned: the Fred Hollows Foundation, the Cancer Council, endless charity raffle tickets and others that I can't recall now. (No way am I ever going to re-open those files.) I cherished discovering your secret open-handedness.

The four young friends staying in the public *albergue* were unable to cook their dinner as there were no pans in the smart kitchen. I told them I'd go and ask at the church, but I was unable to make myself understood. It's not a universal situation to be asked by a stranger who doesn't speak your language if they can borrow one of your saucepans. I went back and suggested Spanish-speaking Lisa should ask. She managed to find someone to lend them a pot. They suspected humbug between the *albergue* owners to make pilgrims use the restaurant.

EMAIL: Thanks so much for all your letters!

I just have to tell you the sequel to O Cebreiro. I randomly slept next, and I mean next, to a Spanish man called Manuel whom I'd met on the way. He is about thirty-four and teaches Spanish in high school. I thought he was nice when I met him on the walk. When he went to climb onto the bed he said, 'Oh no, you have no blanket!' And jumped down to find one for me. I said I had already asked and there were no spare blankets. So he took some sort of rubber thing out of his pack (not what you are thinking) and said, 'Sleep on that, you'll be warmer.' I was wearing a T-shirt, a skirt, a nightie, a cotton jumper, two pairs of socks and had my raincoat ready if I was too cold. It was fairly cold, but I had sort of accepted it would be a crap night with fifty-six others. I was doing my impersonation of being asleep, but Prue could tell you I was faking it because I wasn't snoring, when I heard the zip of his sleeping bag go down and I thought, oh no, here comes trouble. Manuel softly put his sleeping bag over me when he thought I was asleep. How lovely is that? The men on this walk are especially not irritating (apart from the cyclist).

Mostly I like to walk alone, but I've met many great people from everywhere, sometimes in the evenings or having a break in a café. Now I speak English slowly and simply with a Spanish accent. IDIOT! The Spanish people smile when I try to speak their language. I'm not a natural.

I try and remember how generous Lew was to people and how sweetly teary he was when people were kind to him and put that into practice on this walk.

Today I was walking for a while with Sonia who secretly is a physiotherapist, but this is not the place to let people know that is your job. We'd been seeing apple trees laden with fruit and using her walking sticks I hit two apples down. They were out of this world, crunchy, juicy and tart.

I have about 107 kilometres to go. I'm not sad to finish. I think it's the right time, probably five more days. Yesterday I felt light and happy and realised I'd not cried for Lew all day.

I had dinner with an extra lovely Brazilian vet. She spoke from her heart, which most people do here in a gentle unassuming way. We had such a great night. This morning I put on my freshly washed dry clothes and was so simply happy. And then today I was walking and cried and cried for my Lewy. I realise he never could have done this walk because his knee was not good, but maybe he could have done circles on his bike and gone ahead and sussed out the most delicious restaurants and vinos.

You know, everyone said when we were in the province of Galicia it would rain and rain. It hasn't happened. Just like they said the hills were so steep the next day and they were fine, or going down the mountain would be shocking and it wasn't. You just have to take and enjoy if possible each experience as it happens, which is very Lewy. Still a bit homesick …

I wanted to lie on my living room floor and be licked by hyper-happy Molly-Dog, rub my nose in the fur of Louie-The-Cat who smells like sunshine, and kiss all the photos of Lew-The-Human. My home …

Rain

Barbadelo – Gonzar: 28 kilometres

Out the door I went in the teary rain. I was never one of the first. I walked down the hill through a dark green park with looming trees. And off I went from Barbadelo like a curly-pathed ant not sure whether to go uphill or down.

The rain turned massive, straight down and strident. I stood under a tree in the drowning light and realised there was a pilgrim close by silently sheltering in a shed doorway, and then another so still under a tree like me. Feeling spooked I decided to walk on (easier to be brave in front of other people). After half an hour I found a café, but it was too soon after breakfast so on I went, nearly the wrong way until a richly weathered Danish man leaned out of the café and said, 'The other way!'

The rain eased and I became saunatised so I took my raincoat off.

Much later, hunger was gnawing and there was no lunch in sight. I came around the corner of a gently downhill windy path and there was a striking *albergue* and hip café right in the middle of forestry-nowhere. This place was so unexpected, it was as if I were in a dream.

With my lunch I had Santiago cake. It's made from almond flour, which gives it its singular flavour, and the shape of the cross of Saint James of Compostela is left undusted by the icing sugar on top.

While daydreaming in the café I saw Anke, dreadlocked Daniel,

French Canadian Carl and Welsh Lisa again, coming through the forest looking very merry and reminding me of Robin Hood. I bought Carl a large cup of milky coffee as I was worried that he was a bit broke. He was walking with a long stick that he'd found in France. He'd tied four feathers to the top and each day he carved another notch on his staff. He hoped to take it home with him, but was concerned that the airline might not allow it. His voice was like Jeff Bridges'. What courage to have taken off on his own at eighteen and be having this adventure. He said he was leaving Lourdes on foot when a priest called out to him, 'Bon Camino!' So that was where Carl regarded his Camino began.

I really enjoyed the day's walk. My brain was firing with good thoughts, fresh ideas, and the landscape was radiant. Everywhere were curving country lanes, stone walls covered with lichens and mosses, wide greyed wooden gates, and chestnut and oak trees with acorns dropping haphazardly. I walked up The Best Lane with fascinating lichen-spattered dry-packed stone walls on either side. The steep path was made from smooth rocks the size of giant mangoes with narrow granite stepping-stones that I kept to. They were some distance apart so you had to jump, as well as l…e…a…p some bigger gaps. *I felt extraordinarily happy.* I would've skipped if my pack hadn't been so weighty. It was raining, my raincoat made me too hot, my feet were wet and muddy, my skirt and hair soaked, and yet I was filled with JOY. Fifteen minutes before I'd been crying for Lewy.

Some apple trees were now laden, or carpeted below with flyblown fruit, and when you walked past there was an unfamiliar squishy smell of squashed overripe apples. I witnessed a live demonstration of how cow poo materialised in the main thoroughfares when I saw an elderly man and his smiling dog herding cows through the village.

So much camera workout. I captured some eye-catching country gates. They had flat pieces of weathered wood on the vertical, but each piece of wood on the horizontal was curved, earthy and sculptural. The lichens were also mighty lavish and all luxuriating in the rain – light bluey-grey curly and crispy, late middle-aged feathery pastel blue, powdery lime green and pulsating deep green mosses.

I photographed varied and interesting tiny houses on stands that looked like Buddhist shrines (if I knew what Buddhist shrines looked like), but I think traditionally these were for storing corn. Some had a cross at the front highest point of their miniature pitched roofs. I also took a photograph of a giant metallic blue-black slug. I'd seen huge leopard slugs in Australia, but this was larger, flashy and European-looking. A Lamborghini of slugs.

The squat carved stone signposts were counting down to Santiago every 500 metres, which was intrusive, although they also indicated the place you were walking through and it was an agreeable change for me to know where I was. I photographed the 102 kilometres sign, and wanted to capture 100 kilometres, but somehow missed it. I managed to see the one for 99.5. The Danish troop later emailed me their photo of the stone marker for 100 kilometres. It was covered in graffiti.

I crossed a huge non-ancient bridge before Portomarín, which was scary – just four rails between me and the river at least 100 feet below, with lots of see-through gaps. The bridge was too long and I had to keep looking straight ahead, occasionally making Maori warrior grunts – the sort I make when moving nasty spiders. I was sure the legal safety railing height in Spain was lower than in Australia.

My choice of bypassing Portomarín because I wanted to keep walking meant I missed some historic and architectural gems. I walked for 28 kilometres, and was weary for the last 4 as I was unable to find a get-off-my-feet café. Luckily I ran into Marianne, Carsten and Daniel.

I walked happily with Marianne until Gonzar. She said she'd detoured the skyscraping Portomarín bridge, no way was she going over it. Although my feet were cranky, I was glad of her company and picked up my pace. She had kindness in her merry eyes, and she spoke English with some sweet variations, like 'back-sack' for either 'backpack' or 'rucksack', and writing 'beautiful' as 'beauty-full'.

Because we were close to Santiago, the *albergues* became more expensive. Our elemental *albergue* in Gonzar was built around a courtyard. The walls and floor were made of stone, and we slept in timber bunks under brown woollen blankets. Only five of the fourteen beds in our room were filled. The place was run by an extended family of friendly grandma and grandpa, unfriendly husband and wife, and the children were rascals. Funnily enough they acted like we were an intrusion in their home, possibly because we had to traipse through their living room to arrive at our sleeping quarters.

I took a thoughtful photo late in the day of Bertol, the Danish man who'd saved me from going the wrong way. He was sitting on the grassy ground in the steep afternoon light, leaning against the stone wall of a building and absorbed in his reading. His fabulous face looked like it had been hewn out of hardwood.

I had a drink with Marianne, Carsten and Daniel and craggy Bertol in a former petrol station, now a not-so-suave bar. We sat at a table in the place where you would normally park your car to fill it with petrol. Carsten had bought a drink for Danny and Bertol and was embarrassed he hadn't bought one for me. He joked that they always bought drinks for students and pensioners. A little later he bought me one. I believe it was a student he mistook me for.

You could see in Carsten's good-natured expressions that he was looking for an amusing way to see the world and to share these perceptions with those around him. I liked these three people. They were warm, energetic and devoid of neuroses. It was the second time Carsten and Marianne had walked the Camino and I could understand why.

Φ

Gonzar – Ponte Campaña: 21 kilometres

It was now three months since Lewy's life had ended. I set off on my bleary own around 8.40 am.

I stopped for coffee and cake, and met a sociable retired local woman who'd spent her working life in London employed by

Cambridge University. When I told her I was a painter she kindly dashed off to find a catalogue of a painter friend to show me. The work was accomplished, but my priorities had been ambushed – of far greater visual impact was the fact that the bathroom had no loo paper and its rubbish bin was overflowing with horrible things. This was a big problem in the cafés on the Camino and in many *albergues* in the mornings. They needed a Zealous Despot to be specifically in charge of soap, paper towels and loo paper. I always carried tissues. And yet I'd had no sickness, upset tummy or whatever. Living in our unfinished house with no bathroom for six weeks had tempered me.

Santa Magdalena Chapel, Ventas de Narón

I came upon an exquisite tiny church, Santa Magdalena Chapel, at Ventas de Narón. Carved upon each of the three planks that made up its small arched door were a scallop shell, a communion goblet with wafer and a crucifix, all simple and powerful. Four evenly spaced trees flanked the entrance. There was a chain by the door that you could pull to ring the church bell. Sadly the church was closed, so I couldn't talk to the God I'd been imploring. Was he generous and just to have given Lew such happiness for four years before he died? Or was he unbearably cruel to have let Lew die when he was so happy? I was wrestling with contradictions again.

It was raining heavily when I stopped for lunch. Afterwards I used the café's internet and was cheered by emails from encouraging friends. I had much more energy to go on and the walk was beautiful. The rain started to ease and the intimate scale of the country lanes was magic. Again the mosses and lichens were gorgeous. And … it was only 60 kilometres to Santiago.

Φ

EMAIL extracts from Nick: I love your emails. Very inspiring. I read them to Jess whenever I received one. We are very proud of you.

Tasmania was fun. We also decided to come and see family, so now we're in Melbourne … We're seeing Claudie tonight.

The truly inspiring parts of Tasmania that we saw were the alpine country around snowy Cradle Mountain and the surrounding world heritage national park areas including Lake St Clair, the western mountains and the pristine plateaus in between. Despite being a relatively experienced and cynical traveller I was amazed by how ancient, pure and dramatic it was. I'm not used to Australian landscape like this … The lichen I was liken. It was lichen on lichen. (That's my boy!)

The fauna seemed to be enjoying themselves. We saw lots of wombats in the wild, wallabies and birds. We saw Tasmanian devil road-kill, which was reassuring, we said, 'Aaaaw, that's nice, they must not be endangered if they are getting killed on the roads here.' Road-kill was a recurring theme for the whole trip …

We did a one-day trek and it was beautiful. Alpine rainforests leading to snow-covered granite plateaus next to dark glassy lakes, then spiky mountains above.

You can do a 5-day overland trek through the world heritage forests from Cradle Mountain to Lake St Clair (or vice versa), which would be totally amaaazing – like Lord of the Rings but better. I want to do it. Lots of love, Nick x

Ф

ALL the churches that day were locked, which was strange and unnecessary as this was supposed to be a pilgrimage. There would be no sweet prayers and no soft candles. The Zealous Bathroom Essentials Despot could deal with this situation also. The shy and quiet woman at the Ponte Campaña *albergue* said the church there was locked and only opened on Sundays. I went searching for it, as I was ready to climb down a chimney if there was one, but I couldn't even find the church.

I'd planned to walk 26 kilometres that day, but I'd had more than enough by 22 kilometres. My never iffy back was, and I was nervous it could go kaput. The *albergue*, Casa Domingo, had heaps of character, with wooden tools and chairs mounted upon the interior stone walls.

The dear Danish people said, 'Take this bed, and then you can sleep with us.' There were four to our room and Marianne had put her cardigan on the bed for me to look like it was already taken.

Before dinner, we looked at their smiling and spacious photos on young Daniel's laptop. (Not blond dreadlocked Daniel who was travelling with Anke, Carl and Lisa.) Looking at their photos, flooding sparkling memories came back to me of all the magic places I'd walked through over the last five weeks. I was surprised that someone would bring a laptop on the Camino. But I'd found that most people I'd met had something surprising about them.

The rain outside was torrential, the light heavy and grey. Much of the walk had been hot and dry so it was a refreshing change and added to the texture of the trip. The young and serious *albergue* woman did all my washing and drying for a small fee. I was hugely improved by this and thanked her profusely. I saw the hint of a smile in her grave eyes.

Our dinner was the best of the Camino. We started with two

choices of soup – lentil or potato with vegetables. Then came large oval platters of roast chicken, meatballs, veggies and salad. At our generous feast were two Danes, two Germans, two Italians, one lively and droll Irishman and me. (Daniel had a night off.) The German woman had walked the Camino by herself, but her husband had recently joined her so they could finish together. I loved seeing their happiness. They were constantly touching each other.

I kept looking at photos of us after you died. Always we had a hand on or an arm around each other. There was nowhere else we'd rather be and I couldn't believe how lucky we were. I never took you for granted.

I slept soundly, surrounded by kindness. Marianne said my snoring wasn't bad compared to Carsten. He snored for the Olympics, but luckily she didn't mind.

Φ

Ponte Campaña – Ribadiso: 22.5 kilometres

I set off in the almost dark and ran into a loud, frantic, vicious Alsatian dog. I was only saved when he was pulled back sharply by the end of his chain length. This gave me a bad fright.

Laptop Daniel had kindly followed me to let me know I had taken the wrong turn. When I told him what had happened he said, 'And now you are awake!'

I said, 'And maybe I need to change my underwear.'

By myself, I followed the right path. In the dawning morning gloom, after my fright, it was quite creepy. Acorns, chestnuts and heavy splodges of water were dropping onto the misty, dark, canopied path and made me think someone was following me.

Actually, bad things usually don't happen when you anticipate them. My experience is they race up behind you right out of nowhere. The bewildering unforeseen. I put my hand out and asked Lewy to hold it and look after me. My fear evaporated.

I felt far, far away from home. I wondered if it was all a huge mistake and Lew hadn't died, just gone off travelling, and maybe because this place was so out of the way I just might bump into him?

I don't mind that you let me think you'd died … I did all of your tax. And I have your things for you. I kept the washing up to date too well – I don't have anything that smells of you. Is there such a thing as a happy smell? The smell of you was so good. How much further do I have to trek before I start getting closer to home?

Not so much later, around a bend that delivered me from the murkiness, and as the daylight appeared, I saw a huge rainbow which felt like Lew was saying g'day!

Φ

After a while I met up with English Jane and Tim again and strode with them at their fast pace for a time, but then fell back, happy to unravel my thoughts and take the odd photograph.

Finally, I found a pretty church that was open – I would've been happy with an ugly church. In peace and solitude I lit one big beautiful red and five small candles for Lew.

I walked past a hardware store and saw a fantastic broom. Boy, did I want to buy it, but how absolutely ridiculous to want something like that while doing something like this. I'd also seen some wooden rakes, maybe for pitching hay, that were carved from one piece of forked timber and looked marvellously sculptural.

When my old garden broom wore out, Lew spent a lot of time hunting for a hundred percent Australian-made broom for me. It's bright blue and I love it. I thought Lew would long outlast that broom.

I passed the 50 kilometres sign. The flourishing green countryside was familiar now, with its easygoing cows and forests that were shimmering with lichens. I stopped at another church to pray for Lew, and a priest with a big toothy smile warmly shook my hand. I truly missed touching.

Hugs, cuddles, snuggles, soft kisses, embraces, holding … so often. Sleeping entwined, showering together, even when you drove I had my hand on your thigh. Kisses when off to work, kisses when returning, thank you kisses and little-need-for-sorry kisses. I am so lost without you, Lew. And you became so still and dead and I was scared when I touched or kissed you. How could I have been afraid of gentle, kindly, bonkable you?

There was nothing I could do that would bring Lewy back. If only there was something that I could have done for that darling man who was so happy. I hated that life had ended for him. I was starting to believe it now. It was bloody crappy.

Φ

I crossed the road and stopped for lunch. My unexpectedly polite feet and back thanked me for the break. I checked my messages and was so grateful for chatty emails from dear friends.

Back on the track, I ended up walking with likable Carl. We saw a dear little black and yellow spotted gecko on the road. It was like nothing I'd ever seen at home. Perhaps he'd escaped from the Heaven Dome?

We found in Ribadiso a large public *albergue* beside a stream, rustically made of stone with painted blue window frames and a paved stone courtyard. I had more than a drink with Claudia, Tim and Jane.

Tim and Jane had only recently started their walk, I think from Astorga. They told me they'd lived in Sydney for some time when Jane worked in Australia. I'd seen Tim outside El Acebo earlier in the walk and noticed he had some sunburn on his neck. Unable to restrain the mum in me, I'd told him to be careful of the sun as where I came from it could be a problem. He'd kindly never mentioned that they'd lived in Australia and knew that.

Drinks turned into a good dinner, but I had too much to eat and drink. My stop switch had failed. I almost didn't have a wash as I was too weary, then I thought how erk for the person sleeping in my bed tomorrow, so with much effort I acted my age and had a late shower in the darkened dormitory-style bathroom.

Φ

EMAIL: Hello! I've been bursting to write but no available internet. Yesterday while sheltering from heavy rain I answered some emails, but as the rain didn't stop I decided that this former Scotland Islander wouldn't be put off by a little torrential rain, so out I went. What an idiot I was saying no rain in Galicia (pronounced Galeethia). Subsequently it's been pouring, but it's bloody gorgeous here so it's OK …

Galicia is such a beautiful area. It's tantalisingly hilly with curling paths. Because of the high rainfall, it's full of forests and the trees are covered in lichens. Beautiful feathery pale green, crackly blue grey and dusty bright green, as well as deep green mosses – so very beautiful with the rain and light breaking through. Maybe I've talked about lichens before? I'm writing a diary and talking in my head as I walk so not quite sure if I'm repeating myself, but the lichens are sooo good they're worth mentioning twice.

Some mornings my head is just bursting with the beauty around me, the animals, the wonderful pilgrims from many countries, and my thoughts about Lew that have no satisfactory conclusion, just hopefully an acceptance. Very many, many completely different concepts and feelings.

Today I saw a beautiful soft brown cow sheltering from the rain under a giant chestnut tree, with her mouth opening and closing while drinking the rain.

Last night I stayed at an albergue with many pilgrims I've become familiar with. Some have gone home, new ones have appeared, and some favourites weave in and out of your trip. It's a rich experience.

I've been thinking about how Lew was nine months older than me and how I said to him I was born to make him happy. (Reckless thing for a feminist to say.) In early April we will be the exactly the same age and after that I will always be older. It doesn't seem right or possible.

Some Danish people my age and their 'Camino son' Daniel from

Germany told me a sophisticated European rhyme this morning:
Hooray! Hooray!
It's the first of May,
Fucking outside begins today!
Less than 40 kilometres to go, so two more nights out of Santiago.

Ф

Ribadiso – Arca: 22 kilometres

It was only just light when I left, but everyone else had already gone. The days were definitely becoming shorter. I posted a birthday card to my Dad, who gives the best hugs.

I was glad to bump into Claudia and we walked together for some time. We stopped for coffees and met up with Austrian Stephan and his friends Ottie and Arno. It was so good to see vibrant Stephan again.

When I accidentally locked myself in the bathroom, I could hear Claudia quite panicked for me. Having lived in a house with three teenagers, being locked in the bathroom by myself still has some appeal. Before leaving on my own, I secretly paid for Claudia's breakfast – the things you learn from Basque people. And hooray, it wasn't raining!

Because my argumentative feet and dodgy back were up to their old snipey tricks, I was distracted and so squandered the joy of walking through dappled forests and pretty covered-with-canopy lanes.

The afternoon was well-stocked with animals. In a fairy-tale garden, while a caramel and white spaniel blissfully slept, different-coloured rabbits were nibbling and chooks were pecking on the green, green grass. I passed grazing russet-coloured sheep. I came upon a gentle grey mare and her foal. For a little while I gazed as they grazed. They smelt grassy and I loved the sound they made when they blasted air through their noses. I liked watching them swishing their tails, but it was confronting that they were hobbled.

In a crowded café I ordered a ham sandwich. The flavour of *jamón* is sensational and I would serve it piled high on Spanish crusty bread in the Heaven Dome.

Our destination was looming. It gave a cadence to the café. A sort of effervescing excitement as if something big was making its way through. Pilgrim heads were humming with their own private considerations.

For two days there had been hordes of plantation eucalypts planted in countless rows, which to me looked out of character. I love the way they grow in Australia with their scattered and transparent canopies. In this part of Spain they grow taller and thinner, a sort of prescribed super-model version. I walked through an area where they'd been harvested and was taken aback. Enormous trees ripped down and dragged along the ground by harsh chains. Their branches were split, broken and torn in complete unanticipated devastation, the earth's sense of purpose stolen.

Oh, Lewy! It reminded me of when you died.

What were the Australian trees doing here without all our sunshine, and why were they so ripped apart? Trees were not meant to be horizontal. And what was Lew doing in that hospital and why was he dead? I did know the answers to those questions, but I was struggling to accept them. What did I think went on in the countryside; and didn't I know all human life ended?

I'd found it grievous going that afternoon and the rains for the last hour were a pain in the bum. I'd intended to walk about 24 kilometres so there'd be only 16 kilometres to Santiago, but I only managed 21 and then I hunted down a hotel in Arca (I think that was the name of the torrential town) and crashed.

For the first time I didn't look around the town I was staying in. My back was spoiling for a fight and shuddery, so in another first I downed some paracetamol. I had a shower, but not before scalding myself by mixing up the taps. I was nervous to have a bath in case my back buckled and I couldn't climb out.

I felt a little better after, and even turned on the television and watched some silly Spanish soap opera set in the past. I couldn't follow the plot and found the good-looking, ultra-clean, super-thin and overly made-up actors really grating. I was disheartened, unreasonable and dilapidated. Well, so much for not complaining. I thought I'd covered everything, but at least I was on my own.

The bedside light in my room kept flickering. I yearned that it was Lewy saying hello. I'd had plenty of lights flickering on the walk. Please be Lew …

Hello, sweet buddy. Are you smiling at me saying, 'Fabie, it's not so bad and you've done well.' I'm not as brave as you are, Lulu. How did you manage it?

Querulous footage

End Of The Line And End Of My Tether

EMAIL: Hi guys, well, I'm about 20 kilometres from Santiago de Compostela. I have stopped for the night and I have to tell you I'm quite low. My back is sore. It was foul this afternoon; I thought it was going to totally spasm out of control. My backpack weighs 10.95 kilos, which explains my back's querulousness. I shouldn't be carrying more than 8 kilos.

Somewhere along the way my personage has lost 2.3 kilos. (I hope some dope doesn't return it to me.) I was wearing my sodden chunky shoes and socks when that info was revealed, but I'm irritated there isn't less of me.

My feet are also very sore in a temporary way. My treasured walking shoes are on their last legs so to speak. Tomorrow when they deliver me to S de C I will thank them very much and then throw them out. They also took me around Central Australia and way up north, where we thought 9.6- and 10- and 8-kilometre walks were big.

I was determined not to complain, just like Lew never complained, but sadly I feel fairly crap and it just seems to be spilling over. And maybe this is also because this magical goodbye walk to Lewy is almost over. No momentous dreams of Lew, no mystical experiences, lots of beautifully quiet times to think and lots of prayers to simply ask that Lew be taken care of, so many lovely candles to light and lots of pushing myself physically to help the emotions to settle. And a finality that is chilling.

I certainly don't think I have developed a walking disorder and won't be able to stop. And I plan to spend a few days at S de C and regroup and try and make more peace with senseless things.

I do hope you have enjoyed my humble jumble (Hugh's words) of thoughts and experiences on this wonderful walk.

Lewy's birthday is on 13th Oct. Have a big fat drink and a toast for him if you have a chance.

Darling Nick and Jess are expecting a baby in about six months, so how good is that! Lots of love and much appreciation for all your emails.

Φ

Arca – SANTIAGO DE COMPOSTELA!: *20 kilometres*

I slept around the clock and was considerably repaired, especially my back, for my last walking day. And grateful that it was overcast but not raining.

The walk wasn't as striking – it was too well-trod. I walked through many small villages, and saw some sheep peering out of a doorway. They seemed to be saying, 'Oh, we don't think we'll go out in this weather.' I was glad to be solitary – to sift through my thoughts and emotions.

Along the Camino I'd visited cemeteries on the outskirts of towns and villages, or peered through their locked iron gates, and thought that somehow the living and the dead seemed more integrated. I stopped at a closed church with the most cared-for cemetery surrounding it, with lots of fresh and plastic flowers. I was heartened to see such a beautiful cemetery on my last day. So much time had passed since many had died. A stab in my chest. I hated this so much – time was racing for me too and dragging me away from my boy.

There was a laminated child's drawing placed on top of one of the graves. The picture was exquisite and had writing beneath, which (in Granada Jane's later translation) said:

If only you were here to make the world a better place
Forever in our hearts: Mummy, Daddy, Me – Pixas

Child's drawing in a cemetery

I really appreciated visiting that decorated and beloved place. Here was physical evidence of the living having included the dead in their lives. I liked that. A lot. Maybe when I was home I could paint something about Lew on the back wall of my house, facing the tiny garden where we'd enjoyed all those carefree times.

The chestnut trees were gorgeous, but again the eucalypts dominated. Maybe they were stringybarks, as masses of long strips of bark were hanging down from their trunks. I picked up a nut to check when I was home; you couldn't mistake the smell. I preferred the difference from home of oak and chestnut trees.

I had a final Camino lunch in a crowded-with-young-people café. There were many more people that day. Let them go ahead. I needed to be alone, but when I was, unexpectedly I felt isolated.

A Destination

My excitement started to bubble as Santiago drew near, but I was disappointed with myself for being so exhausted. So much for riding high and galloping onwards. I saw golden corncobs drying, and many pairs of sneakers hurled up and trapped in power lines. I guess we're all trapped in something.

And finally ... S A N T I A G O.

I was elated and thankful, but the outskirts of the city seemed a long way from the cathedral. As I was plodding along, Claudia and three friends warmly called out and bought me a white wine. We happily sat in the street near some waste-disposal bins looking like a super-fit bunch of winos. It was terrific to see her and be less isolated. I walked with them towards the cathedral, but fell behind.

And so.

By myself.

I entered the Cathedral of Santiago de Compostela.

Inside it was magnificent. A wondrous cosmos of light shafts, beauty, space, and human utmost.

Lewy, Lewy, where are you? I'm so sorry you're not here.

I've been thinking of one of the dearest things you said to me. You'd been in a difficult relationship, which ended before we met. One day I asked you, 'Did you ever want to give up as I wanted to when my first marriage was ending and life was so shitty?'

'No,' you said, 'I always knew one day I'd meet someone wonderful and be as happy as a man could be.'

Φ

I was overwhelmed from the ending of the mighty Camino walk. There would be no more wanderings in awesome Spain to counterbalance my sorrow and I would miss living with only the necessities that were contained within my backpack. But physically I had definitely reached my and the Finale. My legs and feet were entirely spent and meekly asked if I might buy them, at some stage that was convenient to me, no rush, some anti-inflammatory drugs.

I walked out the main entrance of the cathedral and down into grand Obradoiro Square, where I saw lots of friends which was very affecting. Kisses, tears, hugs, photos and joy all around. So many people from all over the world and so friendly; some already there and some just arriving. A truly big and moving experience.

At the Oficina de Acogida al Peregrino (Pilgrims' Reception Office), not far from the cathedral, I had my credential stamped for the last time and was given my certificate of completion. The Santiago stamp was unusually dull compared to most, which was disappointing when you considered it was our destination. I love irrationally my credential with all its varied bold and washed-out coloured stamps.

I was dazed and outside my own skin, so I found a comfy *hostal* near the cathedral in the oldest part of the city. In this area, which was all made of greyed stone and that day not overlooked by a stony sky, there were marvellous medieval winding-up-and-down streets and no cars.

I slipped out to have a most welcome dinner on my own. Afterwards, I climbed many flights of stairs and entered my attic bedroom. I was transfixed by the textured and tiled view of rooftops from my windows. It was heavenly to fall profoundly and peacefully into sleep.

And like Lewy's Precious Life it was all over.

Detail of a pilgrim credential

Santiago de Compostela

The next morning, I cleaned every trace of dirt from my shoes, expressed my heartfelt gratitude to them, kissed each one goodbye, and softly placed them in the bin in my room. No longer would my small toes peep out of either side. I didn't want to burn them at Finisterre. They could rest in a rubbish heap somewhere outside Santiago, hopefully with the sun and the rain upon them and eventually covered by a blanket, perhaps very dense, of other human scraps. I was sad and indebted at the same time. I'd so cheerfully walked with Lew in Central and Northern Australia wearing those shoes.

I callously went off to buy new walking shoes, some red and some green socks, and a woollen jumper as I was chilly. It was enjoyable fluffing around and not taking everything so seriously.

I arrived at the cathedral at seven minutes to twelve for the noon

Mass and it was already spilling over with pilgrims. There were no seats available so I stood near a huge column in one of the transepts, flouting the histrionics from my feet and legs. A humbly dressed in black and white nun sang sooo beautifully during the Mass in a rich deep contralto voice that I started to cry. My heart swelled and echoed along with her voice in the huge space. Lew would have loved her singing, which seared one's soul.

Over their white robes the nine or ten priests were wearing tomato-red chasubles with large elongated white crosses on them. The opulence of their clothes contrasted markedly with the nun's. They looked striking, as did the hefty display of palest green big round chrysanthemums in front of the altar. Behind all was a typical magnificent gilded sparkling *retablo* of Spanish indulgence.

A priest listed all the different nationalities of the pilgrims who had arrived in Santiago that day. The service, although in Spanish, was poignant. At the end, eight men in deep maroon robes and broad hats hoisted with thick knotted ropes the gigantic silver 53-kilo lit incense burner, the Botafumeiro, until it was high enough to swing in enormous swooshes back and forth through the ceiling space of the crossing. It looked powerful, a mighty generosity indeed, and the air smelt heady. In the good old days, when washing was rarer, the incense would have been a Godsend. I had a great up-close view from where I was standing. It was very theatrical and people clapped at the end.

I saw Anke in the cathedral and took her to lunch with Carsten, Marianne, Laptop Daniel, Weathered Bertol, Erik and Inge. We had sandwiches and coffees in a captivatingly atmospheric restaurant that overlooked the street. The place looked like a scene from a 1930s Agatha Christie novel. Before lunch I took a photo of Carsten's, Marianne's and Anke's feet. They were wearing sandals with socks. I told them in Australia that was a tragic thing to do. Carsten pointed to my red socks and said, 'In Denmark that is a tragic thing to do!'

After a while, I left. I was used to walking, and I had angst in my pants and wanted to see the city. I found myself in a park on a hill which looked back to the cathedral, square and surrounding buildings, framing them with leafy green branches. The view gave me some perspective.

Santiago de Compostela Cathedral

The day before, Claudia had been gently crying in the square, saying the cathedral was so beautiful. I didn't agree. From the outside it was rather a mouldy and golden lichen-covered Baroque extravagance. But this façade apparently covered a Romanesque masterpiece, and certainly the huge and marvellous interior with its Romanesque archways and lengthy colonnades was extraordinary.

In the enormous square next to the cathedral was a magnificent *parador*, which used to be a place for pilgrims to sleep, but now was for rich tourists, which didn't quite seem in the spirit of the Camino. Nevertheless, despite my negativity, the views were overwhelming in all directions and helped give me my bearings.

I headed off to the Contemporary Art Museum. I felt a bit hollow and unreal and sometimes cold because it was over, but I kept bumping into pilgrims I knew, which was warming. We'd smile and wave; a wordless perfect understanding.

I was walking around a simplistic show, only giving it cursory glances, still dazed by the culmination of everything, when I realised the words of a woman sitting in the middle of the room typing were being projected onto the wall. She was typing something to the effect of: *The woman in red is not paying much attention and is walking away.* So I went and sat on the stairs around the corner and wrote on a piece of paper: *The woman in red has just walked over 750 kilometres across the north of Spain because her husband has recently died*, and handed it to her. We smiled at each other.

Φ

I met up with Marianne, Carsten, Daniel, Bertol, Inge and Erik for dinner and great company.

Inge and Erik had walked the Camino together, but they were not *together* together. Erik's wife and Inge's husband had fallen in love and left them, so Erik and Inge decided to walk the Camino jointly to try and sort out their own lives. What a brave thing to do. They were so not playing the victims, but you could see much hurt in their eyes, especially Inge. I have a photo of Erik laughing at one of our humorous and comradely dinners. You can see his pain if you're unlucky enough to be familiar with such things.

I woke early on Dad's birthday and did my washing. It was good to be able to hang clothes dripping wet in the shower, like all my dark thoughts. It was gloomy and rainy and quiet, not like the huge celebratory noise of the previous night. This contrast was typical of Spanish cities. A little allegory for no longer having Lewy in my life, and at that moment it was okay.

I had to go out and see some of the wonderful things that humans could achieve. Everywhere I was still searching for the joy. So I walked to the cathedral's museum, which overlooked Obradoiro Square, and it was touching to watch from on high more pilgrims arriving at their final destination. I walked around the cloisters and inside the museum, where, as well as some fine sculptures, there were tapestries, including some outstanding ones designed by Goya, one of my favourite painters.

I went to Mass again – it had been so moving the previous day. I went early and was able to sit in the nave about a third of the way down, next to two Norwegian girls. I loved meeting people from different countries. Sadly I never met anyone from Finland.

The cathedral was already quite full. I saw Hildie come in and I joyfully waved and called out unrestrainedly. We gave each other big kisses and hugs. There was no room for her to sit with me, but later in the service, during the Sign of Peace, she came up the aisle and gave me another big hug and a kiss. Made my day! It's a beautiful tradition, and in other churches a chance to warmly greet the Spaniards. Lew would have loved it.

Again the nun's singing was breathtaking. Pure, strong and deep. Devoid of artificiality, she looked nothing like the people we see on our televisions. Before I left the cathedral I went looking for her. When I found her I thanked her full-heartedly for her powerful singing.

You always said Catholic women were kind and generous. Poor Lewy Baby. You're going to miss out on so much.

Making Peace With Senseless Things

I looked back on those crowded thoughts and feelings that had been crushing me before and during the walk. I'd been searching for answers, and realised that many of my questions had no answers. I had to accept that life is made up from a myriad of qualities and some of them are abysmal. I had to become used to it and find my way again.

Lewy wouldn't come back. It was a pitiless reality that he didn't have long enough in this life. And that still worries me.

He suffered horribly at the end, but it could have gone on for longer. Bravo to his Dad that Lew inherited from him a fragile heart. It was a gift when he died that saved him from more torment.

It is tragic that someone dies when they are so happy, but also a great good fortune that they have found their happiness.

I'm very thankful that I was blessed to be with Lewy as he was dying. I was able to tenderly embrace him and croon those heartfelt words to the man who loved hugs. If only we could have been so much older …

After he died, why couldn't I have snuggled into bed and wrapped myself around him? I wish I had that enfolding memory. For me, the Big Things have been like this. I believe I'll respond in a certain way, but when they actually happen my reactions aren't always what I'd expected.

I did look after Lewy well in that hospital; his illness just galloped faster and faster than either of us could keep up with, at the end just one breakable thing after another. Still the smallest things were worrying. Why hadn't I filled his room with flowers? It just wasn't a flowery time ... but I yearned that I had.

It still hurt to think about some doctors ... but they're human. I'd forgotten that I'd learnt in high school that intelligence and common sense do not always travel in the same person. And some persons aren't as intelligent as you think.

I hoped I would accept that I went against Lew's wishes to be revived. I understood that if he had been brought back he would probably be in worse pain and with perhaps more broken ribs. I guess it was straightforward; we both just hoped with all our hearts that he wouldn't die.

Much Cheers for all the precious memories we made, particularly those lush travelling adventures. I'm especially glad that Lewy went to Paris, because he simply adored it.

There were four things that gave me the most comfort: Lewy was truly a happy man; he loved me dearly; he knew his love was mightily returned; and our feelings were steadfast because we were deeply grateful to have found each other.

I miss Lewy so much and I don't want to come to terms with that. It just is.

For me, pushing and pushing myself physically on the Camino, to be out in the rich landscape of northern Spain, to be still and contemplative in those sacred churches, to leave behind most of the trappings of my life, and to sometimes commune with a number of gems of humanity, enabled me to survive the worst of my sorrow. From inert hindsight, I should have slowed down during my last week of the walk, because it was on those enchanted pathways, and not in the destination, that the most consolation was to be found.

What had I learnt?

I believe: just throw yourself into life; be able to be still and enjoy the peace; and probably kindness is the most important quality.

Life can be sooo long or way too short.

Goodbye, Goodbye, my Beautiful Darling Lewy.

Φ

Before meeting up with the usual suspects, I had a drink and some green olives sitting in Platerías Square and imagined how much simple pleasure Lew would have taken in being there. How we could have added one more memory to our collection of happiness.

How I ached that Lew could have had more time. Extra cuddles. Added kisses. Further kindnesses. And a lavishness of love. Fifty-three years were not enough.

The day I would become the same age as Lew was the same day my first grandchild was due to be born. After that date, I would always be older than my darling man. How strange. I felt young, there was much to do, but one thing's for sure: sly time would pass and swiftly.

I had a beaut final night with Daniel and the Danes. I was lucky they'd included me in their fun. That evening I felt that some of my burden had lifted and for the first time my heart had truly lightened. It was true: life did have much to offer.

I woke before the dawn and welcomed the utter peace of the streets in the old part of town. The ground was deeply wet. I went into the cathedral one more time, as it was open despite the darkness. A priest was giving a German Mass in one of the side chapels. There was lots of singing, but it sounded uninviting to my judgemental ears.

I lit four candles for Lewy in another little chapel with the simplest of altars. Some were over the top, full of hyper-angst, but this was just right.

My Boy ... My Boy!

Lewy would introduce me as 'My Girl'.

It was cold, it was dark, it was quiet, it was still, it was heavy, as I said goodbye to my generous, gentle and brave beloved.

Then I walked through the empty colonnaded interior of the cathedral for the final time, and down, down into the silent misty square.

Loose Ends

Our plane took off through fog, but it was so clear and fresh above the clouds, beautiful and unbounded. Peering into the endless sky I wondered if Lew was floating around out there. A hundred years ago I might have thought, *if only I could be above the clouds I might find my boy* … In another hundred, could the doctors have saved him?

I stayed with Granada Jane and her family in Spain; and Dad's two sisters, Janet and Margaret, in the south of England. I was thawed by their love, warmed by their kind-heartedness, grateful for their patience, and able to sustain looking outwards. And lastly, fastly and not leastly, Precious Prue managed to catch up with me for a weekend in London before I caught a flight back to Sydney.

In the sky, 35,000 feet up, a glorious rainbow this morning.

A greeting from you?

Why do rainbows have such an air of hope about them?

I'll be okay, Lewy. Will you …?

I gazed out the window at the marvel of a soundless and soulful infinity and thought about the tiny speck that was my home. There would be no drippy yellow arrows to show me the way. And Lew's gentle warmth, always around me, would be no longer.

In a month's time it would be the Summer that Lewy didn't make it to.

☧

Little Hugo entered this world nine months and one day after Lew departed. A new life. How magical. And Hugo's whimsical timing also brought me a humming consolation.

He was born radiating a strong sense of his own self, his definite nose pushed to one side as he had been resting upon it, upside down, poised in his mother's womb. Biding his time, waiting to join us. Gradually his precious nose restored itself to its rightful position.

It was quietly gruelling for me to go back to the same hospital that, with only a pinch of exceptions, was so careless with Lewy's final days.

Jess, after a long and stubborn labour, said, 'I'm glad you're having a positive experience here. It's a good and healing thing.' She spoke in the way a joyful new mother does, for everything was now right with the world.

'Yes, darling,' I said, 'that's true.'

Well, I wanted it to be true, but silently I wondered if I would ever forgive this place. Actually that's not quite what I thought either, but I'll take my cue from Hugo and show some poise.

☧

Before Hugo was born, I started to write, and to write, and write and write. A leaden yearning for my husband was gouging at the confidence and peace I had gained from the Camino. My closest friends had been stirred by my travel ramblings and had taken off on their own adventures. Writing took hold of me. I would wake and start scribbling around 6.30 am, and oh so swiftly it would be 1.30 in the afternoon and, 'I really ought to get out of my pyjamas'.

Several years later, I returned to painting, frustrated by my writing inexperience and the numerous rejections from publishers. I painted in black and white as if I were still in a world of words on paper.

Eventually colour returned to my pictures. I painted themes of friendship, death, sorrow, walking, angels, the unexpected, and magical creatures appeared in my work. I moved away from solely decorative works as my subject matter changed to a darker moodier vision.

Flight

A year ago I stopped painting and returned to writing and a black and white existence, in the ardent hope that Lew's story could be shared.

Φ

The year after Lew died, Prue returned permanently to live in Sydney after thirty years of living overseas. She simply said that the last time she'd left us, she left her heart here. So we are able to play Scrabble together and, more importantly, we still have those chortling and choking times when we believe we are stunningly hilarious.

Three years later, our darling Dads, both called Peter, died within six months of each other. We knew just how the other felt.

I didn't crumble when Dad died, because I was thoroughly thankful that he'd had such a full, long and happy life. But poor Mum …

Φ

Since Lewy's death, the giant magnolia in our garden has flowered seven times, with magenta and white flowers as big as floppy dinner plates. In the last month of spring, the now massive jacaranda tree is a leafless opacity of vibrant mauve flowers. When it fills with kookaburras in the early mornings it appears to be laughing heartily. It reminds me of the misconceptions of my childhood.

I am not so grateful for the legacy of sleeping with a mouthguard. I wasn't able to lose the teeth-clenching habit and am peeved to have to wear at night something that makes me look and sound Neanderthal. And it appears that if I'm truly serious about weight loss, I'll have to walk from the tip of Chile to the top of Canada.

But I'm mighty appreciative that Hugo has a darling brother called Charlie and that for quite a few years I was known as Gwanny.

Hugh and Aimee worked for a year in the Northern Territory and then travelled the world. We have been enchanted by his colourful tales of his escapades at home and overseas.

Claudie still loves Bertie Beetles, but they are sadly only available once a year in showbags at the Royal Melbourne Show. She is now married to her comedian, Simon. As you may have gathered, he will be an essential addition to our family.

Louie-The-Cat has departed this world at a ripe old age. But I have lots of holes in my flyscreens, scratches on the couch and thread-pulls on my bedspread to remember him by.

I'm still thoroughly blessed with Molly-Dog, whose personality of relentless good cheer is a perpetual tonic.

Oh, there is so much for me to be thankful for, Lewy, but since you left us, life has never been as lush. I am not forgetting you and the sizzling, sumptuous, sweetest life we shared.

Φ

Lewis, 25th June 2009

Acknowledgements

I want to tell you unequivocally that I thought Dr Kindheart an angel. And so were the Home Nursing Service and the ridiculously overworked hospital nurses. I would hope there is a really lush place for them in the Heaven Dome.

But it is important that you stand up for yourself if you do not agree with a medical opinion or stance – at least better than Lewis and myself did.

To all of our friends and family, whose love and support delighted Lewy beyond words and enabled him to bear his illness and suffering with such grace, and enabled me to get back on my feet – as my grandmother used to say, 'I looks to yous and I bows'.

For invaluable writing help and advice, thank you to Prudence Frinzi, Jane Isaacson, Simon Keck, Dr Kindheart, Ursula and Peter Laverty, Ian McDonald, Paul Munro, Beth O'Driscoll, Nicola O'Shea, Gwyn Perkins, Helen Piper, Marie-Claire Spurlock, Keith Stevenson, Claudia Tory, Barbara Tuckerman and Tony Voss.

And a heart full of thank yous to the kindness of strangers.

Adiós amigos

www.ingramcontent.com/pod-product-compliance
Lightning Source LLC
Chambersburg PA
CBHW040327300426
44113CB00020B/2677